BW

smudge this pg 7-02

DATE DUE   3/02

DEC 2 7 2002		
ILL 3-26-03		
ILL 5-8-03		
GAYLORD		PRINTED IN U.S.A.

Canoe Rig

The Essence and the Art

Sailpower for Antique and
Traditional Canoes

Written and Illustrated by
Todd E. Bradshaw

**Edited by Peter Spectre
and Jane Crosen**

Design : Darel Gabriel Bridges

Printed in Hong Kong

A WoodenBoat Book
www.woodenboat.com

ISBN 0-937822-57-4

Library of Congress Cataloging-in-Publication Data
Bradshaw, Todd. 1952-
Canoe rig : the essence and the art : sailpower for antique
and traditional canoes / by Todd Bradshaw.
p.   cm.
ISBN 0-937822-57-4 (alk. paper)
1. Canoes and canoeing.   2. Sailboats.   I. Title
VM 353.B66 1999   99-33078
623.8'62—dc21   CIP

Contents

Contents

Contents

The Front Part of the Tip of the Iceberg

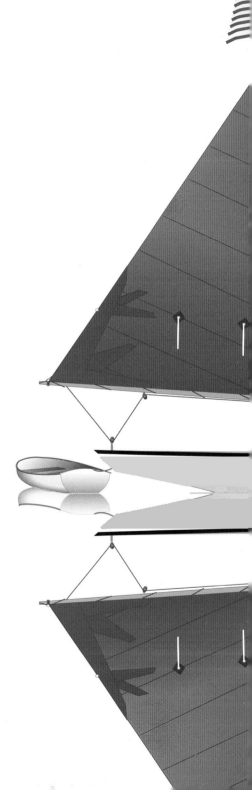

DEDICATION
To my father the artist and my mother the English teacher,
who encouraged independent thought, taught all of their
children the importance of communication skills, and didn't
ask any questions when I'd return from a whitewater trip
with both ends and half the deck ripped off my boat.

ACKNOWLEDGMENTS
The author wishes to thank Ralph Frese (The Chicagoland
Canoe Base), the Grant family (Sailrite), Roger Winiarski
(Bristol Bronze), and Robert Lavertue (The Springfield
Fan Centerboard Co.) for their patient assistance.

IN MEMORY OF CHRIS MERIGOLD

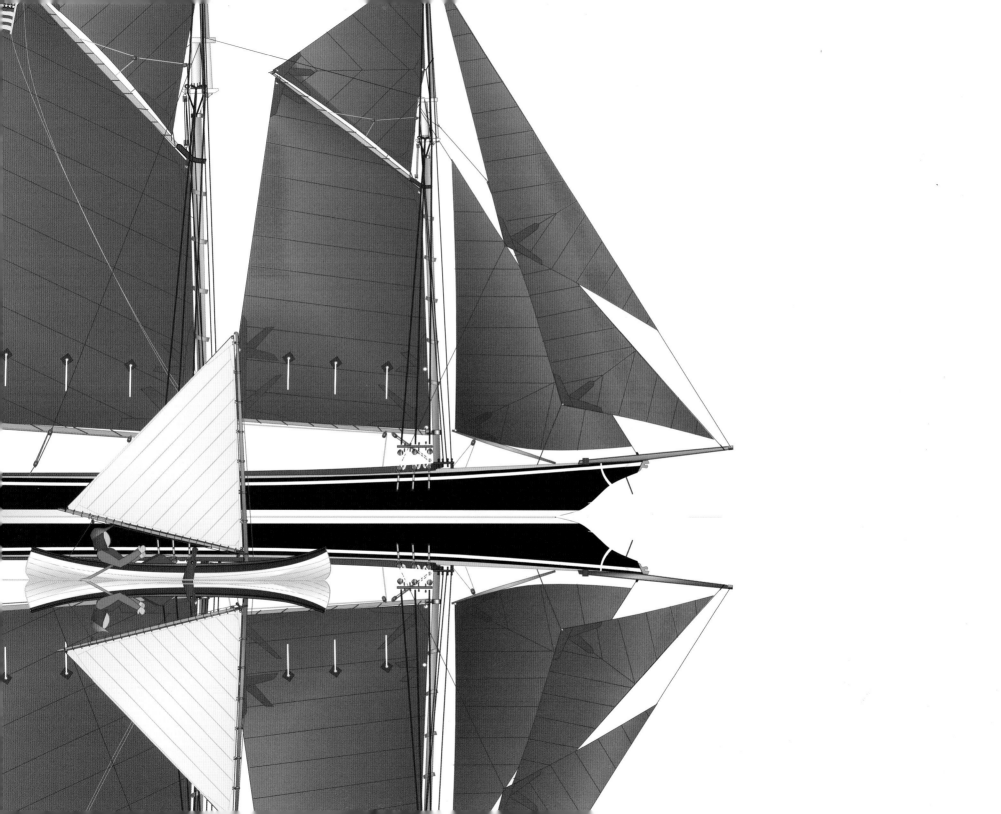

The Old and the New

To say that canoe sailing is a fringe element of a relatively quiet industry would not be an understatement. Many of the people I know in the canoe business are still wondering if they should have kept their real jobs. Sailing equipment for canoes, when available, is relegated to a couple of lines on the back pages of their catalogs.

Canoe building, as an industry, has always been small, but canoe sailing was once a fairly large part of that industry. Today, it is kept alive mostly by those who spend their winters in basements, sanding, varnishing, and restoring the old boats from canoe sailing's glory years, and by a fairly small group of racers in modern boats.

As a long-time canoeist, currently practicing as a sailmaker, I have been lucky enough to get the chance to build replicas of some of the old, tattered cotton sails that once were the power sources for what are now antique canoes. The diversity and ingenuity displayed in these old rigs continue to fascinate me. Most of these sails aren't particularly valuable, in terms of money, but they are testimonials to the days when sails were made by craftsmen, not by the clock.

Though it is still possible to build museum-quality reproductions of these old sails, most of my customers want to sail their boats, not put them in museums, and have budgets that govern the number of hand-sewing hours they can afford. So we strike a balance. Materials are modern, but made specifically for traditional recreations, and most of the

fabrication techniques are, at least, based on traditional sailmaking. The result is a sail that took a little more time to sew, laced to wooden spars usually built or restored by the canoe's owner. It's a mix of old and new with the intention of making something that looks as if it's supposed to be there, not as if it were borrowed from a modern dinghy.

I am happy to say that today we seem to be having a resurgence of interest in canoes built specifically for sailing and in sailing conversions for standard models. For many years, the sport has been dominated by racing. Small groups of sailors in very similar boats, with nearly identical rigs, have kept canoe sailing alive, but strict, class-racing rules tend to stifle development and creativity.

I deal with the touring sailor, not the racer; the fact that new ideas are being developed and old ones dusted-off for another try is encouraging. Variety and experimentation are what interest me most, and the touring canoe is where the variety is and always will be. I like the idea that a canoeist can add a reasonably inexpensive and easy-to-build sailing rig to his or her canoe and have the only one like it in the world.

This style is reminiscent of the days when sailboats, sailing canoes, and iceboats were known by their names, not their model numbers or the mold they came out of. I certainly don't want my sailing canoe to look exactly like the one I just passed, going the other direction. I'm willing to take a few calculated risks in the design process toward that end.

The antique canoes that I have built sails for are interesting because they are all different. We live in an era when the aspiring canoe sailor has to choose between a very minimal rig that both looks and performs as if no one bothered to design it first, and a modern multi-colored rig that sails well but owes its heritage more to a Windsurfer than a canoe. I think there is room for something different—something classic, something functional, something elegant.

Elegance looks pretty good on any canoe, regardless of age. This book is a compilation and an explanation of some of the methods, techniques, and even tricks that can be used to hang a sail on a canoe with elegance...and with style.

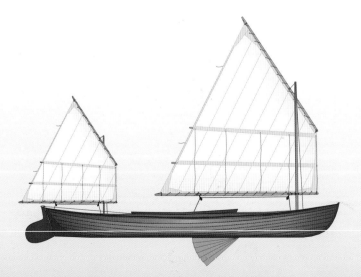

Canoe Rig: The Essence and the Art

Anyone who has ever taken an art class has probably had to keep a sketchbook. It functions as a place both to practice your drawing skills and to develop and store ideas. It is the artist's "file cabinet." In the cabinet are bits and pieces, concepts and details, some highly developed, others still in the "what if?" stage. Some may be accurate depictions of existing objects, while others are pure fantasy, held together only by their ink and a hint of promise.

So it is here. My intent is not really to add another book to the pile, to tell you everything you will need to know to build a spar, or a sail, or how to sail. There are plenty already out there, and many do their job beautifully. I will, however, offer options, observations, and enough basic information on construction and use to give you a foundation upon which to build, with emphasis on the things that make rigging a canoe for sailing different from other sailing craft.

Here, we will concentrate on ideas. Some have been turned into reality by the hundreds over the years. Others have yet to be tried. The history of canoe sailing seems to be full of variety, experimentation, and ideas. Tradition will be respected, but not necessarily the law. I'm not a canoe historian, but I've seen a lot of old boats and tend to remember interesting solutions to problems and construction details. Traditional methods and style function best here, because they produce the most beautiful results; when combined with the small scale and relative economy of outfitting a canoe for sailing, beauty is affordable.

There is no reason that a canoeist, wishing to sail, should be limited to the unfortunate, industry standard—a 55-square-foot lateen sail with blue-and-white stripes strung on skinny, aluminum spars—just because no one in the canoe industry seems to remember how to make anything else.

The following chapters will offer a basis on which the reader can put together an interesting, functional sailing rig, suitable for a traditional canoe, that will put most commercially available rigs to shame, both on and off the water.

We'll start with the good old 55-square-foot lateen rig, but made the right way. Then we'll cut the canoe in half and inventory the various parts of the sailing rig and their functions. We'll look at a variety of different sail plans and investigate the components needed to make it all work, with an occasional side trip for obscure but interesting stuff.

Most canoe sailing rigs were originally adapted from small sailboats and dinghies, and many of the rigs that you will see here can also be used to power skiffs, prams, peapods, and other small boats. With two good hands and a reasonably fog-free mind you should be able to build anything in this book. I'll draw the pictures; you bring them to life. Welcome to my file cabinet.

Chapter One

Catch the Wind

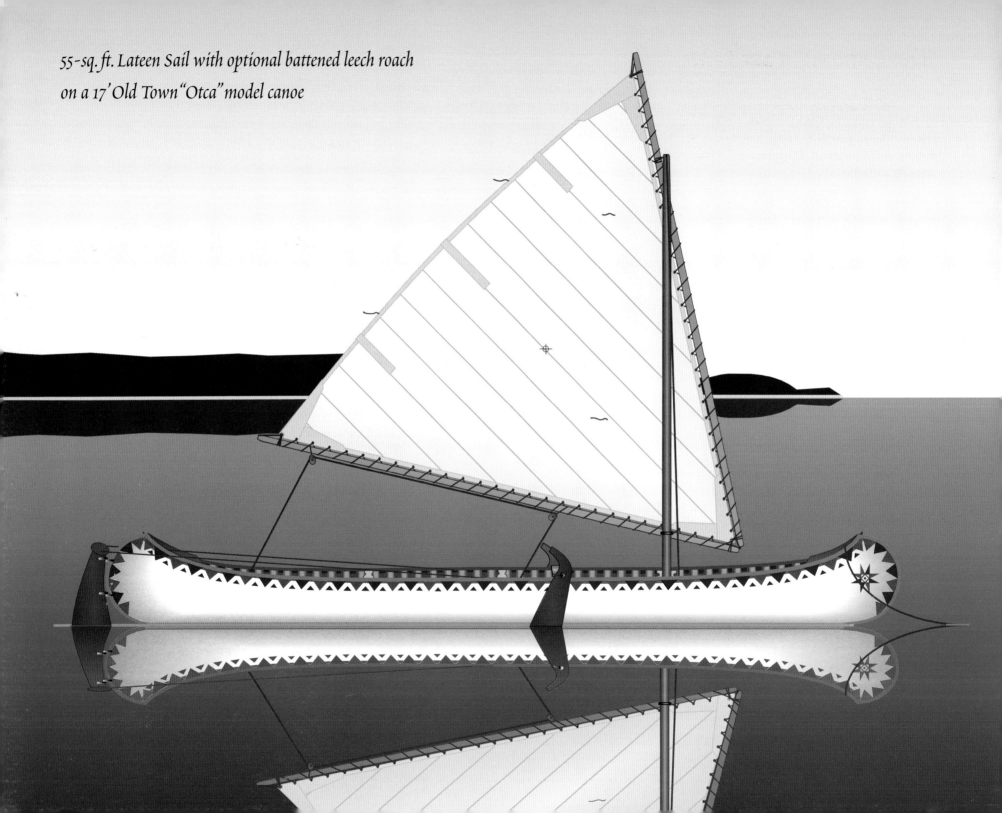

55-sq. ft. Lateen Sail with optional battened leech roach
on a 17' Old Town "Otca" model canoe

The Canoe as a Sailboat

I don't consider a canoe to be an all-purpose sailboat. I'd rather think of it as an all-purpose boat—with sailing capabilities. Even a small sail can be a lot to handle in windy conditions. Failure to keep this in mind, and the open nature of the canoe, can mean a long swim to shore towing a swamped boat…or worse.

Many of the sail rigs on these pages, especially those with twin sails, can develop a lot of power. Because a canoe has a faster, lighter, and narrower hull than most dinghies, it takes more skill to sail one. It also requires more discretion regarding weather. The same wind and waves that you may routinely paddle through without event can be quite a different story when in an unburdened boat with 40 or 50 square feet of sail up!

As a paddling craft, your canoe is a "displacement hull." It parts the water at the bow, slips gracefully through it, and neatly puts it back together at the stern. A long, narrow hull with pointed ends makes a good displacement hull, requiring minimal effort to move it through the water.

If the canoe is sleek enough, and the paddlers strong enough, the boat may approach "hull speed," where the water streamlines around the hull. Hull speed is as fast as that hull, with that amount of weight in it, can go as a displacement hull. To go any faster, it would have to climb out of the dent it makes in the water and skid across the surface, like a water ski. This is called "planing." The reason you don't see canoes planing across the surface of your local river is that planing takes about four times the power as that necessary to achieve hull speed. A paddle just isn't efficient enough to make a canoe plane, but a sail is.

Don't expect to spend most of your sailing hours skimming along the wave tops, because most of the time, even under sail power, canoes are displacement boats.

There may be days, however, when a large sail plan and a good wind can give you quite a ride. If you're ready for it, it can be a lot of fun, but work your way up to it. A day with strong winds is no time to be working the bugs out of a new sailing rig.

"Yes maaaam, it is possible to build a wooden rocket. I've got one right there on top of my truck."

About the Illustrations

The drawings in this book were done on a computer. Most of the sail plans are profiles, without perspective. They are working drawings and accurate down to about the width of a line, though this kind of accuracy is hardly needed for a small illustration in a book. Most were originally full-sized sailmaking plans for sails that I have built for customers.

When figuring fabric amounts, sail-shaping, and even the exact dimensions of a sail panel, I consult the drawing in the computer. Adding color, detail, and maybe even background to a blueprint seems like overdoing it, but it lets me see what I'm shooting for, and it's fun.

A Typical Canoe Sailing Rig

See legend for details

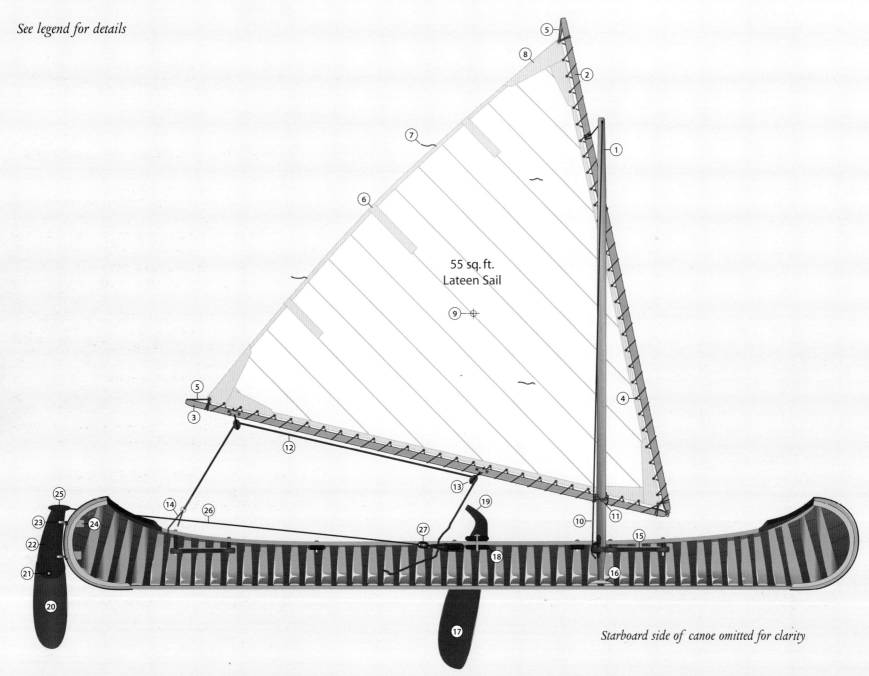

55 sq. ft.
Lateen Sail

Starboard side of canoe omitted for clarity

Legend

Sail and Spars

1 – The **mast**. Generally a sturdy, round-sectioned pole made from spruce and tapered at the ends to reduce weight.

2 – The **yard**, or **upper spar**, a slightly thinner spar that supports the top or leading edge of the sail.

3 – The **boom**, or **lower spar** supports the bottom of the sail and provides a place to anchor sail-trimming lines.

4 – Sails are usually laced to their spars through **grommets**.

5 – The **corners of the sail** are lashed to the ends of the spars, pulling the edges of the sail smooth.

6 – Wooden **battens**, often inside small, cloth pockets, are used to support the "leech," or trailing edge of the sail. They may be as short as a foot, or run all the way across the sail, depending upon sail type.

7 – **Telltales** are small pieces of cloth or yarn, attached to the sail. They function as wind-indicators for adjusting sail trim.

8 – **Corner patches** are extra layers of sailcloth that help reinforce the sail in high-stress areas.

9 – The "**Center of Effort**" is the theoretical center of the sail area. A small mark at the "C.E." as a reference point can help you set up and tune the rig.

10 – The **halyard**, or **halyards** in some cases, are simply lines that raise and lower the sails. They are cleated or tied off near the mast's base.

11 – Most rigs use a simple wooden, metal, or rope **connection to join the mast and boom**. Some are fixed, some are adjustable.

Fittings and Attachments

12 – "**Sheets**" are the lines that adjust sail position relative to the wind. Since this canoe has only a mainsail, it has only one sheet, "the mainsheet."

13 – A pulley, in nautical terms, is called a "**block**." The mainsheet blocks hanging from the boom attach the sheet to the boom and provide low-friction sail-trim adjustments.

14 – The after end of the mainsheet can be tied off to the canoe or can ride on a simple "**traveler**," as shown here. The traveler is just a short line similar to a kite bridle, running across the canoe and tied to the gunwales. The end of the mainsheet is spliced to a brass ring that can slide side-to-side on the traveler. Having a traveler can improve sail shape, at times, by reducing sail twist.

15 – The **mast seat** is a special caned seat that replaces the normal bow seat. The cross bar in the back is extra wide and has a hole in it. The mast is supported by stepping it through the hole. A "mast thwart" is sometimes used instead. Simply a wide thwart with a hole for the mast to pass through, a mast thwart is easy to build.

Canoes using twin sails need two mast seats or thwarts. Often, both seats are replaced with mast seats. Some types of sailing canoe may also have a hole bored in the breasthook (fore deck) for the mast.

16 – The heel of the mast fits into a block of wood that has been attached to the canoe's floor. This is called the "**mast step**" and works with the mast seat, or thwart, to position and secure the mast.

Legend

Foils and Steering Gear

17 –Leeboards are the vertical slabs of wood that hang from the gunwale and slice through the water. They prevent the boat from being blown sideways by creating "lateral resistance." Similar in concept to the keel of a sailboat, leeboards are usually installed on both the port and starboard sides of a canoe, although some rigs have been built using only one board.

18 –The **leeboard bracket** is a removable cross-bar arrangement, clamped to the gunwales. It is usually fitted with sturdy metal angles or wooden chocks at the ends to which the boards are bolted. Often the leeboard bracket consists of two cross bars held together by a couple of big carriage bolts and wing-nuts, sandwiching the gunwales between them. The boards themselves are pinned to the bracket ends with a similar, but horizontal, bolt and wing-nut system—one large bolt per leeboard.

19 –The top end of a leeboard should have some sort of **handle** shape. Rotating the windward (high-side) leeboard on its bolt until it is out of the water reduces drag without much loss of lateral resistance. For rig-tuning and beaching, being able to change leeboard angle is also quite helpful. The handle makes adjustment easier.

20 –Though some canoe sailors steer with a paddle, high-performance and singlehanded rigs are much easier to control with a fixed **rudder**. The rudder blade is the canoe's steering foil. The lower section (#20) is usually designed to pivot up for beaching and down for sailing, and may be rigged with lines and cleats to keep it down or raise it up.

21 –This is the **pivot bolt**, which allows the rudder blade to swing up, clear of the water.

22 –The **upper part of the rudder assembly** is commonly made of two slabs of wood that sandwich the blade. It should be sturdy to prevent the blade from twisting.

23 –Pintles and **gudgeons** are the metal parts that form a hinge between the boat and its rudder system. Pintles are attached to the upper rudder assembly; gudgeons are screwed or bolted to the canoe's end.

24 –Blocking, secured inside the hull, may be needed to provide a strong attachment for the gudgeons. Most canoes, both old classics and modern composite boats, are not really strong enough to take the strain of the rudder fittings without reinforcement for long.

25 –The **rudder head** or **yoke** forms the steering arms that protrude on either side of the top of the rudder assembly. The steering ropes are attached to these "horns."

26 –The **steering rope** is generally a loop of soft-handed line that runs from the port horn of the rudder head, forward to a block near the port side of the center thwart. It then crosses the boat and runs along the thwart to another block, mid-starboard, and then runs aft to the starboard horn of the rudder head. Steering is accomplished by pushing/pulling the rope where it runs crosswise, next to the thwart. A knot amidships provides better grip and a "rudder-straight" reference aid.

27 –Turning blocks route the steering rope and are tied to the center thwart or sometimes to the leeboard bracket.

The Lateen Rig for Canoe Sailing

The popularity of the lateen rig on canoes is due to several factors. While the sail is fairly large and potentially powerful, the overall height of the rig is not extreme. For a narrow hull, like a canoe, tall, skinny sail plans, such as those on modern sailboats, though aerodynamically excellent, create more "heeling motion" than most sailors desire. This means that the taller rig would cause the canoe to lean away from the wind more than the shorter lateen would.

In any kind of breeze, a sailing canoe will heel, but since the only way for the sailor to counteract this motion and control the canoe is to lean out (hike out) over the high, windward side of the canoe, there are limits to how high a lever arm we want to stick up in the air. Obviously, we also have to think about what's happening on the low side of a heeling canoe. At a certain point, water will start coming in. The low-aspect-ratio (short and wide) lateen rig, with less heeling lever, is better for a canoe.

Many potential canoe sailors are surprised when I mention anything about boat speed. Remember that a sailing canoe is quite different from a paddling canoe. It has the ability to really scoot, and at high speeds things happen fast, which brings us to what is probably the lateen rig's biggest potential fault:

As the canoe heels, the tail end of the boom and sail, hanging out over the side, gets closer to the surface of the water. In a big gust of wind, the end can actually touch the water. If hiking out doesn't bring the boat back up, the sailor must ease out the sail. This allows the top of the sail to twist, thus spilling wind and reducing the heeling power, and swivels the rest of the sail, like a weathervane, to de-power it. If the boom and part of the sail are already skipping along the surface, they can prevent you from being able to ease the sail: the boat might simply sail itself over onto its side in a smooth roll. If you can't ease the sail, changing heading is the only other way to reduce the heeling force on the sail.

Unlike some of the other sailing rigs that we will examine, the lateen cannot be reefed. (Reefing is shortening sail by using a built-in system to furl part of the sail, reducing sail area while allowing the rest of the sail to keep working.) With the lateen rig, the sail area you start with is the sail area you have all the time.

The twin lateen rig (see page 9) is one of the fastest sail plans in this book. It has more area than the single rig, yet it is actually lower.

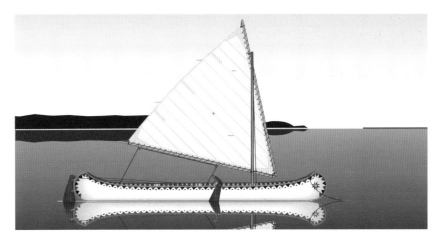

The sailor's job with such a rig is to keep the boat level, fore and aft, as flat as possible, by hiking, and allow it plane across the water. The experienced sailor will find the rig rewarding and exciting; the novice will most likely do a lot of swimming. Observers on shore will get quite a show either way.

You will notice that some lateen sails, such as the single above, have an outwardly curved leech (the trailing edge of the sail). This extra area is called "roach" and generally requires wooden battens, sewn into pockets, to support it and keep it from flapping uselessly. The twin lateen's sails, however, have no roach at the leech. The leeches are straight and may even be cut slightly hollow. Battens are a source of sail chafe and add to the cost of building or buying a sail. The use of roach, then, and the battens to support it, is of questionable merit—especially when you consider that increasing a lateen sail's area may not be the best thing to do on a canoe.

I firmly believe that the battened lateen (common only on canoes) is a fluke related to the canoe business. Somebody created such a sail, and some other company copied it, and then somebody else copied that, etc., without anyone ever really thinking about why, or why not, the sails needed roaches and battens in the first place.

On the whole, though, the lateen rig works well on canoes. It is simple, requires minimal hard-to-find parts, and performs quite well. The 40-to-60-square-foot single lateen rig, despite its limits, is therefore the most common sailing rig used on canoes.

Estimated Performance Guidelines

For medium winds and a typical 16- to 18-foot canoe with various sizes of sails:

75 square feet
You will be hiked out with everything from your hips up outside the gunwale most of the time.

55 to 65 square feet
Hiking will be required at times. Balancing from inside the canoe will often be enough if the winds are steady.

35 to 45 square feet
Unless the wind is gusty, you should be able to move reasonably well without having to hike out. Light-air performance won't be quite as good as with the larger sails.

Under 35 square feet
Used on small canoes and as mizzens on twin-sailed rigs. Might work as a "helper" for tripping.

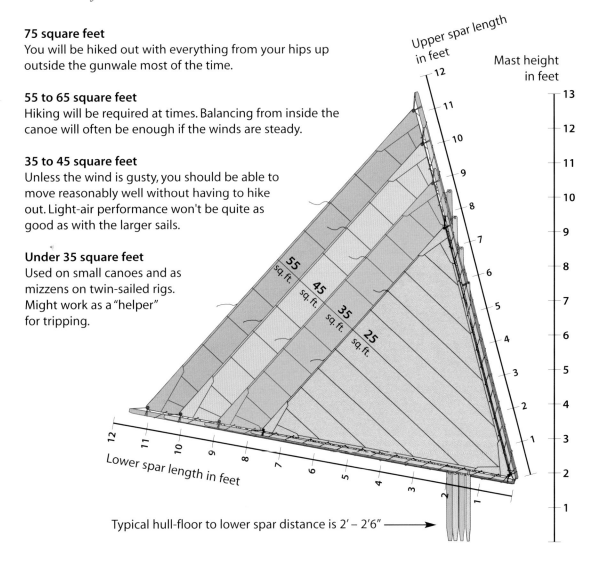

Typical hull-floor to lower spar distance is 2' – 2'6" ⟶

Typical Lateen Rig Dimensions

This chart will give you an idea of spar length, mast length, and sail dimensions for a typical lateen sail. Some people refer to a lateen's upper spar as the "yard" and the lower spar as the "boom." Others just call them the upper and lower spars. Use the labels you prefer. The mast is still the mast.

The largest lateen that I have seen on a canoe was 75 square feet. It would be a lot to handle in any kind of a breeze. With spars about 14 feet long, the rig also would have limited portability.

The halyard is tied to the upper spar to raise the sail. The lower spar is held to the mast by a lashing, a hoop, or a wooden jaw attached to the spar; it is fixed to the spar but free to slide up and down on the mast. The upper and lower spars are joined where they meet by a hinge or link. This link doesn't get much stress, so it needn't be fancy.

Spar diameter varies with wood species, length, cross-section, and sail type. Most canoe spars taper to about 1 inch diameter at the ends and approach 1½ inches in the middle. Masts are typically 1¼ inches to 1½ inches at the top and are 1¾ inches or so at the point of maximum diameter; they are usually tapered steeply below the seat or thwart to around 1 inch at the mast step. The spars should extend 2 or 3 inches beyond the corners of the sail at their outer ends.

The Twin Lateen Rig

An Old Town Canoe Company catalog from the 1960s showed an Otca with this type of sail rig scooting along under perfect control. The sailor sat on the windward gunwale, just behind the leeboard bracket, hiking out with his toes hooked under the leeward gunwale.

In a breeze it would take some skill and athletic ability to sail this boat well—but what a gorgeous thing it would be to see on the water! Many twin-rigged boats were fitted with two caned seats with holes in the seat frames for the masts and were actually sailed "stern first."

30 sq. ft.

45 sq. ft.

C.E. total

High-performance 75-sq. ft. Twin Lateen Rig on 17′ Otca

Chapter Two

Where Wind and Water Meet

Make It Go!

Since canoe sailors have varying amounts of sailing experience, it would be wise to devote a few pages to a bit of basic sailing. There are plenty of good instructional books devoted entirely to sailing small boats, and most of their information also applies to canoe sailing. I recommend that new sailors read one or two of these books. For our purposes, I will provide a simplified, quick course, more as a means of understanding the performance and use of different types of canoe sails than as an attempt to teach the finer points of sailing.

Picture yourself standing on the south shore of Paddler's Pond, having just finished assembling the rig of your sailing canoe. Conveniently, the wind on the pond is always from the north, so you're currently on the downwind side of the lake.

The first objective is to get aboard the canoe and sail to the Pollywog Cafe, which sits on the north shore, for lunch. If we push off and point the canoe due north, not much happens. The sail flaps in the breeze, like a flag, and the boat drifts backwards. It's not until we "bear off," altering our heading about 45 degrees, to either northeast or northwest, that the sail fills with wind and the canoe starts to move forward.

We have just learned the first important rule of sailing: No sailboat can sail directly upwind. Depending on boat design and sail type, there will be a limit to how close to the wind direction you can sail, or how high you can "point," as sailors call it. Some boat/rig combinations point higher than others, but 45 degrees off the wind is fairly typical for general-purpose sailing craft.

We will make lunch, but to get there we will have to sail a zigzag course, heading northeast, then "tacking" to a northwest heading, and then back to northeast, and so on. We will sail "close-hauled," with the sail trimmed in tightly, and feel our highest possible course by watching the sail. If the sail starts to "luff," losing its shape, we have headed up too high and must bear off a bit before the boat stalls.

Once we have figured out how high we can point, we can make another test. Some boats will actually get you to lunch faster if you bear off a bit more (that is, head east-northeast, or west-northwest), ease the sail out a little, and let her rip. You will have to travel farther at these lower angles of attack, but the extra speed may make up for the extra distance. Most catamarans and other multihulls, for example, slow down if they are pointed too high, but they will really move at a lower angle. Many sailing canoes share this feature.

Sailboats that point high and go fast tend to have tall, narrow sail plans. Some of the best will point well into the 30-to-40-degree range and still maintain their speed. We've already established that a canoe isn't a very good platform for trying to counterbalance a tall sail, so with our lower rig we may, indeed, find that a shallower angle of attack and taking the scenic route will get us there in time to get a table by the window.

We can work our way upwind with a series of short zigs and zags with many tacks, or a few long ones with fewer tacks. It takes the canoe a while to get back up to speed after a tack, so the less tacking the better, if we want to beat the lunch rush.

It's also handy to know that today, when we are sailing with a north-westerly heading, we are on the "starboard tack." The wind from the north is coming in over the starboard (right) side of the canoe. By nautical rule, this gives us the right-of-way over sailing craft on the "port tack." (However, if a 160-foot-long schooner happens to be coming at you on the port tack—don't push your luck.)

Should we zag back to our northeasterly heading, the wind will be coming in over the port (left) side of the boat and we will be on the port tack—losing the right-of-way to any boats on the starboard tack.

So far, the wind has been steady and straight out of the north. However, it isn't always so predictable out here on the pond. From moment to moment, both the wind's speed and its direction will vary a bit. Learning to play the directional shifts, in particular, is something that makes a good sailor.

Picture yourself going for lunch on the starboard tack, heading northwest, the wind due north. If the wind were to shift from due north to northeast for a couple of minutes, we could change our heading to straight north—straight toward Pollywog's—and still maintain the same pointing angle in relation to the wind direction. As long as the wind stayed shifted, we could, too.

A wind shift such as this, which allows you to change your heading to a closer course to your intended goal, is called a "lift." Should the wind shift back to due north, we would bear off to keep the sails full, back to our northwesterly course. Using lifts, when they happen, makes the trip shorter.

On the other hand, had we been on the port tack, heading northeast, when the wind direction shifted from north to northeast, we would have found our canoe pointing directly into the wind and stalling fast. To keep moving and maintain our proper pointing angle, we would have had to alter course to due east.

Once we have reestablished our boat-heading to wind-direction angle, we will be fine, headed east. East?…but lunch is north. East is taking us farther away from where we want to go. This is called a "header." Being headed makes your trip longer.

But we can fix this easily. All we have to do is tack. Remember, the northeasterly shift that is heading us on the port tack was a lift on the starboard tack—a lift that will take us directly to our destination!

Out to Lunch

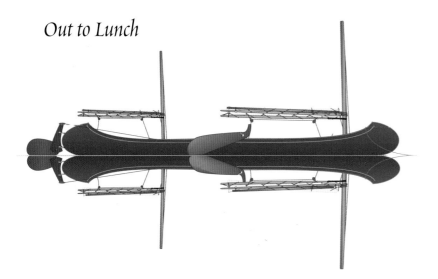

Get Back!

After a couple of frogburgers at the Pollywog Cafe, we're ready to sail again. Our wind is still out of the north. Before we head home, let's check out the east and west ends of the lake. Our course will be perpendicular to the wind direction and is called a "reach." Actually, there are three types of reaches, and they are all pretty fast and fun to sail.

A "beam reach" is square to the wind; in this case, a straight east-west track, and can be sailed in either direction. A "close reach" is similar, but slightly upwind. We will be sailing an easterly or westerly course, but also angling northward a bit in the process—not as high as we were when we sailed close-hauled to get up to this end of the lake, but we can still make some upwind progress.

Since we're already at the north end of the pond, we might choose a "broad reach" instead. Rather than just heading east or west, a broad reach will put us on a southeasterly or southwesterly course. We will be heading home but via an indirect route, with side trips to the east and the west sides of the pond.

To sail any reach, the sails are eased out a bit. The trimmed-in-tight mode that we used coming upwind will tend to stall the boat and heel it over on a reach. The sails, when eased, can develop maximum aerodynamic lift (sails are airfoils, just like a wing). The lift is formed on the convex, downwind side of the sail; easing the sail helps aim that lifting force so it is pulling the boat forward. Rather than using our airfoil to fight its way upwind, we can now use it to generate maximum speed.

On a close reach, the sail might be trimmed almost as much as it was when sailing close-hauled. On a broad reach it would be eased out as much as 45 to 50 degrees from the centerline of the canoe, and on a beam reach it would be somewhere in between.

One way to determine how much to let the sails out on any reach is to ease the mainsheet (the line controlling the sail) until the sail starts to flutter, then trim the sheet in just enough for the sail to fill and start accelerating the canoe.

Just as we did when sailing up the lake, we can zigzag our way back, linking easterly and westerly reaches. On close reaches, we can tack, swinging the bow into, and then past, the oncoming wind and onto our new heading. We can also tack to change a beam reach from an easterly to a westerly heading, but we might want to "jibe" instead.

A jibe is a directional turn, like a tack, but the boat is steered away from the wind, so that the wind crosses the stern instead of the bow.

For example, if you are sailing straight east, with a north wind (you are on a beam reach), and decide to make a U-turn and head west, you could turn to the left (north or upwind—a tack), or turn to the right (south or downwind—a jibe). A jibe usually slows the boat less than a tack and might, thus, be preferred.

If we were angling downwind, sailing a broad reach, the boat would already be pointed somewhat downwind, due to our heading. It would be much more efficient to jibe than to tack, which would require making a looping 270-degree turn onto our new heading.

In high winds, jibing can be pretty exciting. As the wind catches the sail from behind, the boom can swing across very quickly and with a lot of force (that's probably why it's called a boom). There can be a momentary, wild ride as you get the boat under control on its new heading. If you find yourself in windy conditions and a jibe might be a bit hairy, tack instead.

Tacking slows the boat and is much gentler than jibing, even though you may be making a loop instead of a direct turn to your new heading. Tacking is easier on both you and your equipment; any sailor who claims he has never tacked when he might have jibed is lying.

While working your way back on a broad reach, there is one heading/sail-trim configuration that should be avoided: "sailing by the lee." If we were headed southeast, for example, we could let the sail out on either side of the boat until it filled, and the boat would go. But letting it out over the port (left, and also upwind) side is asking for trouble. All it would take is a slight wind shift (to the northeast in this case) to put the wind directly behind the sail. In such an event, before the boat will even slow down, the sail will flutter, the boom will lift a bit, and the sail and boom will come flying across to the starboard side of the canoe, pulverizing anything that gets in their way—particularly, your head.

To avoid the potential hospital bills involved with sailing by the lee, always do your downwind sailing with the boom on the side of the canoe that is AWAY from the wind (south side in this example). That way, it would take a monster wind shift to get behind the sail and give you a headache.

While reaching, just as while sailing upwind, we can take advantage of wind shifts to get to our destination faster, but it's a little different in concept. We can already make drastic changes in heading by aiming the boat and adjusting the sail to whatever reach it happens to be, so we use the shifts for speed.

If our particular canoe sails fastest on a beam reach, pointed east or west, a wind shift might allow us to stay on a beam reach but actually be headed more upwind or downwind, depending on where we want to go. Just as we saw when going upwind, a shift will either put us on a more direct course to our goal, or on one that takes us farther from it. Tacking or jibing to the favored heading may be the best choice if you think the shift is going to last for a few minutes.

WIND

Close-hauled

Close reach

Beam reach

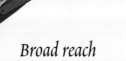

Broad reach

Run

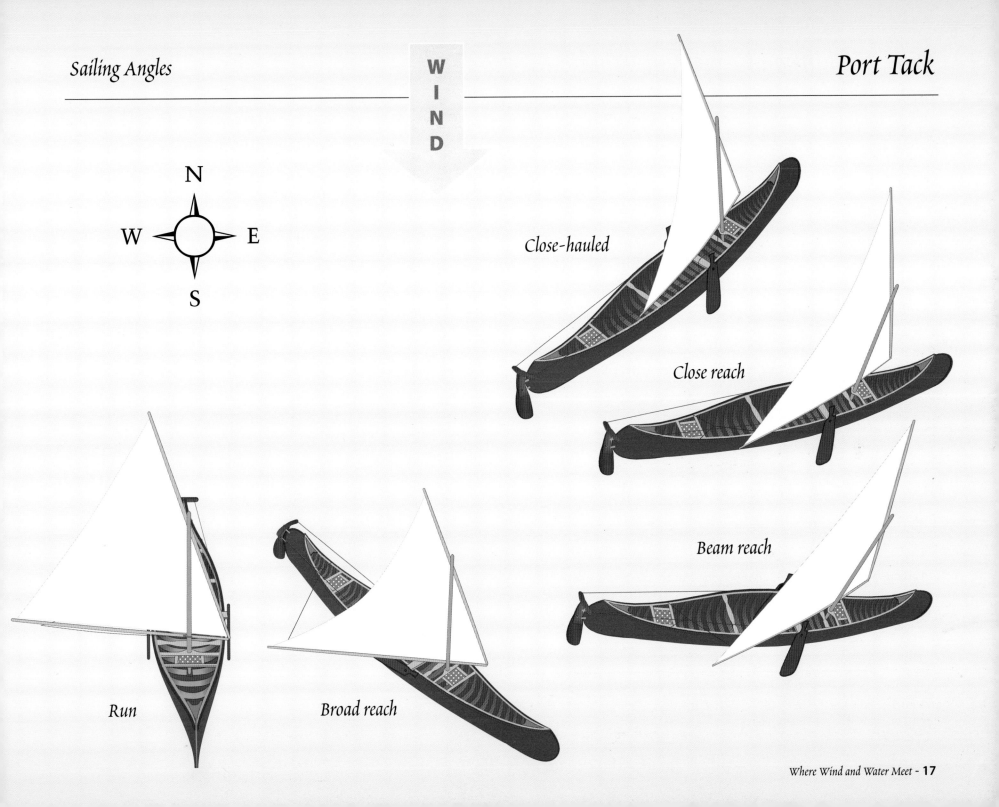

WIND

N
W   E
S

Close-hauled

Close reach

Beam reach

Run

Broad reach

Velocity Shifts and Apparent Wind

An increase in wind speed (velocity shift) can also occur from time to time. At first, it will seem like a change in wind direction. This is because the breeze that we feel and react to while sailing is a combination of the true wind direction and the boat's heading, as the boat moves through the wind. This is called the "apparent wind."

If our wind is from the north and our canoe is sailing toward the west, the wind that we feel, the wind that the sails and the telltales (the small streamers attached to the sail) respond to, will appear to come from somewhere between north and west. If we could stop the boat and check the wind, we would find that it was still from the north, but as we started sailing again, it would again seem to shift slightly westerly. The faster our boat moves, the more westerly our north wind would appear to be.

Iceboats, the fastest sailing craft, can sail many times the speed of the wind propelling them. So fast are these boats that the apparent wind is always blowing in your face (and its really cold, believe me). Since regular sailboats and canoes have to move rather slowly through the water in comparison to iceboats, which skate across a frozen surface, their apparent wind will never shift to the bow of the boat, but it will shift somewhat.

A puff of faster wind—the velocity shift mentioned earlier—can change the apparent wind that both we and the sailboat feel without changing the true wind's direction. Since the apparent wind is an average of true wind and canoe movement, skewed by the relative speeds of both, changing the true wind speed will change the equation. The boat, in turn, may also speed up, because it's getting more wind/power/aerodynamic lift.

Perhaps having to deal with all this is the real reason for the invention of the outboard motor! Don't worry, you will either get the hang of it or learn to ignore it. I know many diehard sailors who wouldn't be able to define apparent wind to save their lives.

The important and surprisingly simple lesson here is that an increase in velocity—changing the apparent wind—will at first seem like a shift in wind direction. Don't be too quick to tack or jibe. Wait a few seconds and then decide whether it's really a directional shift, requiring action, or just a puff that will eventually give you a bit more speed.

What if we had left Pollywog's and our frogburger wasn't sitting too well, and all we wanted to do was get back to the car and seek medical attention? We have already learned that a sailboat can't sail straight upwind, but it CAN sail straight downwind! We could lie in the bottom of the boat moaning, point the bow due south, let the sail out 90 degrees to the line of the keel, and sail home. This is called "running."

Running is usually rather slow and peaceful. The wind that you and the boat feel is the actual wind speed, minus your boat speed. Sometimes, after a windy, spray-filled, upwind leg, turning and running downwind feels as if you came out on an entirely different day.

Here again, boat/sail-rig configuration will determine the actual efficiency of running. It's quite possible in some boats that you may get to the ambulance more quickly by using your sail more as an airfoil, broad-reaching back and forth to go south, than just running straight down, where the sail acts more like a windsock.

Some of the sails now used on canoes and kayaks, and some in this book, are downwind sails only. They can usually be sailed as "high" as a broad reach, but that's about it. They are common for tripping, as they stow easily, and can be used instead of paddles when you are lucky enough to have a favoring breeze.

Obviously, in real life, the wind isn't always out of the north, but these basic sailing principles are the same when the wind blows from any direction.

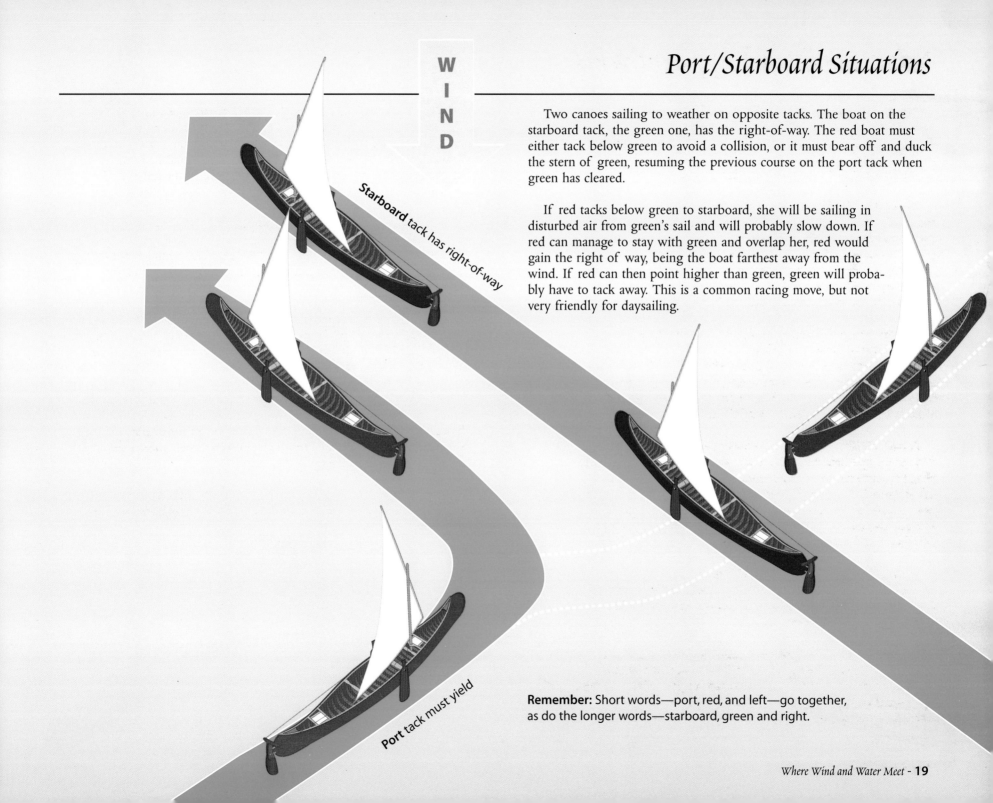

Port/Starboard Situations

Two canoes sailing to weather on opposite tacks. The boat on the starboard tack, the green one, has the right-of-way. The red boat must either tack below green to avoid a collision, or it must bear off and duck the stern of green, resuming the previous course on the port tack when green has cleared.

If red tacks below green to starboard, she will be sailing in disturbed air from green's sail and will probably slow down. If red can manage to stay with green and overlap her, red would gain the right of way, being the boat farthest away from the wind. If red can then point higher than green, green will probably have to tack away. This is a common racing move, but not very friendly for daysailing.

WIND

Starboard tack has right-of-way

Port tack must yield

Remember: Short words—port, red, and left—go together, as do the longer words—starboard, green and right.

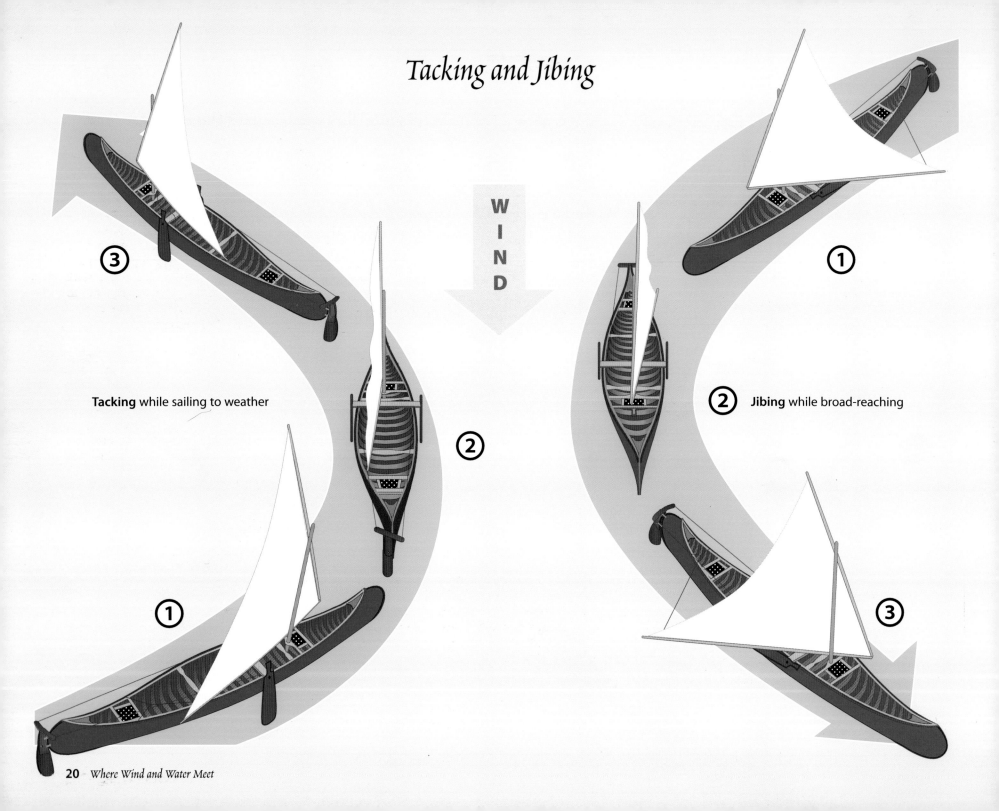

Tacking and Jibing

WIND

Tacking while sailing to weather

Jibing while broad-reaching

Wind Shifts

Destination ↑

This canoe is sailing on a **close-hauled** course, pointing as high as possible, with a north wind. Forty-five degrees off the wind is about as close as most sailboats will sail, so our actual course on this tack is northeasterly.

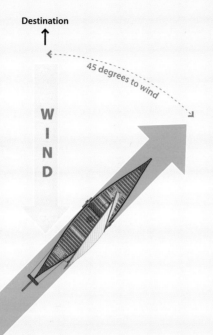

45 degrees to wind

WIND

Destination ↑

45 degrees to wind

WIND

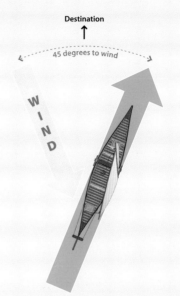

New Course—North-Northeast

Lift

A fairly small westerly shift in wind direction allows us to change our heading—closer to our desired northern objective while still maintaining the same angle to the direction of the wind. We save time and gain distance to weather for as long as the shift lasts. This is called a "**lift**."

Header

Destination ↑

45 degrees to wind

WIND

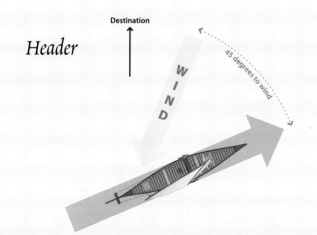

A shift in an easterly direction means we have to bear off to keep our sails full. Our new course is making our trip longer. This is a "**header**." We would be advised to tack. On the other tack, as shown by the boat at right, the header becomes a lift and saves us time.

Destination ↑

45 degrees to wind

WIND

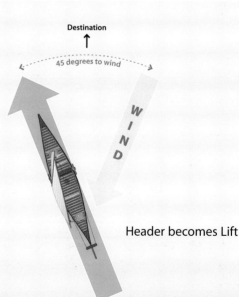

Header becomes Lift

The "Forced Cross"

During one of my more interesting, if not profitable, careers, I worked as a professional hot-air balloon pilot. I flew a giant tomato over college football stadiums for a chain of pizza places. Since I didn't have any money at the time, I was forced to do almost all of my sailing in a Sunfish owned by my brother, who had conveniently moved to the desert and left the boat where there was water.

The sail was pretty bad, so I built a new one out of better fabric and had its shape computer-plotted with the day's most advanced sail-design software. The sail is black, with a hot-pink and lime-green star-cut panel layout. It is probably one of the most high-tech lateen sails ever built and still sails well.

Having nothing else, I sailed that boat in all kinds of wind and waves, and was always amazed by its heavy-weather capabilities. On really windy days, I would modify the halyard to what was called a "Jens rig," named after a well-known Sunfish racer who had pioneered its use.

The Jens rig simply involves tying the halyard of a lateen sail so that it's lashed around the mast, holding the yard close to the mast before it goes up to the halyard lead atop the mast. The entire sail is raised, but in a lower position than usual. This shortens the non-reefable lateen rig and reduces the heeling force on the boat.

Instead of meeting at the usual masthead location, the yard and mast cross 12 to 18 inches lower on the mast, and the boom just clears the deck. The result, also workable in a canoe, is a more controllable boat in high winds.

One problem with Jens-rigging your boat for high winds is boom clearance. Most lateens are rigged with the mainsheet running along the underside of the boom, so when tacking, if the boom doesn't hit you, the temporarily free-hanging mainsheet might try to strangle you.

The Jens-rigged lateen is not the only small-boat sailing rig with this problem. The mainsheet can hang up on your lifejacket or the low boom can come across at high speed during a jibe; both possibilities can be annoying and dangerous. To avoid this some sailors will hang the rig so high that they can nearly walk under it, but those with more experience will know the benefits of a keeping it down where it belongs.

One of the first obvious conclusions about rigs that canoe sailors arrive at is that anything that will contribute to the stability of a 3-foot-wide unballasted sailboat is worth fitting. It greatly outweighs the drawbacks of getting hit in the head or strangled, as long as you can find a means of controlling the risks.

This brings us to what I call the "forced cross," though it really isn't forced, but rather eased. I use a forced cross when I tack and jibe small boats and even when high-wind-jibing our big trimaran. I don't know if anybody else uses the technique, but most canoe sailors should get in the habit. It's easy, it's controlled, and it works.

This seems like a lot of buildup for simply grabbing the boom and the mainsheet hanging from it and bringing them across by hand, before they can bonk or strangle you, but that's it!

At a certain point, during any tack or jibe, the sail begins to luff and the tension on the boom and sheet disappears. During that brief time you can grab the boom and sheet in one hand and swing them over your head to the new side. You can even lift them a bit over your head if clearance is tight.

The forced cross takes less than a second. Then you're ready to concentrate on finishing the tack—without having to wait, ducked down in the bottom of the canoe, for the boom and sheet to wander over or, in the case of a high-wind jibe, to come flying across.

You can't rush a forced cross. If the sail is still catching wind, it may resist mightily, but if you learn when to act, the maneuver will be quite smooth.

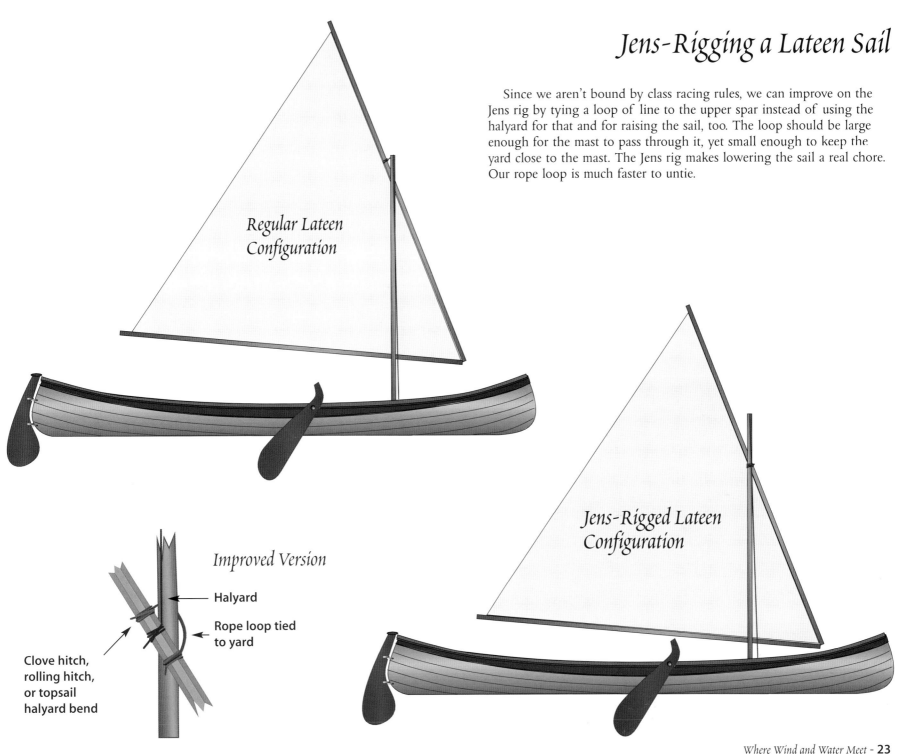

Jens-Rigging a Lateen Sail

Since we aren't bound by class racing rules, we can improve on the Jens rig by tying a loop of line to the upper spar instead of using the halyard for that and for raising the sail, too. The loop should be large enough for the mast to pass through it, yet small enough to keep the yard close to the mast. The Jens rig makes lowering the sail a real chore. Our rope loop is much faster to untie.

Regular Lateen
Configuration

Improved Version

Halyard

Rope loop tied
to yard

Clove hitch,
rolling hitch,
or topsail
halyard bend

Jens-Rigged Lateen
Configuration

Chapter Three

Cloth and Wood

Sail Speak

Before we start comparing sail types, let's look at a couple of sails and label their various parts.

Most of the sailboats that you see these days are "Marconi-rigged." A Marconi mainsail is a tall, triangular sail, like the one shown at right. It can be used with or without a jib and does best set on a hull with a weighted keel to help counter its heeling force. Some canoe sails, such as the lateens, are also three sided, though they are seldom in the shape of a tall, skinny triangle like our sample Marconi.

Many traditional boats use "four-sided" sails, such as the balanced lug canoe sail shown below. The historical transition from the early square sails to the modern, high-aspect Marconis was not instantaneous. There were plenty of variations of both three- and four-sided sails developed during that evolution. Many of these have hung around, especially variations on the four-sided sails, which are quite common on traditional sailboats and canoes—partly for nostalgia, partly because some of them do certain things very well.

As we go through the different possibilities for canoe sails, we'll look at both three- and four-sided options. Regardless, most of the terminology for the sections and parts of sails is the same, though certain models have more parts than others. But, as in the fried chicken commercials, "parts is parts."

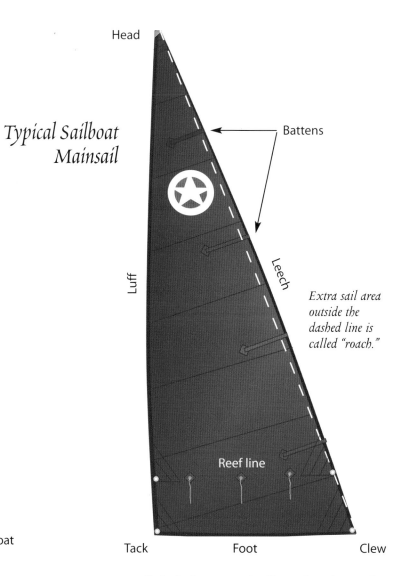

Typical Sailboat Mainsail

Head

Battens

Extra sail area outside the dashed line is called "roach."

Luff

Leech

Reef line

Tack   Foot   Clew

Sails for both canoes and sailboats share the same basic technology and terminology. Canoe sails, however, come in a variety of shapes and types not common to the average sailboat. Their small size, relative affordability, and often the need to stow them aboard has led to a lot of experimentation over the years.

Balanced Lug Canoe Sail

Peak

Head

Leech

Battens

Reef line

Reef line

Throat

Luff

Clew

Tack

Foot

Those Confounded Configurations

Regardless of the vessel it's attached to, a rig is a rig. To the right we have a single-masted craft with only one sail. It is "cat rigged." Many dinghies and canoes are cat rigged, though the shape and size of their single sails will vary. One type of sailboat, a "catboat," is a cat-rigged traditional sailboat developed in New England. The catboat's mast is stepped way up in the bow. A "catamaran," such as a Hobie-Cat, is a twin-hulled sailboat that may be cat rigged but is actually more commonly seen with a sloop rig.

The Cat Rig

The Sloop Rig

At left we see a "sloop rig." This is the typical rig with a single mast, a mainsail, and a jib that is so common on sailboats these days. Jibs can be various shapes and sizes. Many boats carry several different jibsails for different conditions. On a "fractional rig" like this one, the jibstay (the wire that the jib is attached to) only goes partway up the mast. On a "masthead rig" it would go all the way to the top, as would the head of the jib.

The sloop rig isn't common on canoes. It almost always needs additional rigging to pull back the mast to keep tension on the jibstay. It is usually better suited for a taller, narrower sail plan.

The Ketch Rig

On the left we see a "ketch rig," which is common to both sailboats and canoes. Spreading a lot of sail without being too tall reduces the wind's power to force the boat over on its side. This is actually a "cat ketch," because it has no jib. Most ketch-rigged canoes are cat ketches. Most regular sailboats with a ketch rig carry one or more jibs and are therefore considered true ketches.

The Yawl Rig

The "yawl rig" is similar to the ketch, but the mizzen—the smaller, after sail on a ketch or yawl—is very small. Unlike the ketch, which carries a mizzen to provide additional power, the yawl uses the mizzen primarily for balance. Sailboats are designed to balance the power of the wind, captured by the sails, against the resistance of the water. The small mizzen on a yawl doesn't add much power, but it adjusts the point at which the sail power is acting on the hull. This improves the handling and steering of some boats.

On a canoe, using a mizzen allows the mainmast to be moved forward, providing more room in the middle of the boat for the crew.

A schooner has two or more masts, though for canoe purposes, two masts are enough. The after mast is called the mainmast and the forward one the foremast.

Since it has no jib, the rig at the right is a "cat schooner." Though there are a few big cat schooners, most large craft with a schooner rig carry at least one jib and often topsails set above the main and foresail shown here.

The schooner is an uncommon rig for a canoe, but not impossible. I show one later in this book that is a rather interesting-looking rig. Like a ketch, the schooner spreads a low and wide sail plan to reduce the heeling lever of the rig.

The Schooner Rig

The Cutter Rig

With a mainsail and two jibs (technically, the inner one is called the forestaysail and the outer one the jib), the "cutter rig" is both lovely and practical. If the wind comes up, you can furl the jib and still have a jib, if you know what I mean. Unfortunately, I have yet to find a good use for a cutter rig on a canoe. Loading the boat with a lot of sail up forward means moving back the mast into the already limited space for the crew. Plus, on some vessels, the jib and bowsprit interfere with the faucet....

It's almost impossible to rig a canoe as a "ship," "brig," "bark," or "barkentine," so I'll spare you their descriptions.

Other Ways

Though for canoes the lateen rig may be the most common, there are many others that have found their way onto canoes in the past and a few that might still. As sailing equipment goes, the components of a canoe rig are quite affordable, which opens the door for experimentation.

The sailing success of any given rig, at least in this book, is a combination of (a) does it work? and (b) does it look good on the boat? You will have to look long and hard to find a sailing book that seems as preoccupied with the cosmetics of rig design and sail construction, but I have always believed that the first rule of boatbuilding is, there is no excuse for an ugly boat!

High-quality work can be beautiful, but bad work never will be. To restore a neglected old boat—spending hours sanding, cleaning, filling, and varnishing—you must be driven by how the boat will look as well as how it will work. I don't consider myself to be particularly vain, but when I go to the launching ramp with a rescued and restored old boat I expect to get compliments…and not necessarily about the clothes I'm wearing!

The remainder of this chapter is a look at the various possibilities for canoe rigs. Most are general-purpose rigs, like the lateen. A few are designed just for downwind sailing, where the sail is as much a wind-catching device as an aerodynamic one. On those days when both you and the wind happen to be going in the same direction, they're a bit more efficient than having your bow paddler hold up his poncho.

Some of the systems require more rigging or hardware than others, but most of the items aren't difficult to produce with available materials. More-detailed descriptions of individual parts and components will follow the overview.

Other than rudder fittings, no sail rig requires the drilling of any holes in your boat, and most canoes could be switched from rig to rig in only minutes.

Which Rig Is Best?

To be honest, I don't know. I'm not sure anybody knows. Anyone who tells you that they think they know is probably lying.

In order to answer the question, we would have to try all of the rigs in various sizes on the same canoe and in the same but varied conditions.

This is the kind of stuff that *America's Cup* syndicates spend millions of dollars doing, and after dissecting hundreds of tank-tests, computer simulations, and real on-the-water trials—you know what?—THEY STILL DON'T KNOW!

All we can do is make educated predictions based upon the characteristics of certain sail types and be glad that our brand of experimentation is a lot more affordable than *America's Cup* contenders'.

Some bottles are best left unopened

Gunter Rigs

The Gunter Rig comes in many forms: single or twin; straight or curved leech; full, short, or no battens. This one is from an old 14-foot sailing Peterborough. We had the spars, and the original sails were still in good enough shape to be measured. As the "mast" is divided into two parts, the rig can be stored in a shorter space than most. This little boat has a lot of sail area, so we added a line of reef points on each sail for those times when it's too windy for carrying full sail. The luff of each sail (the leading edge) is fitted with rings that slide up a metal rod attached to the after side of the mast. The heel of the topmast slides up the same rod and then swivels up to vertical on small brass hinge fittings. The sails are laced to the topmasts and the booms. It wouldn't be too difficult to duplicate this system today, but some gunter rigs are a bit simpler and less "hardware intensive." In all of them, the mast is divided into two sections, which make the rig more portable than a single, longer-masted rig would be.

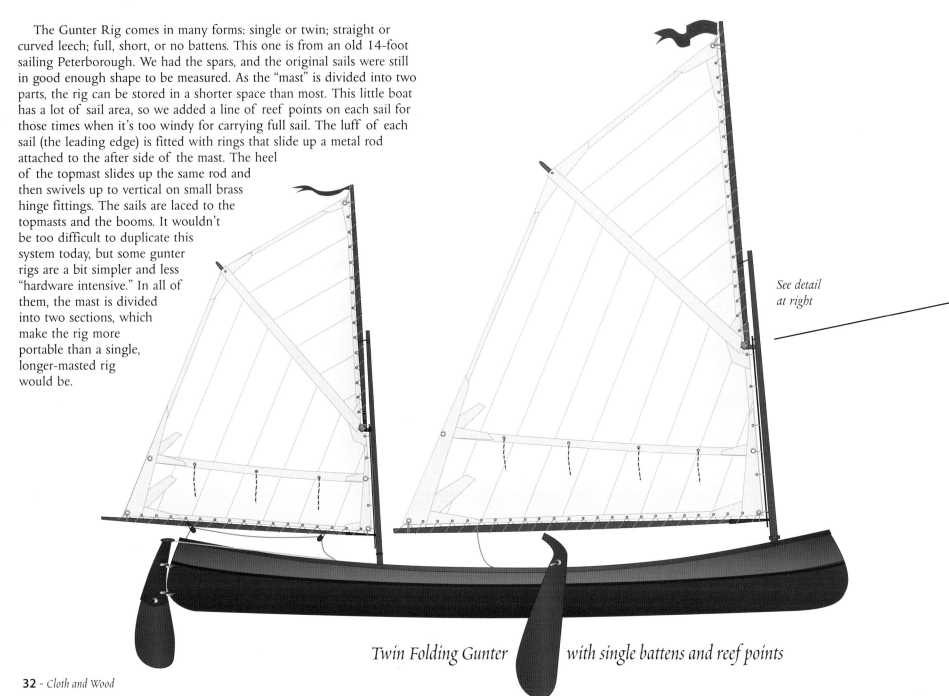

See detail at right

Twin Folding Gunter   *with single battens and reef points*

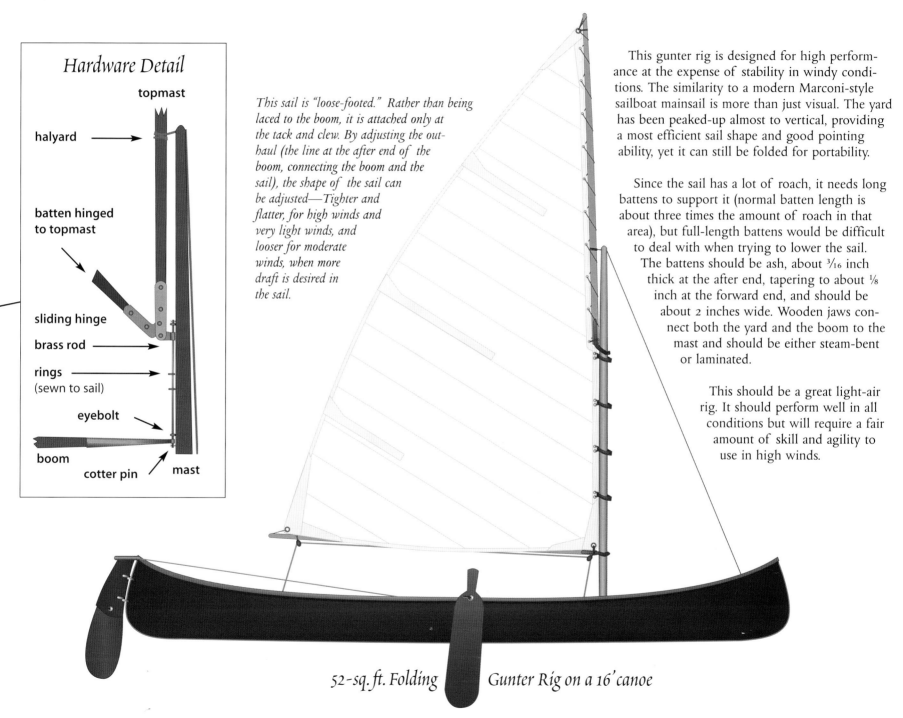

Hardware Detail

topmast

halyard

batten hinged to topmast

sliding hinge

brass rod

rings
(sewn to sail)

eyebolt

boom

cotter pin   mast

This sail is "loose-footed." Rather than being laced to the boom, it is attached only at the tack and clew. By adjusting the out-haul (the line at the after end of the boom, connecting the boom and the sail), the shape of the sail can be adjusted—Tighter and flatter, for high winds and very light winds, and looser for moderate winds, when more draft is desired in the sail.

This gunter rig is designed for high perform-ance at the expense of stability in windy condi-tions. The similarity to a modern Marconi-style sailboat mainsail is more than just visual. The yard has been peaked-up almost to vertical, providing a most efficient sail shape and good pointing ability, yet it can still be folded for portability.

Since the sail has a lot of roach, it needs long battens to support it (normal batten length is about three times the amount of roach in that area), but full-length battens would be difficult to deal with when trying to lower the sail. The battens should be ash, about 3/16 inch thick at the after end, tapering to about 1/8 inch at the forward end, and should be about 2 inches wide. Wooden jaws con-nect both the yard and the boom to the mast and should be either steam-bent or laminated.

This should be a great light-air rig. It should perform well in all conditions but will require a fair amount of skill and agility to use in high winds.

52-sq. ft. Folding   Gunter Rig on a 16' canoe

Leg-o'-Mutton Sail

Despite its peculiar name, the Leg-o'-Mutton Sail is really a low-aspect (not too tall and skinny), jib-headed (pointed at the top) predecessor to the modern mainsail that most sailboats carry. The leg-o'-mutton has been used on whaling boats, iceboats, and surf dories. A small version of it can look pretty good on the right canoe, too.

The mast is about 13 feet long and tapered. The boom is joined to the mast with a set of wooden jaws and is rigged with a simple downhaul to keep it from climbing the mast and to adjust tension on the sail's luff. The sail is attached to the mast with wooden hoops that slide up and down, and to the boom with "robands" (small, individual ties).

The same basic sail shape can also be used with a gunter rig by dividing the mast into two sections and redesigning the sail's luff to allow for the jog around the folding or sliding-joint assembly as seen on the previous page.

This simple rig still presents a very classy package with a saltwater surfboat flavor. It's different from the average canoe rig, yet still looks as if it's supposed to be there.

I think the trick is matching the rig's shape to the boat's shape. In this case, even slight changes to the shape of the rudder and the leeboard help sell the package.

The sail, with roped edges and hand-sewn corner rings, echoes the saltwater look and is stronger as well.

The mast is raked slightly aft (it leans back) to keep it from looking as if it's falling forward and to move the C.E. (center of effort, to be discussed later) back. The mast step was positioned accordingly.

The taller-than-average sail plan has more heeling lever than most canoe rigs, but should sail quite well, especially in light air.

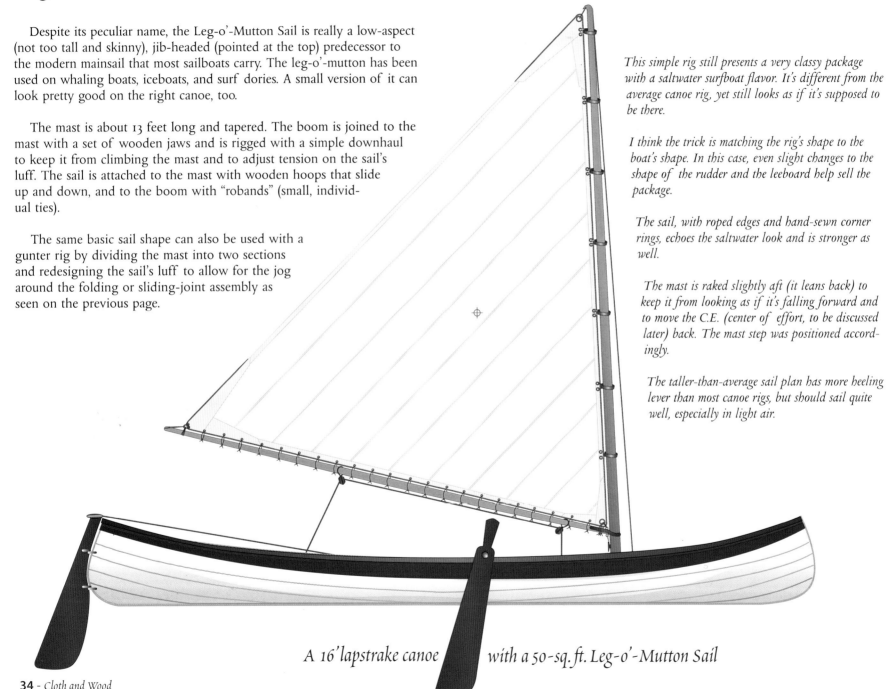

A 16' lapstrake canoe with a 50-sq. ft. Leg-o'-Mutton Sail

The Gaff-Cat Rig

This Gaff-Cat Rig was designed for a friend who wanted to put a small gaff sail on a canoe and stick it way up in the bow, like a catboat, to get it out of the way. The problem with this is that if the wind is anything but "light," the boat will always want to turn downwind and run away. With the addition of a tiny lateen mizzen to the stern, the balance of the rig should be much better and will probably make the boat easier to control, despite the increase in sail area, and not much of the interior of the canoe will be obstructed.

Better balance was one of the main reasons that many traditional sailing canoes had twin sails. Another, as we see on the twin lateen rig, was to increase sail area for performance without having to increase mast and sail height and the "heeling power" of the rig.

The small wire forestay and spreader strut on the gaff sail's mast are to prevent the mast from bending due to sheeting and gaff loads.

This boat will sail better as a "yawl" with a small mizzen aft to help balance the helm. A gaff cat with a swallow-tail!

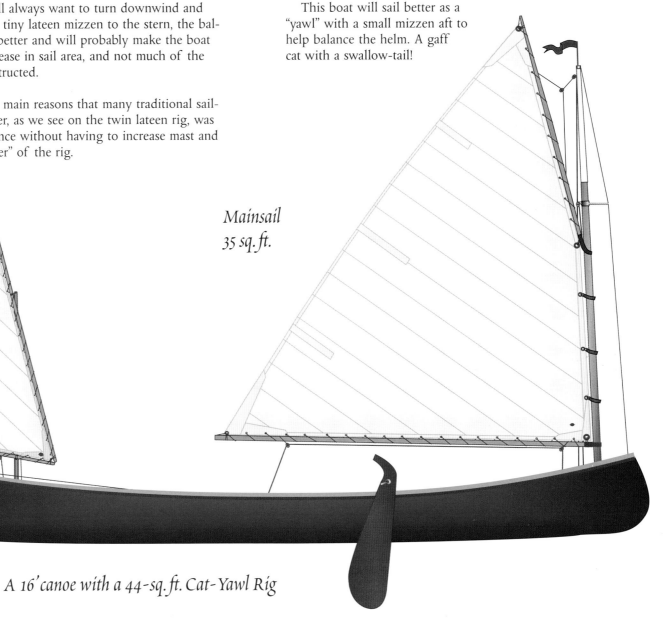

Mizzen
9 sq.ft.

Mainsail
35 sq.ft.

A 16' canoe with a 44-sq.ft. Cat-Yawl Rig

Bat-Wing Sails

The Bat-Wing Sail uses full-length battens to support a large leech roach and is quite distinctive in appearance. The two on this boat are essentially modified gunter sails. The mast/topmast system is similar to the gunter rig showed previously but has been built without metal parts.

The battens can ride inside fabric sleeves, but those in this plan are of thin, varnished wood and are laced, or tied, to the outside of the sail, on both sides, through small grommets—Chinese junk-style—which is partly responsible for this rig's unusual look.

It is possible to lower the sail and reef out the bottom slab in high winds. It would be worth the effort to rig both throat and peak halyards: the former to raise the sail, and the latter to adjust the topmast angle and the sail twist.

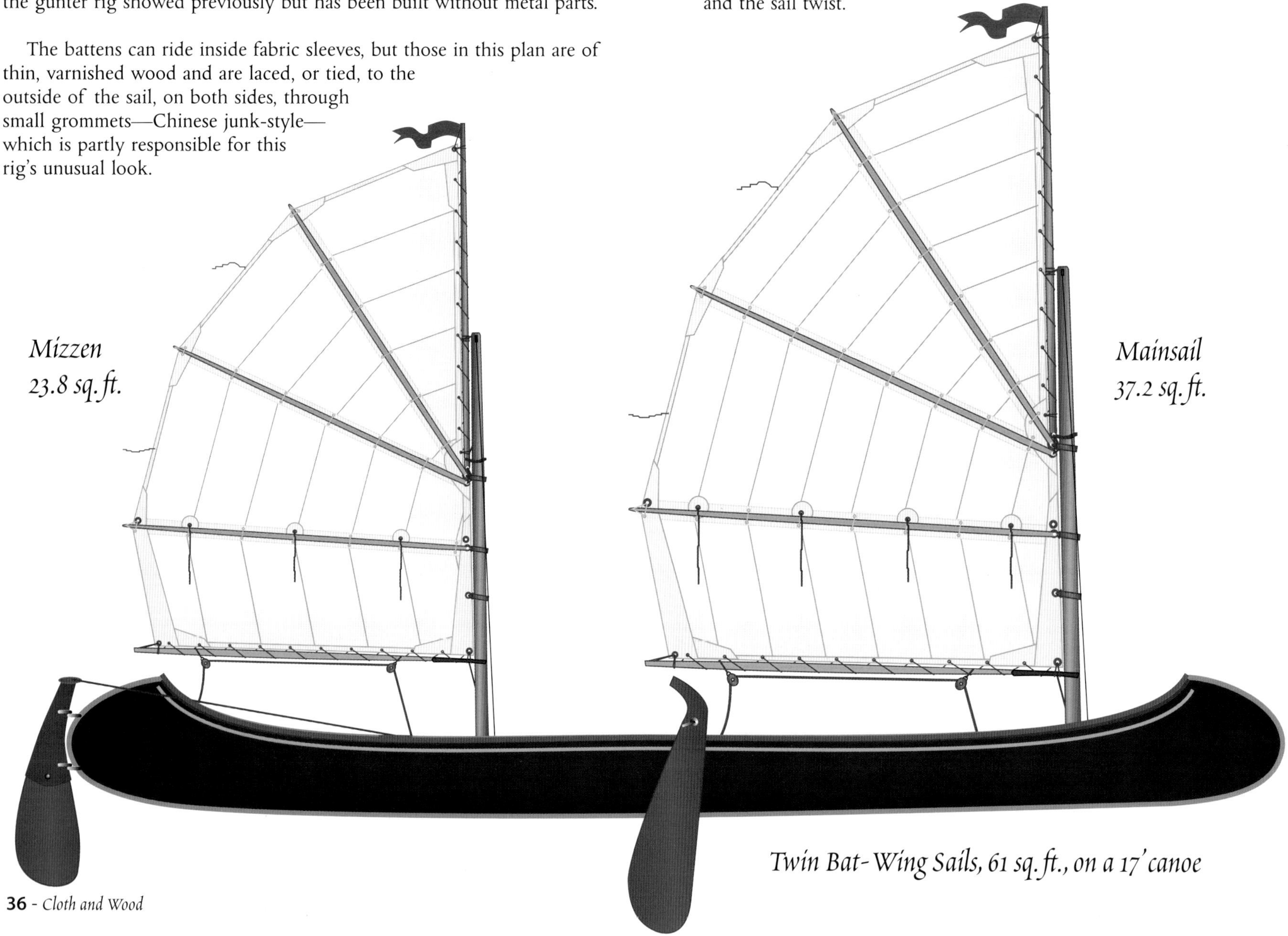

Mizzen
23.8 sq. ft.

Mainsail
37.2 sq. ft.

Twin Bat-Wing Sails, 61 sq. ft., on a 17' canoe

Bat-Wing Variations

Here we see three different bat-wing configurations. The top canoe has more sail area due to the extreme roach along the leeches. There is actually more roach area than standard measured sail area, which is the imaginary triangle from the tack to the peak to the clew. Since bat-wings have so much roach, I usually calculate the actual area of each section, batten-to-batten, and add them up to determine the true, total area of the sail. Adding area to the top of a sail allows it to catch more wind, but it can cause extreme amounts of twist and may require heavy battens for support.

The two boats at the bottom have modified bat-wing sails, with the battens spread along the luff (rather than fanning out from a single point) and more normal roaches. The black canoe's sails are each made from four major panels, seamed beneath the enclosed batten sleeves. Though not as fancy-looking as the narrow-paneled sails, these would be easier to build, and the battens would still show through when the sails are back-lit.

Maxi-Roach Bat-Wings.

Four-Panel, Modified
Bat-Wing sails with sleeves for battens.
Arrows indicate the threadlines of the panel fabric.

Not a true bat-wing, but very similar.

The Balanced Lug Rig

The Balanced Lug is one of several styles of lugsail rig, having a mast and a yard (the upper spar) that hangs at an angle from the top of the mast and extends partially forward of it. A balanced lug has the sail's leading edge parallel to the mast, forward of the mast, and has a boom. Some lug rigs don't share these features.

Having at least part of the sail area on either side of the mast (or on either side of the boat when the sail is eased out to go downwind) and supported by both a yard and a boom helps make it more controllable—hence "balanced."

Balanced lug rigs were common on early decked sailing canoes. Many of these canoes were fairly small solo boats set up more like a kayak than a modern canoe. They were used for canoe-tripping and racing.

Twin, Balanced Lug Sails with batten reefing

Some of these boats had a centerboard that folded like a fan into a box built along the keel.

Here is the same boat with two more options, but both still use balanced lug sails. The sail on the left came from a drawing by Christine Erikson that appears in *The Sailmaker's Apprentice*, by Emiliano Marino (International Marine Publishing Company, Camden, Maine). If you are interested in building or just understanding traditional sails, this book is required reading—the absolute best of the lot! The sail is a fully battened, balanced lug built in the Chinese lugsail style. I drew it out for measurement because I liked its "paper-lantern" look. It would be a very striking sail to put on a varnished wooden canoe.

The second sail is a battenless, vertical-cut, balanced lug in tanbark-colored Dacron. This is a simple, no-nonsense working sail. Notice that the mast will interfere with the shape of the sail on one tack. This happens on most lugsails, lateens, and a few other sail types. Though you would think it a potentially serious performance problem, on the water it doesn't really seem to be worth worrying about; you generally don't even think about it while sailing.

The Sprit Boom Rig

The Sprit Boom Rig is one of the simplest sail rigs around. The sail can be attached to the mast by lacing or a sewn-on sleeve, and the sprit boom itself is little more than a stick. The sprit boom is attached to the clew (after corner) of the sail and held close to the mast, in front, by an adjustable line—usually called a "snotter"— that pushes it back and down.

By adjusting the lashing's tension, you can easily and quickly adjust the sail's draft from deep to none. After the sprit boom has been dropped, the sail can be furled by rolling it around the mast.

Some people have even built curved sprit booms, so that the sprit boom doesn't interfere with the shape of the sail on one tack. The most advanced versions of these have twin, curved, wishbone sprit booms and are called "windsurfers"! Also feasible in a twin-sail rig, the sail's panels could be laid out as vertical-cut, cross-cut, or miter-cut as shown here.

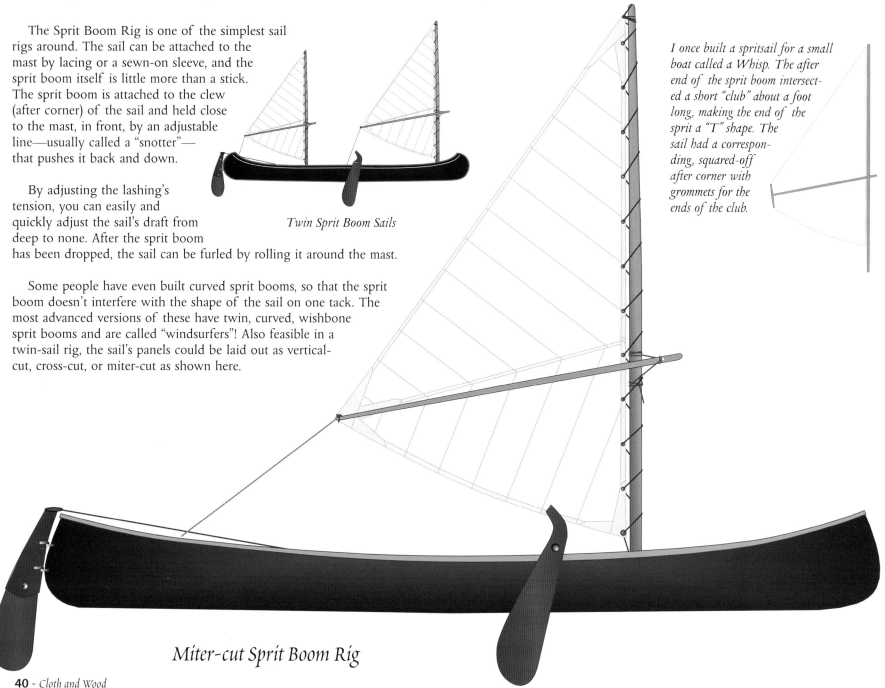

Twin Spirt Boom Sails

I once built a spritsail for a small boat called a Whisp. The after end of the sprit boom intersected a short "club" about a foot long, making the end of the sprit a "T" shape. The sail had a corresponding, squared-off after corner with grommets for the ends of the club.

Miter-cut Sprit Boom Rig

The Sprit Rig

The Sprit Rig is one of the most popular traditional rigs and is often the rig of choice for small dinghies. Its simplicity and effectiveness, and the fact that a sail hitting you in the head hurts a lot less than a boom would, makes it a good choice for any small boat. The luff of the sail is laced to the mast, and the sprit props up the peak. Sprit tension is adjustable via the line or block where the sprit and mast meet.

Spritsails are usually equipped with a "brail," a line that runs around the upper half of the sail, through a small block near the masthead, and down the mast. Pulling and cleating the brailing line collapses the sail and sprit against the mast: a very fast and effective way to furl a sail.

For those interested in a simple, easy-to-build-and-assemble sailing rig, the spritsail coupled with paddle steering is excellent.

I saw these leeboards in an old Chestnut Canoe catalog. They are rather unusual in shape and have a handle that reminds me of a goose.

Tying off the halyard to a bow thwart or the fore deck as shown here can sometimes help to support the mast.

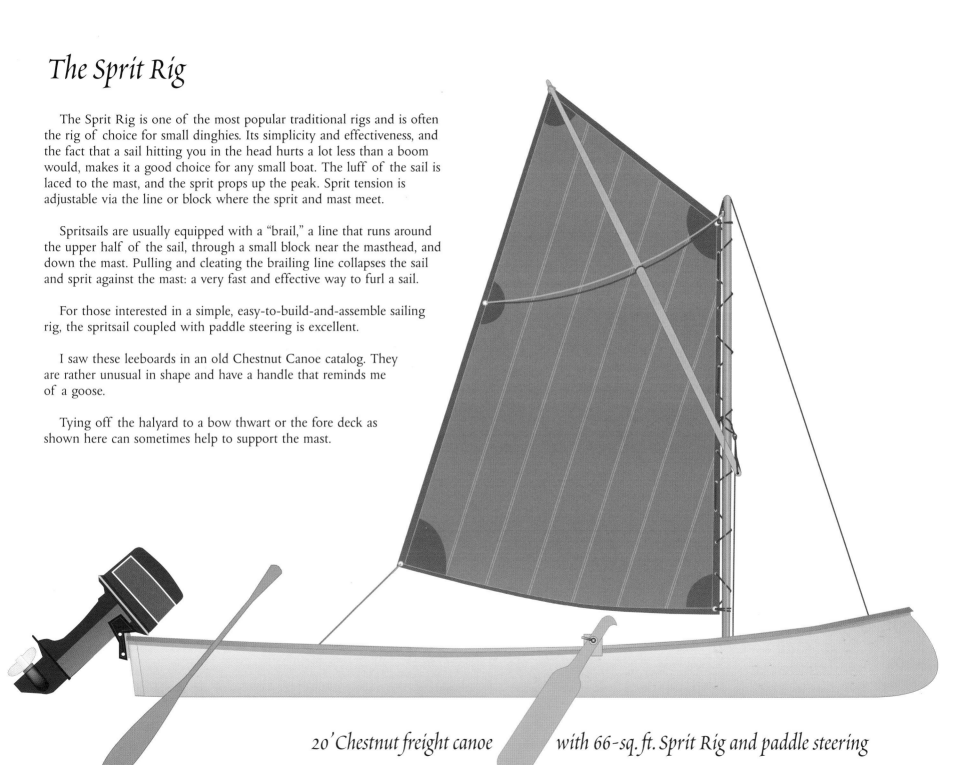

20' Chestnut freight canoe   *with 66-sq. ft. Sprit Rig and paddle steering*

The Standing Lug Rig

The Standing Lug Rig is one of the more traditional sail rigs and is used on a variety of small craft. It is user-friendly, reasonably efficient, and reef-able, and will come down in a hurry—should the need arise.

The yard is raised by a single halyard and kept close to the mast, up top, by a rope loop, usually fitted with parrel beads. Strung on the loop, these beads act as wooden ball-bearings when raising or lowering sail.

The boom may have either jaws that straddle the mast or a fixed mechanical gooseneck fitting connecting it to the mast.

Most standing lug sails are vertically paneled. Panels 10 to 15 inches wide would be a good choice here.

If you are building a lugsail, or having one built for you, it is a good idea to reinforce the un-supported leading edge (the luff) by roping that portion of the sail. Sewing a short length of rope onto or into the edge between the spars will greatly increase strength and durability of this somewhat vulnerable area of your sail.

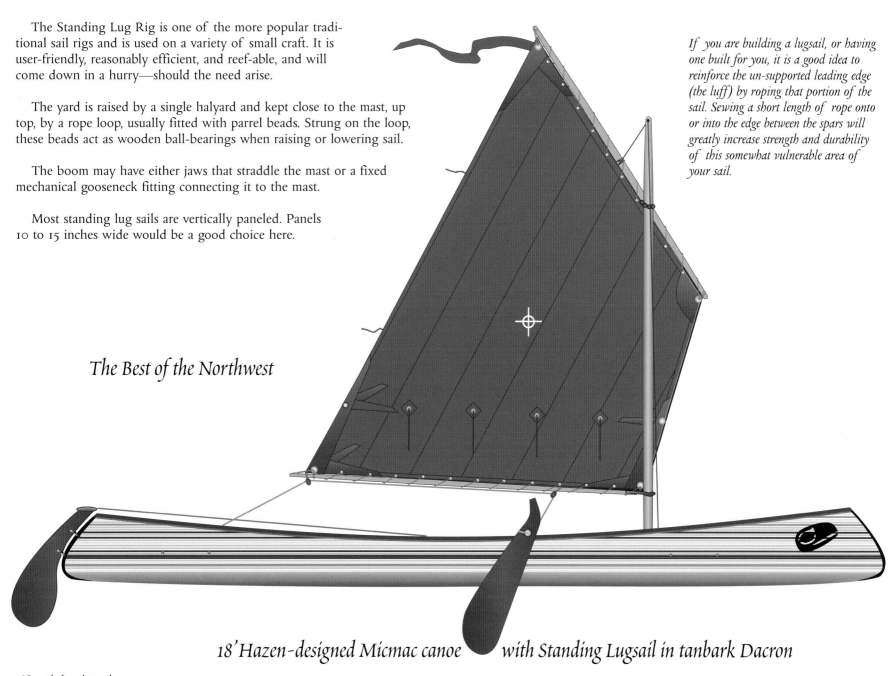

The Best of the Northwest

18' Hazen-designed Micmac canoe *with Standing Lugsail in tanbark Dacron*

The Wood-Strip/Fiberglass Canoe

Adding a sail rig to a strip canoe is often easier than it is on a wood-and-canvas boat, especially if you are building the canoe yourself. In new construction, blocking for rudder gudgeons, mast supports, and hardware can be designed into the plan, rather than be retrofitted. You may have to beef up the gunwales a bit, at least in the area where the leeboard bracket will clamp on, since many strippers are designed with minimal gunwales to save weight. Reinforcements can be attached with screws, epoxy, and, dare I say, even fiberglass if necessary.

No, a stripper rigged for sail won't be a true traditional boat, but it will still look great with wooden spars and a traditional sail. Though many traditionalists turn up their noses at these lovely composite canoes, by now they have been firmly entrenched in the sport for twenty-five to thirty years.

The strip canoe drawn here was custom-built for me in 1975 by Wilderness Boats Inc. of Carlton, Oregon. It was not as traditional or as pretty on the inside as my Old Town Guide is, but it was light, very seaworthy, and the fastest tripping boat that I have ever seen.

On its first trip across Ontario's Quetico Provincial Park, we were stopped several times by rangers—not because we were doing anything wrong, but because they had heard that the boat was in the park and wanted to see it! One ranger even jumped, fully dressed, from the dock into chest-deep water to help me put on the spray skirt.

David Hazen's book, *The Stripper's Guide to Canoe Building* (Tamal Vista), is still available and worth reading. However, modern epoxy resins should be seriously considered as a replacement for the polyesters Hazen used in the 1970s and recommends in the book. But wood is still wood.

Hazen's book includes plans for two double kayaks and half a dozen canoes. Having paddled or built most of them, I can tell you that the 17- and 18-foot Micmacs are the gems of the lot—great, all-purpose boats. Unfortunately, nobody in the East thought anybody in Oregon knew anything about canoes. The most easterly Wilderness Boats dealer was in Illinois—me. But make no mistake about it, Hazen's ravens can still fly. Build one with Sitka spruce strips and epoxy resin, Hazen's double-bar portage yoke, and caned seats instead of the suggested canvas slings, and you will have a superb boat.

Tanbark

In the days when tannic-acid-based preservatives were applied to cotton sails, they usually turned a dark, reddish brown color, mimicked by today's tanbark-colored Dacron. This cloth is commonly used for traditional-style sails on boats of all sizes.

Remember, sails were dunked in preservative only after they were completed. If you are building, or having a tanbark sail made for you and wish it to look reasonably believable, the entire sail, including the edges, roping, etc., should be the same color. I even pre-stain the hand-sewing thread that I use for corner rings and finishing when I build a sail from tanbark Dacron. Your sailmaker might fight you on such a fine point, because it's a lot more work for him to make all the sail's parts in a matching color, but it's nevertheless a lot more correct.

The Sloop Rig

The Sloop Rig, with a mainsail and a jib, is the most common sailboat rig, but it is rare on canoes. To get a jib to work properly, we almost are forced to brace the mast with shrouds and a forestay to keep the jib luff from sagging to leeward. Fitting a jib also tends to require moving the mast aft, eating up more of our already limited crew space. This canoe has a self-tacking jib on a club boom. Total rig height is only about 10 feet, so it won't be a great pointer, but the rig is an interesting concept and has a certain charm.

The jib halyard and forestay are combined. The halyard ties to the sail at the head, runs through a block shackled to the masthead, then down to the bow deck, passing through brass rings on the sail luff. It then runs up to the tack, pulling down on the jib, and is tied off or cleated.

I borrowed this rig from a group of peculiar old iceboats called Great South Bay Ice Scooters. Like this canoe, they had big jibs, small mains, and short rigs. The interesting part is that they had no steering gear.

By adjusting the sheets and thus the pressure on the sails, the crew could make the boat head up or bear off as desired, though apparently such a system sometimes lacked a bit of precision. The same concept might work on a canoe—without having to bolt rudder fittings to the boat. The latter alone might make eliminating the steering gear worth trying. A rudder could always be added later if the system didn't pan out.

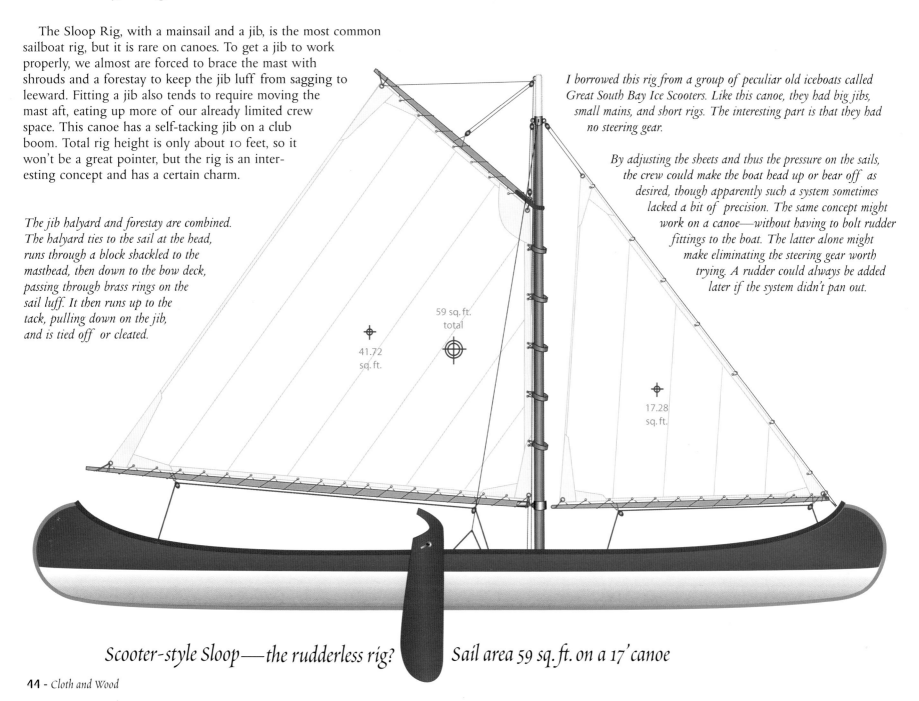

59 sq. ft.
total

41.72 sq. ft.

17.28 sq. ft.

Scooter-style Sloop—the rudderless rig?   *Sail area 59 sq. ft. on a 17' canoe*

Gaff Sails, Schooner Rig

This twin is technically a Gaff Schooner, as the larger mast—the mainmast—is aft. I wanted to see if I could put a schooner rig on a 17-foot Otca canoe without making it look stupid. The center of effort is slightly higher than that of the twin lateen, but the sail area is substantially less. The foresail is boomless, and the leeboard bracket and mainmast thwart are combined into one unit. This rig is a good candidate for laminated, hollow masts to reduce weight aloft while keeping the masts as stiff as possible to take the strains of the gaff sails without bending too much.

The masts are raked, and therefore the placement of the mast steps must take that into consideration. I'm not really sure why anyone would need a canoe/schooner (canooner or schoonoe?) but it would probably sail pretty well and definitely would be quite unusual.

Oh, well…

To help control mast bend and rake, and take some strain off the mast step on days when the wind comes up, it might be a good idea to add a stay connecting the mast heads and running down to the bow deck.

52.87 sq. ft. total

31.26 sq. ft.

21.61 sq. ft

A 17′ Otca canoe rigged as a Gaff Schooner

Squaresails

A Square Rig is not the most versatile or efficient, but it does have a certain charm. When I first drew one on a canoe, I instantly thought, "This looks like a Viking ship!" (another boat that I've always wanted, though it's pretty far down on the list of what to build next). If your idea of canoe sailing is to take advantage of the breeze when it favors you, a squaresail might work well—and make an aesthetic statement at the same time.

A stubby mast, a yard laced to the top of the sail (wider sails might sometimes need another one or a pole to spread the bottom corners), and a few feet of rope, and you're ready to set off for Greenland! If the wind comes up, let go the halyard and drop the sail to the gunwale. Reefing is possible, as are various sail sizes, though I think I'd rather err on the small side.

If you really want to be salty, you could furl the sail to the yard and hoist it aloft. After all, what is a Viking ship? A great big sailing canoe full of really hairy guys!

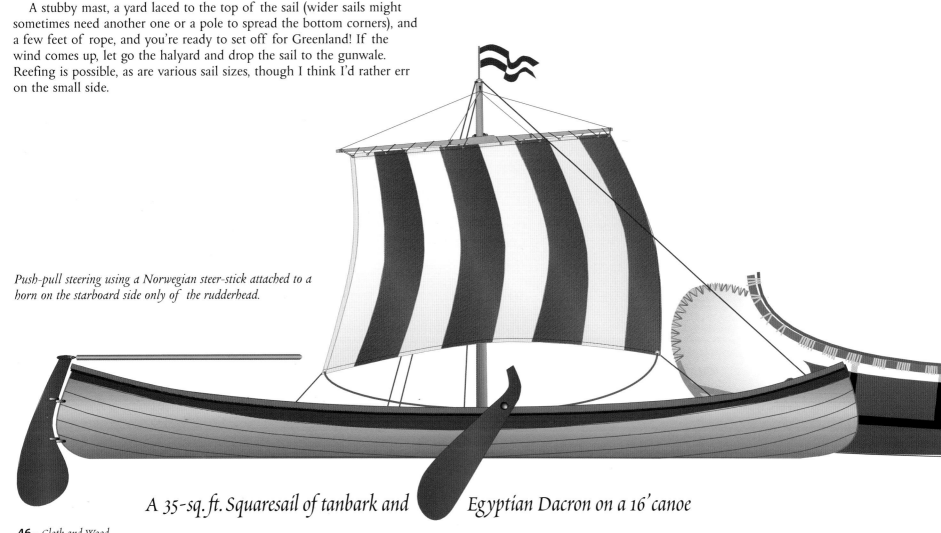

Push-pull steering using a Norwegian steer-stick attached to a horn on the starboard side only of the rudderhead.

A 35-sq. ft. Squaresail of tanbark and Egyptian Dacron on a 16' canoe

Voyageur-Style Square Rig

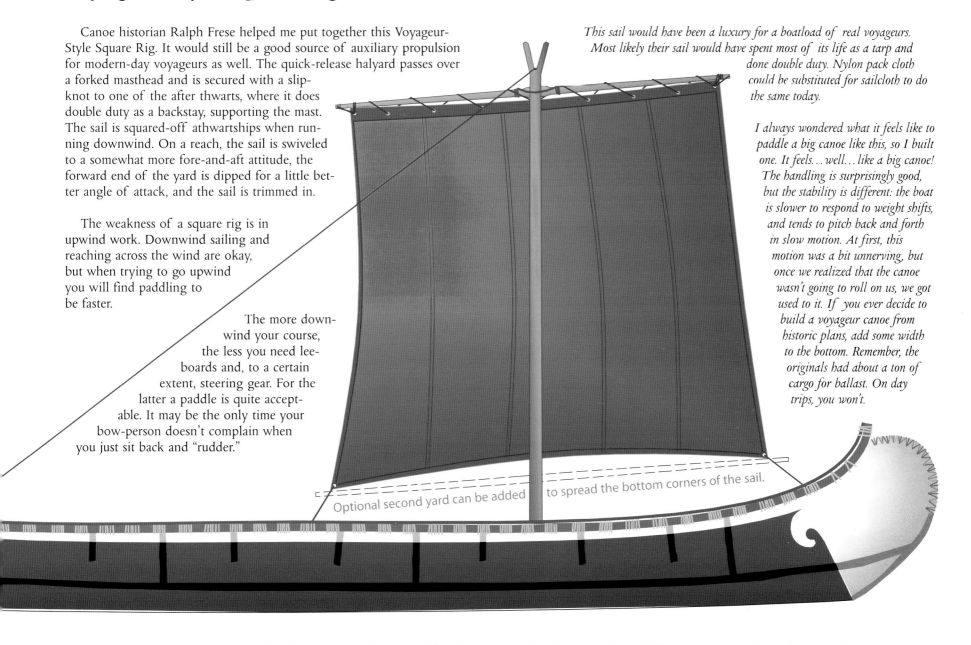

Canoe historian Ralph Frese helped me put together this Voyageur-Style Square Rig. It would still be a good source of auxiliary propulsion for modern-day voyageurs as well. The quick-release halyard passes over a forked masthead and is secured with a slip-knot to one of the after thwarts, where it does double duty as a backstay, supporting the mast. The sail is squared-off athwartships when running downwind. On a reach, the sail is swiveled to a somewhat more fore-and-aft attitude, the forward end of the yard is dipped for a little better angle of attack, and the sail is trimmed in.

The weakness of a square rig is in upwind work. Downwind sailing and reaching across the wind are okay, but when trying to go upwind you will find paddling to be faster.

The more downwind your course, the less you need leeboards and, to a certain extent, steering gear. For the latter a paddle is quite acceptable. It may be the only time your bow-person doesn't complain when you just sit back and "rudder."

This sail would have been a luxury for a boatload of real voyageurs. Most likely their sail would have spent most of its life as a tarp and done double duty. Nylon pack cloth could be substituted for sailcloth to do the same today.

I always wondered what it feels like to paddle a big canoe like this, so I built one. It feels…well…like a big canoe! The handling is surprisingly good, but the stability is different: the boat is slower to respond to weight shifts, and tends to pitch back and forth in slow motion. At first, this motion was a bit unnerving, but once we realized that the canoe wasn't going to roll on us, we got used to it. If you ever decide to build a voyageur canoe from historic plans, add some width to the bottom. Remember, the originals had about a ton of cargo for ballast. On day trips, you won't.

Optional second yard can be added to spread the bottom corners of the sail.

North canoe with tanbark Squaresail, rigged for downwind sailing with paddle steering and without leeboards

Baidarka Fan Sails

These interesting downwind sails were featured in George Dyson's book *Baidarka* (Alaska Northwest Books). They caught my eye because they were so "organic" looking. A kayak—which is what a baidarka is—being propelled by such a large seashell conjures up visions of Captain Nemo himself, sitting at the helm. If you've ever wanted to see a guy build a beautiful, basically quite traditional kayak from aluminum tubing and recycled stop signs, get Dyson's book. It's fascinating!

The Fan Sail would work on a canoe as well as on a kayak. The mast is inside the center sleeve, and battens occupy the remaining sleeves. Wedges can be reefed out in pairs (port and starboard), starting at the bottom. Fully reefed, only the two center panels would be catching the wind.

The fan rig is simple but elegant in design, portable, and adjustable. When the wind is at your back, the fan could be a good reason to put your feet up and enjoy the view. Captain Nemo would approve.

Steered with a paddle, no leeboards required for downwind sailing—this rig is easily stowable for tripping.

A Fan Sail on a canoe, viewed from the bow

The V-Sail Rig

The V-Sail Rig is sometimes used on tripping canoes and kayaks as an easy way to get a break from paddling. It is strictly a downwind rig and won't point any higher than a broad reach, but if the wind is heading your direction, it will only take a few seconds to set up. The tack corner is tied down to a thwart and the spars are held up by wind power. The sailor holds the sheets and can swivel the sail a bit to help catch the best wind and adjust the sail's effect on the boat's movement. Using this rig is almost like flying a captive kite.

This is a very easy sail to build and would be a great first project. The spars can vary from the size of a broomstick to that of a closet pole, depending on how big you want your sail to be. A little taper, especially at the top ends of the spars, looks good and keeps the flying weight down for better performance.

The sailcloth could be lightweight nylon or regular Dacron sail fabric. I think I would favor the stretch resistance and durability of the Dacron, even though it's heavier.

If it's carefully made, this rig will be pretty classy and look quite respectable on a traditional boat, even though it's much simpler than most of the canoe rigs we've looked at.

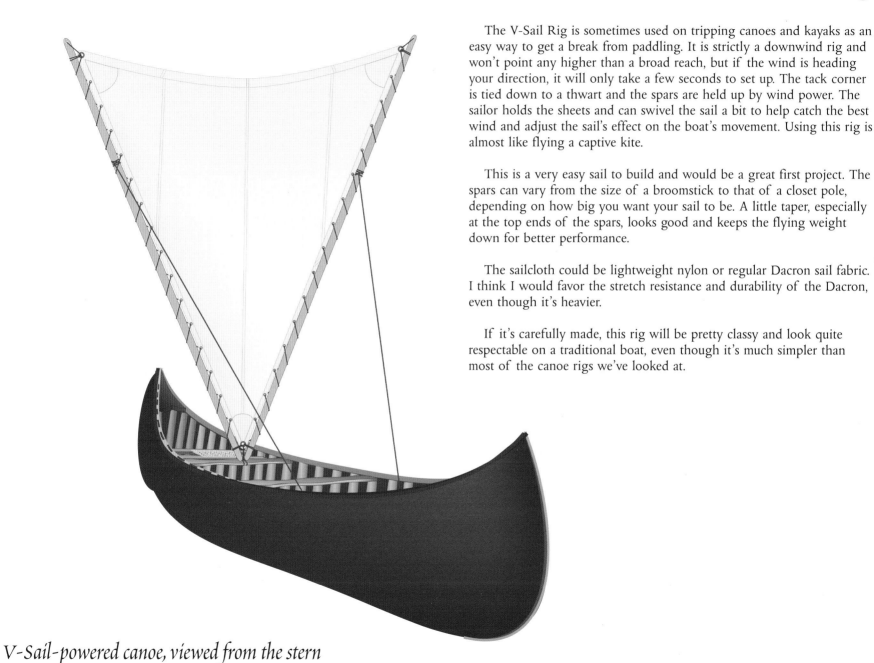

V-Sail-powered canoe, viewed from the stern

The Symmetrical Spinnaker

A nylon Symmetrical Spinnaker isn't particularly traditional, but its ease of use, quick construction, and stowability (the entire sail will stow in a bag the size of a grapefruit) makes it worth including in our selection. Building a spinnaker is a fun weekend project. If you have one plotted and cut out for you by one of the sail-kit companies, it could easily be built in a day.

Though the sail could be built from fabric-store ripstop nylon, real spinnaker nylon is better because it will be about half the weight, more stable, and less porous. Four-ounce Dacron strips to be folded over the edges and three grommets are the only other components required. The seams are basted together with sailmaker's double-sided tape and sewn with a single zigzag stitch or a three-step zigzag (three straight stitches form each zig or zag).

The mast is small, but it should still be fitted through a mast thwart and a step, as with most other rigs. Adding a pair of simple shrouds (light lines from the masthead to the gunwales, aft of the mast) will help support the mast and keep it from bending. The halyard runs through a hole in the masthead and will quickly raise or lower the spinnaker. Jibing is just a matter of swiveling the sail from side to side with the handheld sheets, attached to the lower corners of the sail.

The spinnaker is strictly a downwind sail, but it's easy to build, easy to stow, and fun to use.

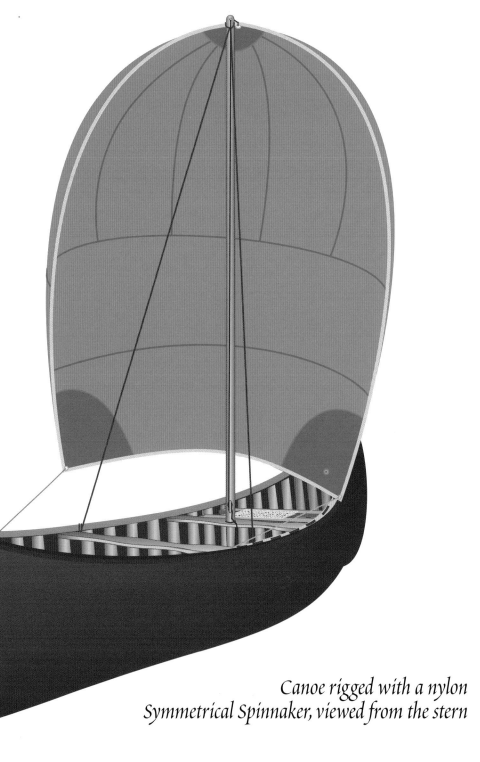

Canoe rigged with a nylon Symmetrical Spinnaker, viewed from the stern

The Asymmetrical Spinnaker

The Asymmetrical Spinnaker is as antique as last week, but it is a bit easier to singlehand than its symmetrical cousin. It works somewhat like a jib, with its forward (tack) corner attached to the bow by an adjustable line. The sailor controls the sail by the sheets, which are both attached to the clew (after corner) and used one at a time. The sail, rather than swiveling to jibe, turns inside out as it passes through the foretriangle on its way to the other side. Since only one sheet must be handled at a time, paddle steering is a bit easier than with a symmetrical spinnaker.

Once you have figured out the proper shapes or purchased a pattern for them, these sails can be cranked out pretty quickly at a reasonable cost. Making small spinnakers can be habit-forming, especially if you temporarily toss tradition out the window and start playing with color combinations. I keep my patterns on the computer, and have been known to waste hours popping various colors in and out.

Sometimes called a cruising spinnaker, the asymmetrical is not as good for sailing straight downwind as the symmetrical model. It will usually reach a bit higher, though, and relies on the "go farther, but faster, and get there sooner" principle. It uses the same mast, shroud, and halyard system as the symmetrical spinnaker, and needs in addition only the ring or block on the bow for the tack line.

The panels fan out, matching the weave of the fabric to the stress put on the sail by the wind.

A radial-cut Asymmetrical Spinnaker, viewed from the stern

Birds of Paradise

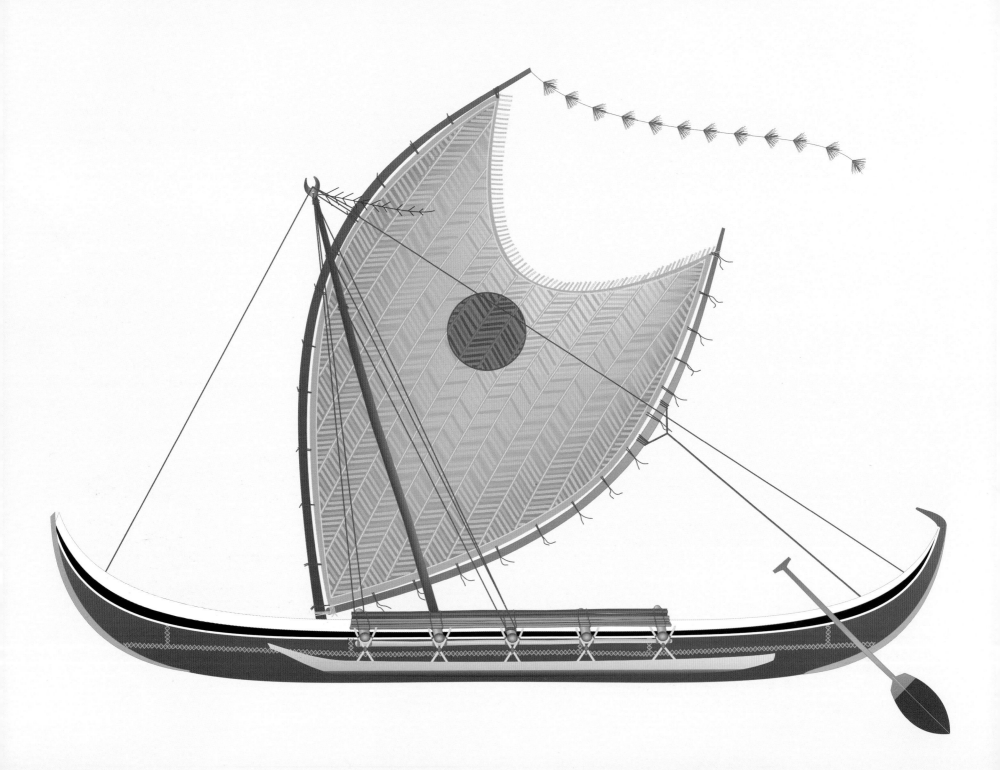

The Other Side of the World

When we think of traditional sailing canoes, most of us conjure up visions of a pretty wooden boat from the early 1900s, built by craftsmen in New York, Maine, or Canada, gliding along on the power of the wind. A picturesque vision, no doubt, but in a way it shows us how limited our dreams can be. What if I could show you a sailing canoe that was faster, much more stable, and able to handle water rough enough to make old-time canoe-builders like J. Henry Rushton turn green? What's more, a canoe that is more on a par, historically, with birchbark canoes than Old Towns? Would you be interested? Impressed? At least curious?

To see one, leave North America, turn left at Hawaii, and head for the South Pacific—birthplace of the outrigger canoe. Using "primitive" navigation skills (these guys are so good, they'd make a homing pigeon take notice), the islanders have been wandering the Pacific for eons in sailing canoes. Though these boats don't show the highly finished look of a late-nineteenth-century Rushton or Peterborough canoe, as long-distance traveling craft they are probably better designed.

I've always liked the idea of the outrigger canoe—narrow, fast hull, kept upright by a floating counterweight, rather than by paddler balance and waterline beam. As a sailboat, the outrigger canoe offers a different and exciting alternative to the typical North American canoe, which requires the sailor to hike out while trying to sit on the narrow gunwale.

Granted, the outrigger has its own drawbacks. Outrigger canoes are more cumbersome due to width and more parts. They don't maneuver in tight quarters as well as a regular canoe, and they tack slowly, sometimes with difficulty, compared to their western counterparts. A narrow hull is going to be less maneuverable and less buoyant, so a longer boat may be necessary to carry the same load. But when you apply wind power, that skinny hull can really go!

Single- or double-outrigger systems—the double forming a trimaran—have been retrofitted successfully to sea kayaks and North American canoes to take advantage of the added stability and sail-carrying ability that their broad base imparts to the package. Several such systems, ranging from pretty crude to pretty sleek, are currently available from modern canoe manufacturers, though most of them have a definite "training wheels" appearance that just won't go away.

In general, I prefer my multihulls to start out as multihulls, not as something else that has been retrofitted, so I started looking for information. Unfortunately, I didn't find much. Most of what I could find had bad drawings, if any, and vague text. After distilling what I found and blending it with my experience sailing and studying multihulled sailboats, I realized that anyone wishing to try sailing an outrigger canoe is probably going to have to design and build their own boat.

Such a project is about half engineering and half sculpture, and the handful of guys designing really successful catamarans and trimarans are truly gifted, but a couple of canoe prototypes? I'll take a shot at that... It's only a canoe... right? So I sat down at the computer, ignored any political or cultural boundaries, and roughed out a couple of preliminary drawings for modern yet traditionally based recreational sailing canoes with outriggers. These designs are surely "mutts"—a bit of this, a bit of that—but I find them pleasing to look at, probably worth the time to loft full size, and, perhaps, eventually worth building. They are presented as "brain food" and will perhaps inspire someone else to build or design one of their own—a sailing canoe from the other side of the world.

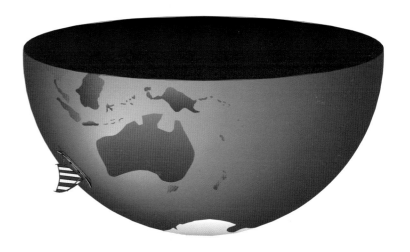

20' Outrigger Sailing Canoe "Bird of Paradise"

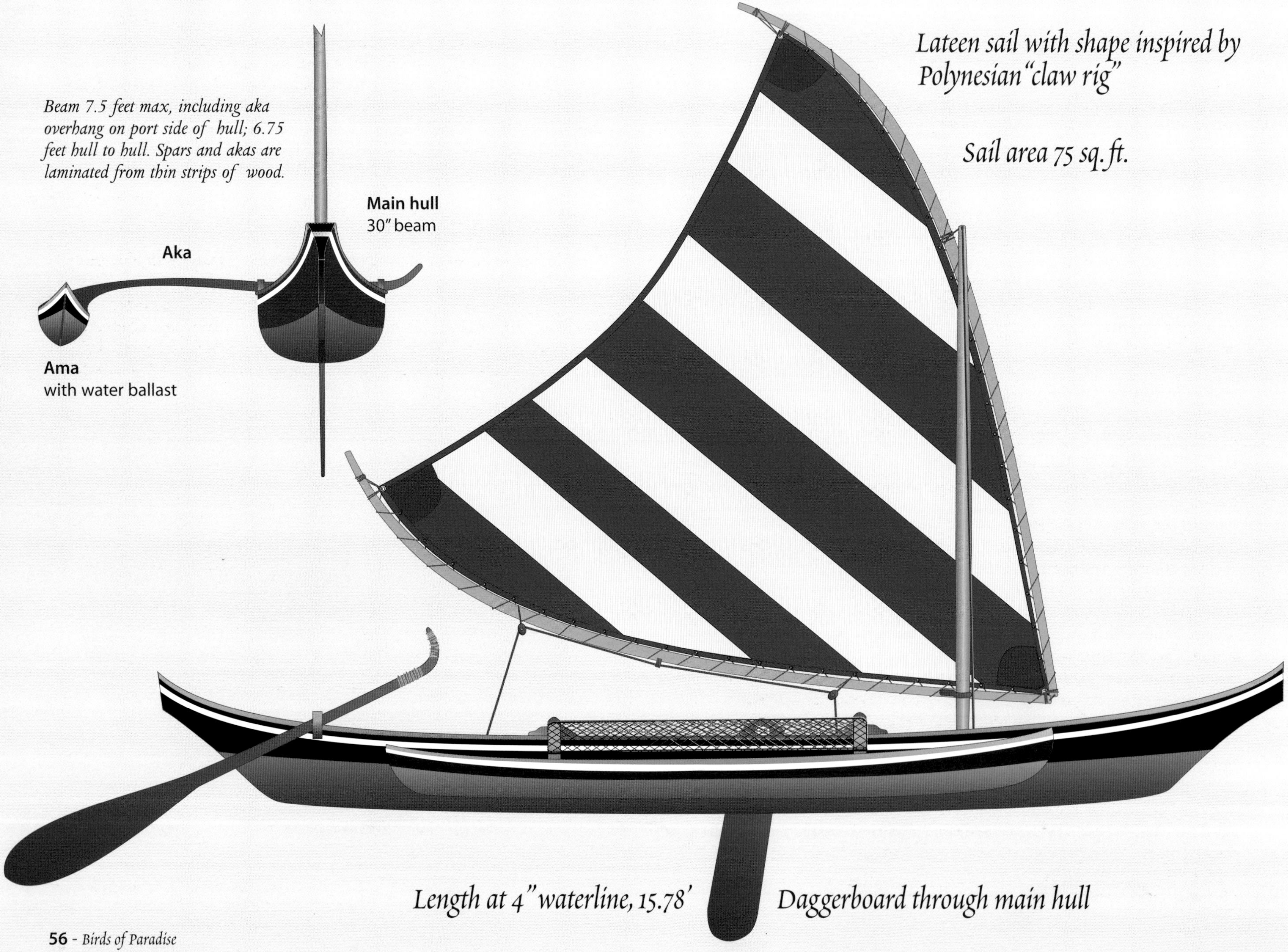

Beam 7.5 feet max, including aka overhang on port side of hull; 6.75 feet hull to hull. Spars and akas are laminated from thin strips of wood.

Main hull
30" beam

Aka

Ama
with water ballast

Lateen sail with shape inspired by Polynesian "claw rig"

Sail area 75 sq. ft.

Length at 4" waterline, 15.78'

Daggerboard through main hull

Bird of Paradise

In Wisconsin, where I live, most of us know almost as much about tropical island life as the guys who invented Hawaiian Punch. Even so, the trim, asymmetrical look of this outrigger canoe earns it a place in the "build this eventually to see what it can do" file. She has a sweeping sheerline, high ends, and long overhangs, things that don't really do much on a boat—except make it beautiful. Things that are conspicuously absent from most modern fiberglass sailboats.

On one tack, the buoyancy of the ama (outrigger) adds stability. On the other tack, the variable weight of the ama's water ballast—and crew weight as needed on the net between the akas (the crossbars that join the hulls)—does the stabilizing. Though a rudder could certainly be attached for steering, it is not easy to design one that looks as if it's supposed to be there, so a steering paddle/oar is used with a side-mounted chock to help with leverage.

The hull and ama could be strip-built, or cold-molded with diagonal layers of veneer, or possibly formed from compounded (bent) plywood. Also, they could fairly easily be redesigned for multi-chine construction (stitch-and-glue) or hard-chine, plywood construction. The canoe should paddle pretty well and be relatively fast under both paddle and sail. I did not go to extremes on hull or rig design in an effort to have a general-purpose but visually eye-opening boat. For speed, the main hull could be narrowed to the 20-to-24-inch range and the sail area increased, but I was shooting for something with a bit more room than a narrow hull would provide and the capacity to carry two to three weekend islanders.

The boom, yard, and akas are laminated to shape and need to be quite sturdy. They would take some work to build, but it would be rewarding: glue up a pile of strips, using every clamp in the county, and later turn that uneven, glue-covered mess into a graceful, flowing shape. While you're at it, better plan on building the steering paddle, too. With that "Little Bo-Peep" vertical stabilizer for a grip, one like it won't be found in your local canoe shop.

I stuck a lateen sail on this canoe, because it is simple and most of us can figure out how it works pretty quickly. I curved the spars like those on a traditional South Seas claw rig; this makes the sparmaking job tougher, but it does major things for the cosmetic appeal and uniqueness of the whole package. A true claw rig could be fitted, instead, by tying down the tack (where the boom and the yard meet forward of the mast) at deck level, lengthening the mast, and moving its base out to the ama, about where the forward aka and the ama meet. The mast would then lean forward and in toward the main hull, forming an asymmetrical, bipod structure with the yard. The masthead-to-upper-spar lashing (halyard) would stay about where it is shown on the yard. It is a weird-looking arrangement but is said to work pretty well. I chose, instead, to borrow the claw's cosmetics and apply them to the more familiar lateen configuration.

The basic shape of this canoe's hull and parts could probably be scaled up or down to produce canoes of from 14 feet for a solo boat (which would almost have to have a rudder and tiller, with extension, so the sailor could stay amidships) all the way to 60 feet for a cruiser without much change in shape—though I think a shorter twin-masted rig would be much easier to handle on a large boat than a 550-square-foot lateen! Now there's a scary thought....

The Pacific Proa "Witch Way"

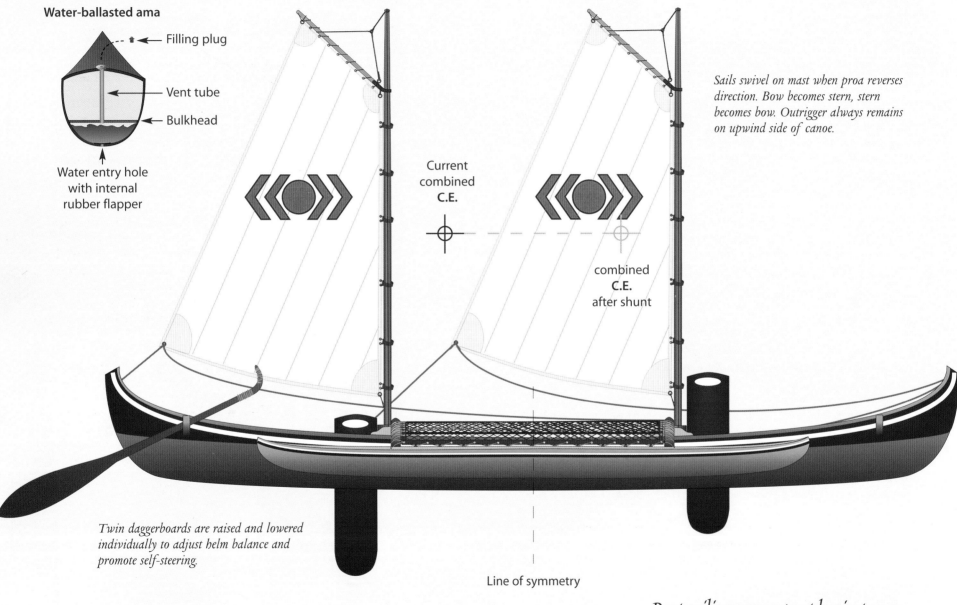

Water-ballasted ama

Filling plug

Vent tube

Bulkhead

Water entry hole with internal rubber flapper

Sails swivel on mast when proa reverses direction. Bow becomes stern, stern becomes bow. Outrigger always remains on upwind side of canoe.

Current combined **C.E.**

combined **C.E.** after shunt

Twin daggerboards are raised and lowered individually to adjust helm balance and promote self-steering.

Line of symmetry

Part sailing canoe, part brain teaser

The Proa

Witch Way is another outrigger canoe, similar to Bird of Paradise, but its operation, under sail, is radically different. This is a proa, specifically a Pacific proa. Everything at one end of the boat—hull shape, mast placement, sail, and steering gear—is a mirror image of that at the other end. Witch Way sails in both directions. If you're sitting in the bow on one tack and don't move, you'll be sitting in the stern on the next tack.

Actually, proas don't tack; rather, they "shunt." We can understand this by looking at the profile drawing of Witch Way and pretending the boat is underway. The temporary bow is on the right and the boat is moving toward the right. Since the ama is always carried on the windward side (upwind) on a Pacific proa, we know that the wind is at our back as we look at the page. We are ready to shunt!

First, we steer a reaching course, perpendicular to the wind. Easing the sails out completely, we let them swing away as the canoe slows down and comes to a stop. While we're briefly stopped, the proa blows downwind a bit, but because of its shape it remains more or less square to the wind. The steering paddle is moved to the other end of the boat where the helmsman relocates, or if there are two people aboard, one at each end, the crew can become captain and the captain become crew as roles are reversed.

The sails are trimmed in, this time on the page-right side of the masts, and the boat starts to move from right to left. The entire shunt could be accomplished in 20 to 30 seconds. As the proa comes up to speed, course can be altered to more upwind or downwind, depending on where you want to go. The proa makes its way around the lake with this back-and-forth see-saw process.

Designing a proa is a real mental exercise. The boat itself isn't really difficult—it's the sail plan. Getting the center of effort of the sail plan to relate properly to the center of effort of the hull, regardless of which side of the masts the sails happen to be on, is nearly impossible. (Center of effort, center of lateral resistance, and other naval architectural terms will be defined and discussed in detail in Chapter Six.)

To make it all work, we actually make the hull's center of lateral resistance adjustable. You may have wondered why this canoe had two daggerboards. They provide most of the actual lateral resistance and are used together to fine-tune the C.L.R. By having varying amounts of wood sticking down into the water, and trimming the sails individually as needed, we can make the boat nearly steer itself in the direction we want it to go. The helmsman and paddle are only necessary to correct for wind shifts.

As I said, this is a Pacific proa—outrigger to windward. There are also Atlantic proas. Their outriggers are to leeward instead. The advantage of the Atlantic-style is that the ama's buoyancy helps resist the narrow hull's tendency to tip over.

On the Pacific proa, there will need to be some weight on the ama to resist tipping. Crew weight on the net and water ballast inside the ama are the obvious choices; they are adjustable for best performance. This ballasting is similar to hiking out to balance a standard sailing canoe, but it is much more comfortable for the crew. For maximum speed, we want the ama to barely touch the water or actually fly just above it, reducing wetted surface area and drag. This can't be done on an Atlantic proa, where the ama is always in the water and the harder the wind blows, the deeper the ama goes and the more drag it creates.

Atlantic proas also have a tendency to turn during the stopped phase of a shunt. The main hull catches more wind than the ama and wants to be on the downwind side. During the shunt, there is plenty to do without having to worry about the boat spinning around. Our Pacific-style boat already has the big hull downwind, so it will tend to blow sideways while we're busy doing other things.

"Shunting" a Proa Upwind and Downwind

Upwind travel

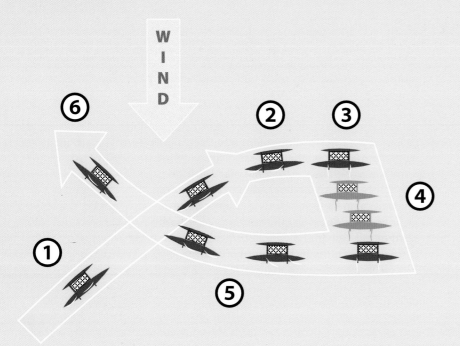

1. Sail upwind, close-hauled, sails trimmed in.

2. Bearing off on a reach.

3. Sails eased all the way out; boat coasts to a stop, square to the wind.

4. Slight drift downwind while crew moves to new stations.

5. Sails gradually trimmed in; proa moves off in new direction.

6. After regaining speed, the sails are trimmed-in to close-hauled, and course is altered for maximum gain to windward

A Pacific proa's ama is always carried to windward.

Downwind travel

1. Sailing downwind on a broad reach, sails eased somewhat.

2. Course changed to beam reach, square to wind.

3. Sails eased all the way out. Proa comes to a stop, then drifts downwind as crew moves to new stations.

4. Sails are trimmed, proa moves off in new direction.

5. Sail trim completed, proa picks up speed.

6. Bearing off on new heading and easing sails for broad reach.

Witch Way Paddling Stations

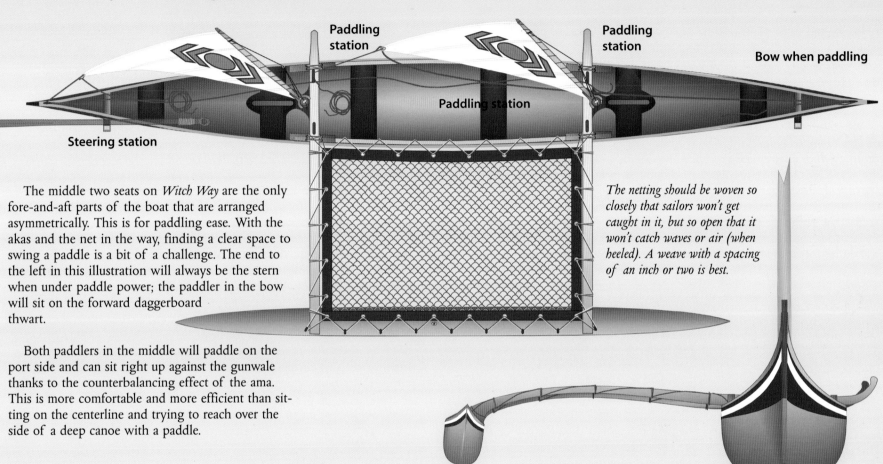

Paddling station

Paddling station

Paddling station

Bow when paddling

Steering station

The middle two seats on *Witch Way* are the only fore-and-aft parts of the boat that are arranged asymmetrically. This is for paddling ease. With the akas and the net in the way, finding a clear space to swing a paddle is a bit of a challenge. The end to the left in this illustration will always be the stern when under paddle power; the paddler in the bow will sit on the forward daggerboard thwart.

Both paddlers in the middle will paddle on the port side and can sit right up against the gunwale thanks to the counterbalancing effect of the ama. This is more comfortable and more efficient than sitting on the centerline and trying to reach over the side of a deep canoe with a paddle.

The netting should be woven so closely that sailors won't get caught in it, but so open that it won't catch waves or air (when heeled). A weave with a spacing of an inch or two is best.

The Flagpole Principle

If we could hang a big mainsail on a flagpole and sheet it in tightly, sooner or later a gust would come along that was strong enough to exceed our pole's strength and limited ability to bend, and down would come our flagpole.

Adding amas, akas, hiking nets, and water ballast to a boat does wonders for stability. We create a boat that stays within about 10 degrees of upright, but unlike a monohulled sailboat, our multihull can no longer lean over in a puff, spilling excess wind and taking strain off the rig. We have essentially created a sleek, waterborne flagpole.

We deal with this by sailing conservatively, shortening sail early, and using oversized hardware and fittings. Even though a multihull may be much lighter than a comparably sized monohull, its structure and rig must be stronger. Weakness in design, construction, or components carries the risk of catastrophic failure.

About Witch Way

Proas tend to be platforms for experimentation. They are often the boats of choice for those attempting to break the existing sail-powered speed records. Most of these extreme boats will only sail in one direction, unable to shunt and head back the other way. Instead, they are towed back for the next run.

When I doodled-up Witch Way, I wasn't the least bit concerned to design a boat to break the 50-knot speed barrier, but rather, to see if I could produce a reasonably practical day-sailing proa that looked traditional and wouldn't be too much of a handful to sail. The final profiles are sort of Polynesian/Norwegian/Algonquian (great nautical minds think alike in any language). I envision this canoe to be about 25 feet long. That may seem large if you are used to a 16-foot Old Town, but length adds speed, increases stability, and lessens the effects of crew weight on fore-and-aft trim. Remember, too, that all proas have fairly narrow hulls. A bigger boat has more room to move around in while shunting and sailing.

With Witch Way, as with Bird of Paradise, the ama has a water-ballast tank built into its bottom, with a sealed air chamber above. Every cubic foot of water in the tank will give us better than 60 pounds of ballast on top of the ama's own weight. When we hang the ballasted ama 7 or 8 feet out from the center of the main hull, it creates a lot of leverage—just the same as having a bunch of fat guys sitting on the gunwale.

Once the boat is in the water, the plug is removed from the top of the vent tube on the deck. Air leaves the tank through the tube and water flows in an entry hole in the ama's bottom and into the ballast tank. When the desired amount of ballast has been added, the air plug is replaced. I added an internal rubber flap over the water entry hole for fear of watching the water run out of the ama while it flies. It might be unnecessary but can't hurt for good measure. It does, however, mean that a string or wire from the flap, up the vent tube, would be needed to lift the flap for draining the tank. There are many ways to build a water-ballast system; this seemed simple and required minimal hardware.

Compared to Bird of Paradise, the ama on Witch Way has a rounder bottom. Bird uses the ama's V-shaped cross-section to increase the canoe's lateral resistance. I wanted the daggerboards to do as much of the resisting as possible on the proa to give the adjustable-lateral-resistance theory the best chance of working. These boards are big—about 4½ feet long—and my guess is that, under sail, the after board would be down all the way and the forward one down just enough to hold course and balance the helm. I have also considered moving the daggerboards to a position just inside the akas (fore and aft). This would put the stern board below the sail plan's center of effort and might eliminate the need for using both boards at once. It would, however, leave an awful lot of boat sticking out beyond the forward board, without much lateral resistance and possibly subject to blowing off course in the wind.

I have always liked the look of the narrow-topped gaff sails on some of the Polynesian-inspired catamarans designed by James Wharram. I doubt that there is anything Polynesian at all about a gaff rig, but somehow they look good.

I did away with the booms for three reasons. First, it eliminates two head-knockers in a fairly narrow boat. Second, the booms only really improve sail shape when running downwind with the sails eased way out. Multihulls are generally much faster broad-reaching back and forth to make progress downwind, rather than running straight down. On a proa, we don't want to lose our ama-to-windward attitude for safety, so we don't want to point the boat dead downwind in the first place.

At the sailing angles that this canoe will use, the sails will never be so far out that their lack of booms will be a major sail-shaping problem—which brings us to reason three: Should the boat get overpowered to the point of risking capsize (the crew falls overboard, the ama falls off, the skipper falls asleep, etc.), cracking the sheets and letting the boomless sails way out will produce horrible sail shape, rob the sails of their power and lift, and, I hope, bring the heeling boat back to a more normal angle.

The best rule to follow when sailing a Pacific proa is: "When in doubt, let it out!" The rather short gaffs will also tend to twist off to leeward in a puff, spilling wind and helping depower the sails somewhat, just as the new "square-topped" mainsails on modern, racing boats do.

Making a gaff sail that can spin 180 degrees on its mast is a challenge. Hoops around the mast are used to hold the luff to the mast, just as on most gaff-riggers. These will spin easily, as long as there are no spreaders or other obstructions to stop them. The gaff jaws, with a parrel, will also spin—as long as you have eliminated the throat halyard, which usually pulls up on the jaws.

Eliminating a halyard means that the peak and throat halyards have to be combined into one, and it must pull from the top or from the leeward side of the mast and oscillate back and forth as the boat shunts—all without getting tighter or looser as the boat changes direction. A "spinning" mast cap with a fairlead on top seems to be the best way I have found to deal with a single halyard. The tail of the halyard could be led over the mast top and down to a cleat somewhere on the ama side of the mast step, keeping the halyard from interfering with the sail.

Since we only have one halyard, I think I would be inclined to make the junction where the halyard meets the bridle (attached to the gaff) fixed, rather than use the typical sliding or rolling arrangement.

It would take some experimentation to get right the tension between pulling up on the jaws and in on the peak, but once it was done, we would be set. Having a short, stiff gaff will also make the job easier. The downhaul cleats to the leeward side of the mast so it can maintain even tension as the sail spins; it would probably be set after the sail has been raised. Without a throat halyard, and using a minimal system for both halyard duties, the downhaul becomes the major luff-tensioning device. If need be, it could even be slacked off during a shunt to help get the sail and gaff to spin around the mast, and then it could be reset…as if you weren't already busy enough.

Freestanding hollow masts, as stiff as possible, would be my first choice for the spars. A bit of discreetly applied internal carbon fiber might be worth the extra expense. The masts are just under 14 feet long; they are stepped on the keel and pass through a chock on the aka at

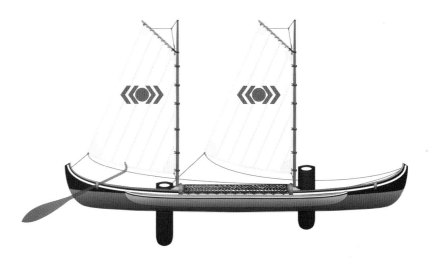

gunwale height. If needed, a pair of shrouds could be attached to a band just below the masthead. Each mast could have one wire running to the nearest ama tip and another anchored mid-ama.

Both sails have twin sheets leading to their respective cleat locations for sailing in both directions. Working the sheets resembles trimming and tacking a jib or asymmetrical spinnaker.

Carrying 87 square feet of sail, Witch Way is rather modestly powered, but remember that its narrow hull should move easily through the water. Any proa has a certain amount of vulnerability to capsize, so there's no need to press our luck. If I want to go 50 knots, I just get in my car.

Wanna turn some heads on your next river trip or sailing club regatta? Show up with a proa, and watch everybody else try to figure out what in blazes you're doing!

Rigger-ous Exercise

As I mentioned before, outrigger systems are becoming a popular option for taming or sometimes supercharging canoe and kayak sailing rigs. Most of these are trimaran configurations, with an ama on each side of the boat, giving a maximum beam of between 7 and 8 feet. Outriggers can create a boat that is nearly impossible to capsize and allow even beginners to sit wide-eyed on the floor as the boat charges along under a larger-than-normal sail plan.

I have seen amas for these systems built from foam cylinders, and from roto-molded polyethylene, plywood, and wood-strip/fiberglass constructions. The foam floats were very crude, the wooden ones looked like mini-sea kayaks, and the poly-amas were pretty nicely shaped, but worked only with the boat they were built for.

Though no one can doubt the practical aspects of adding an outrigger package to a traditional canoe, such add-ons definitely kill the cosmetic appeal of a classic wooden boat, both in its general appearance and in the way that it looks under sail.

A narrow, heeling sailboat, responding to every puff of the wind and the movement of her skipper, is art. A canoe held up by mechanical means, even though the arrangement may be eminently practical and capable of nearly eliminating "pilot error," is a contraption.

This doesn't mean that I am totally against retrofitting outriggers. The only reason to sail a canoe is for fun, and if outriggers make the experience safer and more enjoyable for you, that's great. Just keep in mind that showing up at a classic boat regatta with an antique Rushton Vesper sporting amas made from recycled soda bottles might be considered bad form.

I do have a problem, though, with supercharging a canoe with an oversized sail plan and clamp-on amas. There are a lot of very intense calculations that go into designing a high-performance multihull—righting moment, ama buoyancy, rigging loads, etc.—and I'm not convinced that many of the people designing, building, and selling some of these rigs have done their homework.

My recommendation is not to put any more sail on the canoe than you can handle without outriggers. Then, if you decide you're not in a hiking-out mood on a particular day, you can strap on the training wheels and relax.

The best way to obtain an outrigger system is to buy plans, a kit, or a finished set from one of the plywood sea kayak and canoe makers. Most of the amas have a V-shaped cross-section and a flat or slightly crowned deck. If I were going to build a set, I would be tempted to build them instead with a narrow, flat, rockered bottom and flared sides, like long, skinny dories. I think they might benefit from the extra buoyancy that the dory cross-section offers over the V and be less prone to burying.

The akas should be laminated, quite sturdy, and attached securely to both the amas and the canoe. I would like to see a minimum of around 4 cubic inches of laminations (2" x 2," 1.25" x 3," etc., in cross-section) for the akas on a normal tandem-sized canoe. If you plan to use outriggers all the time, you might also be able to incorporate your leeboard brackets into the system as one modular unit for convenience.

Finally, if you do plan to put amas on your Rushton classic or equivalent—at least carve them to look like swans, or leaping dolphins, or northern pike…a flock of ducks…really fast beavers?

A Typical Add-on Outrigger System

Most plywood amas are built using a deck panel, two side panels, a small triangular transom, and several internal bulkheads to help shape the sides and reinforce the aka attachment points. Screw-in inspection ports can be added to the deck as needed. Amas have a V bottom and are rockered, fore and aft.

If you are designing your own outriggers, make scale models with cardboard and tape to fine-tune the side-panel shape. Typical dimensions are 6 to 8 feet in length by 8 to 10 inches beam. A vent hole ($\frac{1}{16}$ inch or so) should be drilled in the top, or high on the transom, to keep the internal air from heating up and blowing out the seams on hot, sunny days.

On a trimaran-type configuration as illustrated here, we want the canoe to heel 5 to 10 degrees as it sails for better sail shape and proper feel at the helm. The akas should be designed so only the main hull and the leeward ama are in the water at any one time. The windward hull should be flying to reduce drag.

You may have noticed on the drawings of Bird of Paradise and Witch Way that the amas are hung at a slight angle off vertical of 7 to 8 degrees. This helps put the ama, when it's down in the water and the whole boat is heeling, at a more vertical and therefore "steering-neutral" position. A hull on edge wants to carve a turn. We want the steering to come from the main hull and the rudder/paddle systems, not from the amas. Especially on boats with wide hull-to-ama spans, canting the amas is a good idea and will improve handling.

There are several ways to attach an outrigger system to a canoe. If possible, find a system that can be moved fore and aft to adjust for changes in helm balance brought on by adding extra hulls. Always consider drilling holes in the canoe as a last resort, especially in the gunwales, where you don't need to lose much wood and create a weak spot.

Sandwiching the gunwales or thwarts between the akas and sturdy back-up boards, held together by bolts, is often the best option. Leather is the traditional chafe preventer on sailing craft and should be used to protect the boat. It also acts as a nonskid surface to keep the clamped-on parts of the sail rig from wandering around while you are sailing.

BEAVERS?

Chapter Five

Unraveling

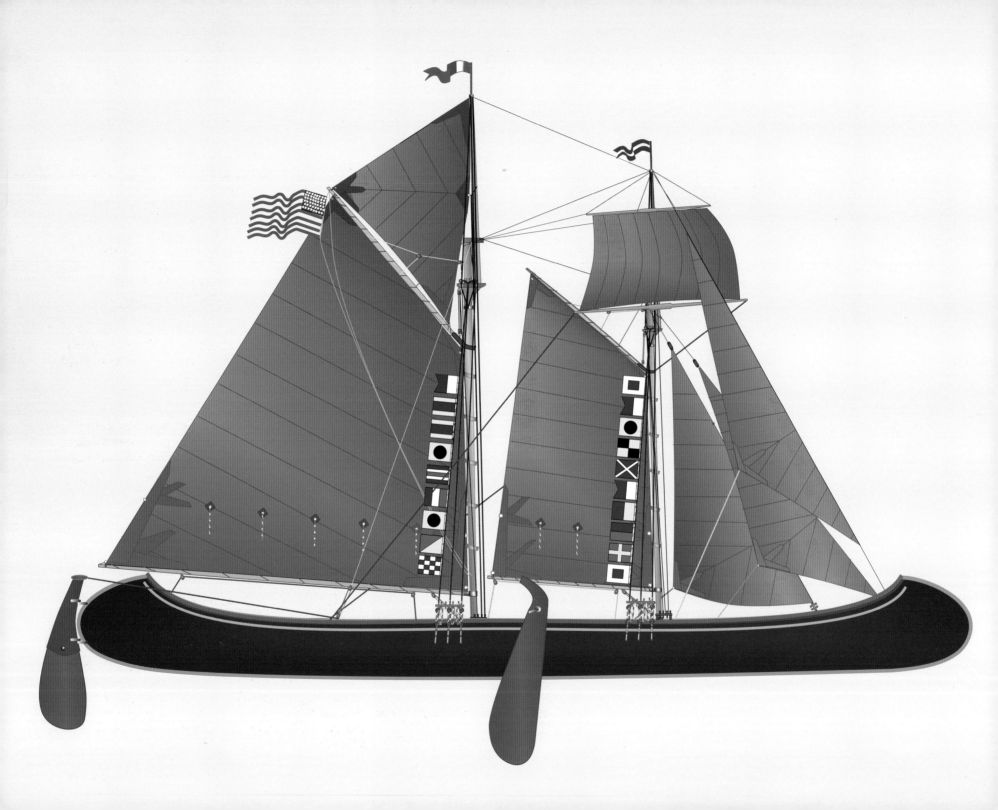

And the Winner Is...

As you no doubt have surmised by now, there are many possible ways to use wind power to move your canoe. It can be as simple as sailing downwind only with a V-sail rig built in a weekend and tied to a thwart, or as complex as an outrigger canoe, where you start by designing and building the boat long before starting on the rig.

The decision of which rig to use has many considerations. All rigs are compromises, as no one has yet designed one that will sail great on all headings, point high, never be underpowered or overpowered, weigh nothing, portage like a spare paddle, and stow neatly under the bow deck when not in use. Oh...and look good on the boat, too. The last one doesn't worry me too much, but the rest will all be compromises that you must make by considering your canoe, your needs, your energy level (both as a builder and as a sailor), and the type of weather that you plan to sail in.

Some of the rig drawings in previous chapters indicate square footage for the sails. This can be modified to fit your situation and/or the configuration of your canoe. Don't be scared off by a 55-square-foot plan if you really think you will be better off with 40. In later chapters I will diagram the basic measurements for all of the rigs and show you how to scale them up or down.

We have already discussed the strengths and weaknesses of the lateen rig. It is reasonably low, simple, and user-friendly. On the other hand, the lateen's 10-to-12-foot-long spars aren't very portable and can drag in the water when the canoe heels in high winds, causing a loss of control.

Other rigs—the tall single gunter and the leg-o'-mutton, for example—have medium boom lengths and will probably not have this problem. Their compromise instead is a lengthened luff. On windy days, more weight on the gunwale will be required to balance these rigs' heeling lever. The nearly vertical leading edges will probably allow them to point higher than the lateen, and on light-wind days the taller sail plans will catch more air because there is usually a bit more wind up higher above the water.

The gunters, with their two-part spar systems, are reasonably portable, but the leg-o'-mutton's long mast can be cumbersome on a trip. Raising and lowering sail on the leg-o'-mutton is a cinch but on the gunter is a bit more awkward.

The sprit-boom sails share the higher aspect ratio (taller and narrower shape) of the gunter and leg-o'-mutton and can actually be laced to the mast in the raised position permanently. The mast, with the sail rolled around it for storage, can be dropped through the hole in the mast thwart and into the step; once the mast is in position the sail can be unrolled and the sprit boom quickly attached. The mast might be a bit long for tripping, but the rig is easy to assemble for daysailing.

Another set of compromises are presented by bat-wing sails and the twin folding gunter rig, which some would consider a bat-wing variant due to the large roach and its supporting batten. With shorter booms, sail area is achieved by adding massive amounts of roach in the leech.

For upwind sailing, roach is not as effective as height in generating "pointing power," so those seeking maximum possible upwind capabilities might do better with a taller sail. A big roach does, however, boost reaching performance, with less heeling lever than the tall rig, so it may be wiser to bear off a bit and let her rip. The top will also tend to sag off to leeward in a gust, spilling excess wind and reducing the rig's heeling power.

The bat-wing, though complex in structure, can be a pretty good general-purpose rig with good portability. To many, it is the most visually distinctive canoe sailing rig as well.

At the beginning of Chapter Three, I mentioned that it was tough to decide which rig is best. By now you probably see what I meant—and we haven't come close to considering all of the possibilities!

The lug rigs, both balanced and standing, and the sprit rig make up the "basic three" for traditional small craft sail design. Though there are many possible structural changes, cosmetic and minor, in each, the sails are simple. They're not too tall, not too wide; you hang them up and go, bring them down and stop. They aren't exceptionally high pointers; they simply provide good, basic, all-purpose sailpower. Those with higher peaks will point higher. Those with lower peaks will heel less and twist more, up top, to dissipate the effects of a sudden gust. Their construction is fairly simple, and they rank in the middle of the canoe sailor's "portability spectrum."

Gaff sails, with their throat halyards, peak halyards, jaws, parrels, and mast hoops, are for "string pullers." I am proud to be among that brotherhood. I love tweaking this and adjusting that, all in an effort to get the best possible sail shape…at least until the wind shifts, when the process can begin all over again. Some designers avoid small gaffers just because of their potential complexity and all that hardware. I must admit that sailing a gaffer is somewhat more involved than just tying a halyard to a yard with a clove hitch and pulling the rope, as one might do with a lateen or lug rig, but it can also be fun in itself. If you share my personality quirks, you might be a good candidate for a gaff rig.

In performance, the gaff rig is about in the middle of the range. High-peaked models with more-vertical gaffs point a bit better than low-peaked, portability is fair, and the booms are medium length. Masts should be a bit bigger in diameter and have no upper taper until above the jaws, which will push forward in use, trying to bend the mast. A gaff rig is a good place to try building a large-sectioned hollow mast, for stiffness.

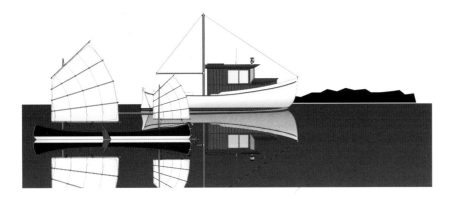

About the only reason to put a square rig on a canoe is that IT'S REALLY COOL. It won't point much above a beam reach, if that, but it will work pretty well downwind. A square sail requires more rigging and hardware than other downwind sails, isn't particularly portable, and needs a pretty sturdy mast to avoid bending, which would look unseamanlike. But square rig is still cool—an unexpected surprise—and should be carried out to the letter: proper sail, properly shaped yard, shipshape and Bristol fashion rigging. It's a reminder of those days when the men were men and the whales were "less fortunate creatures."

The downwind sails—the fan, the V, and the two types of spinnakers—are as much serious tripping tools as they are fun. They are auxiliary propulsion for any day when your shoulders might need a break. With its low center, the fan is probably the most stable of the lot and requires the least amount of attention.

The V-sail is the easiest to build and is the only rig in this book that requires no modification to the boat. As long as there is enough wind to keep the sail up, it will pull you along, though you may be looking for your third hand while trying to tend it and steer at the same time. If your boat is set up for sitting on the bottom and steering with your feet, or if you have a partner aboard, any downwind sail will be easier to use.

The spinnakers, though rather untraditional in spirit, win the "small stick/tiny sailbag" award, and I doubt anyone would look at a canoe being towed down the lake by a colorful nylon flower and think, "Boy, that thing is ugly." If the wind isn't at your back, stow the sail and take comfort in the fact that, unlike every regular sailboat that has ever been built, yours will actually move easily under paddle power. It slices through the water, it glides, it turns—just as if it were made for it! Imagine that….

A Class of Its Own

Some readers who have canoe sailing experience may be wondering why I have ignored the established canoe-sailing classes. For those new to the sport, I should mention that class associations are sanctioned groups of sailors who race nearly identical boats and rigs. Most canoe sailing is governed by either the American Canoe Association or the International Canoe Federation.

Classes include lateen-rigged boats; the Class C Canoe, a boat about 17 feet long, rigged with a fairly tall, Marconi-type cat rig; and the Ten-Square-Meter Class, a supercharged screamer with a big fully battened maxi-roach sail and a plank sticking way out the side on which the sailor sits and tries to counterbalance all that heeling lever.

Sailing races are conducted on a course marked by buoys and designed to test the boats and their skippers on all points of sail. Class rules are set up to ensure fair, even competition by keeping the boats the same. This makes it a canoe race, not a contest to see who can buy the largest collection of go-fast gizmos and fancy equipment.

For small boats, the rules usually regulate all parts of the sailing rig and where they come from. This means that you can't build or assemble your own rig. You send a check, they send you a rig, and you go sailing.

Though I understand the intent of class rules, they have a rather stifling effect on the sport. Too often the touring sailor is stuck buying a class-governed rig, just because nothing else is available. Usually, this rig has aluminum spars and a sail made by a production loft, as fast and as (shall we say) economically as possible. The rig works fine, but it certainly is not much to look at. In fact, it clashes with a traditional boat.

I want my sail rig to be mine. Perhaps the only one like it, anywhere. Something with a bit of imagination—something that may not conform to any class rules, but it'll have plenty of class all by itself.

Eenie-Meenie-Miney

If you were hoping that I will be steering you toward a particular rig for your canoe, you probably realize by now that it isn't going to happen. It's YOUR boat, YOUR budget, YOUR idea of how and why you want to sail, and YOUR decision.

But at least we have categories now, and within each there are options. It is probably safe to match the category to your intended use and pick the style of sail that you most like the looks of. Balance that against your desired level of portability, ease of construction or acquisition, and budget, and you're almost ready to get started.

As long as you don't choose a spinnaker for trying to sail upwind, or a big twin-sailed rig for leisurely afternoon sails in 25 knots of wind, you should be fine. For the price of a small fiberglass sailboat, you could easily build several canoe rigs.

One reason that we have so many possible options on the same canoe is that the rig is movable and the leeboard system essentially makes the hull adjustable—characteristics not common on regular sailboats.

Now that you've seen the sail rigs, it's time to look at the hull and other components, and see how they relate to and work with the sails. So don't make that rig decision quite yet.

I'M STILL WONDERING ABOUT THOSE BEAVER-AMAS

Chapter Six

Lines on Paper

Naval Architecture for the Canoe Sailor

To fit a downwind sail such as the V-sail or one of the spinnakers to a canoe is pretty simple. As long as it ends up somewhere in the forward half of the boat and doesn't constantly knock the bow paddler's hat in the drink, it should tow the canoe downwind without a problem.

To rig a general-purpose sail, however, one that will take us upwind, across the wind, or downwind, requires knowledge of some rudimentary naval architecture. It will be necessary to balance the power of our sails with the hull and its interaction with the water. This balancing act can be subdivided into two distinct parts: balance for stability, and balance for steering and boat control—called "balancing the helm."

Since most canoe-sailing rigs are retrofitted even when provided by the manufacturer, sailing-rig design is somewhat less formal here than for a regular sailboat. You wouldn't imagine a naval architect designing a hull first and then trying to decide whether it should be fitted with sails, or perhaps a motor instead. The primary and secondary propulsion systems are part of design from the start.

Most canoes are designed as paddling craft. If the manufacturer offers a sailing rig, it is usually exactly that—a single rig that can be retrofitted to most of the canoes in their product line. Consequently, certain models may be deemed "better" sailing canoes than others, which may be true, but may just be because that particular sail size and rig works best on certain models. The same rig that overpowers a 12-foot-long canoe may be too small for good performance on an 18-footer.

Here, we have the ability to retrofit our boats with sailing rigs that stand a much better chance of working well, but some of the design work will have to be estimated.

Balancing a sailing canoe for stability is a matter of determining how much sail it will take to propel the boat well, and at what point heeling forces will become so great that the sailor will no longer be able to counterbalance them.

If we were lucky enough to have the boat's lines—the actual, blueprint-style scale drawings of the canoe as seen from several angles—on paper, or plugged into a computer yacht-design program, we could actually figure out how much the hull would heel at various wind speeds and roughly how fast it would be going.

Unfortunately, running the numbers is no easy process and is rarely done for canoes. Paddling-canoe designers assume that the boat will be upright, not heeled over, so they don't need to know much about a boat's resistance to heeling from outside influences, such as a sailing rig. Even if you have the lines drawing, sailing-stability calculations are very intense mathematics, begun by figuring out the immersed volume of your particular hull, at various angles of heel, in cubic inches.

Most of us could probably build the sailing rig in less time than the calculations would take, so the accepted practice has always been to estimate and experiment, rather than to calculate. The finished sailing craft will have definite strengths and weaknesses, and in certain conditions, it could be difficult to control. In others, it might be slow, on the verge of boring; in still others, it may be perfect.

By taking a good look at the boat, the sailor, and the type of conditions that the canoe is intended to be sailed in, you can stack the deck in your favor before building the rig.

It may seem obvious, but designing your sailing canoe to work best in the conditions that you plan to sail in is the most important part of rig design. It will have a much greater bearing on your sailing enjoyment than which style of sailing rig you choose.

By far, the most common question that I hear from canoe sailors is, "How much sail area should I put on my canoe?" It is an extremely difficult question to answer, because of an enormous number of variables that can figure into the answer and because many of these people have had little or no sailing experience.

There is no formula for generating an answer to the above question, but an estimate can be made by asking more questions and listening to the customer's answers.

How long is the canoe?

If we take two 36-inch-wide canoes, one 14-footer and one 18-footer, the longer boat will be quite a bit more stable even though both are the same width. This is because the longer boat has more volume, more buoyancy, which must be immersed in order to heel the canoe.

How wide is the canoe?

Width also adds stability. Paddle a 14-foot-by-36-inch canoe and then hop into a 14-foot-by-27-inch solo canoe: the difference in stability will be obvious.

Most small solo canoes are sailed by sitting on the bottom, amidships, and steering with a rudder controlled by a rope or by foot pedals. Sitting on the bottom will add quite a bit of stability, compared to kneeling on the bottom, or to sitting in a seat for paddling, but the sailor's ability to hike or lean out over the side, using his or her weight for balance, is quite limited.

I'm sure that agile sailors could carefully work their way up to a crosswise position, sitting on the high-side gunwale in strong winds, but getting back in when there was a lull and before the boat flipped over backwards would be quite difficult. This lack of convenient hiking ability will limit the amount of sail area that is comfortable on some boats.

Surprisingly, the shape of the bottom of a canoe—flat, round, shallow arch, or V—which is quite important in defining a canoe's paddling stability, probably won't make a lot of difference in its sailing stability, though it may affect its speed under sail and its handling. A sailing rig has easily enough heeling lever to defeat any transverse bottom shape.

Will you sail alone?

Sailing with a friend is often the best way to learn to handle the canoe. The extra pair of hands and extra weight for counterbalancing the sails can be a big help and a lot of fun. If you plan to steer with a paddle, you will need to be positioned within reach of the stern; having someone forward will make the boat sail a lot better. It is nearly impossible to design a sailing rig to fit a canoe that has most of its forward half out of the water, as it would if you were steering from the stern with no one up forward.

Fitting two people, a leeboard bracket, a mast or two, booms, sails, and a bunch of control lines in a canoe can be an interesting experience in itself. Usually, the initial results are more comical than dangerous, and it will take a while for everyone to learn their roles, but as long as nobody gets a "Captain Ahab Complex" you should enjoy canoe sailing.

Solo sailing is faster, because there is less weight in the canoe and the canoe draws less water. The boat accelerates quicker and turns faster, but the sailor has to do everything simultaneously—steering, sail handling, and balancing the boat—and without getting distracted. On a breezy day, that narrow, open hull can demand a lot of concentration.

What conditions do you plan to sail in?

This is often the toughest question for those who haven't yet sailed. They don't know what type of sailing will be the most enjoyable for them. Ghosting along on a beautiful evening under sail has the same appeal that it does under paddle power, except it is smoother. That same boat on a windy, weekend afternoon, with plenty of waves and motorboat chop, may test your mental and physical abilities just to stay upright. Adventuresome sailing is something you may want to work your way up to, but it is no place to start.

It is pretty easy to look at a profile drawing of a sailing canoe and forget that, unlike most other small sailboats, it really is a canoe! A sailing canoe has no ballast and is half-again narrower than most dinghies. The sailor can hike out, gaining considerable leverage to offset the rig's heeling lever, but he'd better be ready to get back in quickly if the wind dies.

Asking questions and providing honest answers is the best way to attack the issue of sail area and its effect on stability for sailing canoes. The number chosen is still an estimation, but it can at least be based on that particular boat and that particular sailor.

If I were put on the spot and made to assign arbitrary sail-area figures to "average" canoes for general use, they would be something like this:

Small canoes, 10 to 12 feet long—15 to 25 square feet of sail

Medium canoes, 12 to 15 feet long—25 to 40 square feet

Large canoes, 15 to 18 feet long—40 to 60 square feet for average use, 60 to 75 square feet for high-performance use (hiking definitely required)

Big canoes, over 18 feet long—60 to 75 square feet, for normal use

Perhaps canoe sailors should take note of another type of narrow, unballasted sailing craft, the sailboard or windsurfer. Board sailors usually start out with a general-purpose rig; many will eventually build up an inventory of various-sized sails and components for different conditions—all designed to fit the same board. Smaller sails are used on windy days, larger sails for light air.

Canoe sails and spars are simple and inexpensive enough to build that having several rigs of various sizes becomes a viable option.

Balancing the boat for steering—sail-plan design—getting the sail plan and the canoe to work together properly—is a bit more scientific, with less guesswork than that involved in balancing for stability. Sail-plan design uses a few simple yacht-design principles and may require a drawing or two, but no computer and no cubic inches.

The primary tool for sail-plan design is the profile drawing of the canoe and its rig. Most of the profiles that we looked at in earlier chapters were sail plans rendered to look realistic. For design purposes, we assume that the boat will sit level in the water, fore and aft, and be perfectly upright, even though we know it will actually heel over in use.

What we want to determine is where the theoretical center of the wind's pressure on the sail or sails is, and where, fore and aft, the canoe's hull, leeboards, and steering gear resist that pressure the most. Simultaneously, we also need to consider the internal layout of the canoe. Where can we conveniently step a mast, or clamp on a leeboard bracket? It doesn't make much sense to design a rig and then have to move all the thwarts and seats to get it to fit the boat.

The sails will try to push the canoe sideways; the hull, rudder, and leeboards will resist; and the energy, seeking an easier avenue, will squirt the boat forward.

To understand the principle, lay a banana on your kitchen floor (be sure your parents, or spouse and/or kids are out of town). Stomp on the banana, as hard as you can. Note that you created a uniform mess directly under your foot.

Isn't yacht design fun?

Now, take a second banana and cut the last inch of the peel off one end. Stomp on this banana, too, as hard as before.

Gee, this time most of inside of the banana hit the wall, way over there. All that goo from banana number two chose the path of least resistance.

Clean up the mess, and proceed to the next paragraph.

Your canoe is already somewhat like a banana. Adding leeboards and a rudder is like cutting the peel off the forward end. Pressure, not relieved by heeling, will be used to move the boat forward. In addition, the sail isn't just a piece of cloth; it's an airfoil. The downwind side of it will be generating lift. Easing the sail and boom out, away from the centerline of the canoe, will angle that lift. It will still retain some of its heeling power, but it will actually start using its lift to pull the boat forward. You will be sailing!

As someone who had paddled thousands of miles before ever sailing anything, I remember thinking, "Hey, this is pretty neat. You just hold a rope and steer. What a concept."

Our first step in designing a sail plan is to begin determining the canoe's center of lateral plane, or C.L.P., also sometimes called the C.L.R., for center of lateral resistance. In doing this we deal only with those parts of the canoe and its attachments that are underwater and can contribute resistance to our equation.

We start with just the hull. A typical canoe when loaded will draw 3 or 4 inches of water. The profile of most canoes is symmetrical, or nearly so, fore and aft. If we took our profile drawing and with scissors cut out the shape of the hull and then cut away everything above the 4-inch waterline, what we would have left is our underwater profile, a long sliver that tapered on both ends.

If our paper were stiff enough, we could actually balance that sliver, fore and aft, like a seesaw on a knife edge. Since our canoe is nearly symmetrical, the balance point would be very close to the center of our sliver. We have just determined that the lateral center of our symmetrical sliver is, as we might expect, in the middle.

But this is not just a paper sliver; rather, it is a representation of the working portion of our hull profile. We have just found the center of lateral plane, and thus the center of lateral resistance for our hull. Though this determination seems idiotically simple on a canoe, most sailboat hulls are far from symmetrical and therefore this simple method of finding the C.L.P. comes in very handy for them.

In our case, though, we aren't done yet. As anyone who has ever paddled in a crosswind knows, the shallow draft of a canoe hull doesn't really provide much lateral resistance. Stop paddling, and the boat will drift sideways at an alarming rate. For sailing, we will depend on the addition of leeboards and a rudder (or a steering paddle) to provide most of the needed lateral plane.

If we were to add the underwater profile of our rudder blade to the stern of the previously tested paper hull sliver and then re-balance it, we would find the sliver to be tail-heavy. We would have to move the knife toward the stern to get the sliver to balance. The new C.L.P. would have shifted toward the stern of our canoe's now-asymmetrical underwater profile.

That seems easy enough to fix—we still have the leeboards, and they're adjustable, fore and aft. They are also bigger than the rudder and should be a big contributor in the balancing equation, right?

True, but before placing the boards we should probably do two things: place the sails, and decide where we want the final C.L.P. to end up.

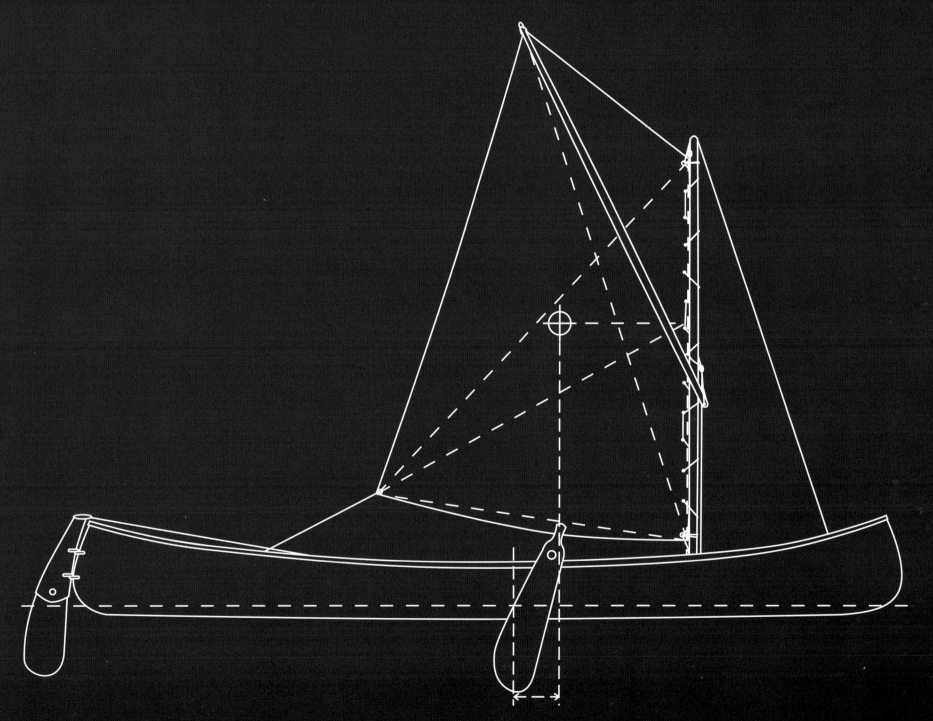

Finding the Center of Lateral Plane

We start with the profile drawing of our hull on a stiff piece of paper or cardboard. Estimating that our loaded waterline will be about 3 inches above the keel, we cut out the profile and cut away everything above the waterline, leaving only the dark sliver.

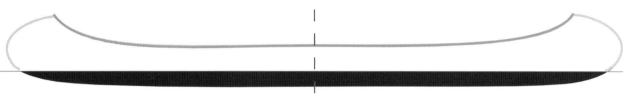

Balancing a paper cutout of the underwater profile of the hull on a knife edge is a simple way to find the approximate center of lateral plane for that hull. Since canoes are usually symmetrical fore and aft, or very close to it, it's easy to see that the midpoint is going to be the C.L.P.

If we somehow connect the area of the immersed portion of our rudder blade to our paper sliver, the balance point of our paper model, and consequently

Once we add the underwater profiles of the rudder blade, or steering paddle, and leeboards to our cutout, we can expect the balance point (and the boat's C.L.P.) to move.

its C.L.P., shifts toward the stern. Further adjustment to the the C.L.P. will be possible as we position our leeboards, but first we have other factors to consider. We will leave the C.L.P. "on hold," as it is here, until we're ready for it.

New C.L.P. with rudder added

Old C.L.P.—hull only

Fitting the Rig to the Canoe's Structure

We would like to be able to step the mast(s) using as much of the existing seat/thwart configuration as possible. The canoe is a multi-purpose boat, and we want it to stay that way. Switching a stock seat or thwart for one with a hole in it for a mast to pass through is not a big deal. Adding a thwart in a place where you wouldn't normally have one just to hold a mast up is usually less desirable.

The most common way to step a single mast in a canoe is to replace the bow seat with a mast seat. The latter is a special caned canoe seat with an extra-wide after cross bar with a hole in it, just large enough in diameter for the mast to pass through it.

Sailing stern   Sailing bow

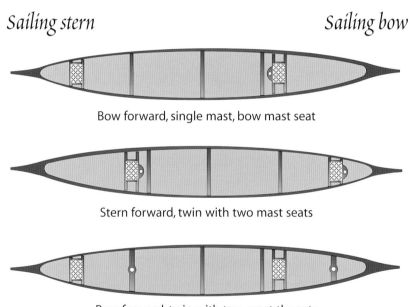

Bow forward, single mast, bow mast seat

Stern forward, twin with two mast seats

Bow forward, twin with two mast thwarts

If desired, a mast thwart—an extra-wide thwart with a mast hole in it—can be used instead. This would replace the quarter thwart, located just behind the bow seat. If you plan to do a lot of high-wind sailing, keep in mind that a mast thwart, bolted tightly under the gunwale, is stronger than a mast seat that has been lowered into position on long bolts and wooden spacers, as in many common bow seat installations.

A block—the mast step—is attached to the canoe's floor, directly under the mast hole in the seat or thwart. The heel of the mast is designed to fit into a depression cut into the block. Most masts taper drastically between the mast hole and mast step, and are only an inch or so in diameter at the bottom, or heel. This allows us to use a fairly small block.

A twin-masted rig will have two mast holes (seats and/or thwarts) and two mast steps. The forward mast on most twins is pretty far forward, so the most common configurations involve either a hole in the bow deck for the mast, an added mast thwart near the bow, or replacing both seats with mast seats and actually sailing the boat with its paddling stern as the sailing bow.

The principal drawback to a stern-first twin is that rudder gudgeons, even nice ones, aren't very pretty, yet they will be bolted to your bow when you're not sailing. Better to stick with bow-first sailing by adding a removable forward mast thwart and stepping the mizzen through the stern quarter thwart. That way, the gudgeons will be on the stern when you're paddling and the boat will look better.

The important point here is that you determine how much sail area you want, which sail style you prefer, and where you can step the masts without having to completely rebuild the canoe.

Calculating Sail Area for Three-Sided Sails

By convention, sails are usually measured as either three-sided or four-sided sails. Multi-faceted bat-wings have more sides than that, but they are usually measured as three-sided sails—as if they had no roach and the leech was a straight line from the peak, at the head of the sail, to the clew, near the end of the boom.

This inner triangle (peak to clew to tack and back to peak) is where the sail gets most of its power and upwind capability. Since a rig's efficiency is generally determined by its ability to sail to weather, or windward, this is the most important part of the sail.

On a bat-wing, where so much of the sail is roach, you could probably justify measuring the actual sections and adding them up. You will be trying to counterbalance all of that area while reaching, so it may be a better way to determine how much sail to put on the canoe. But for the design on paper, we'll follow tradition and use the standard measurement triangle.

There are two methods for measuring triangular sails. On a sail where the boom is more-or-less perpendicular to the mast, we can multiply the luff measurement (tack to peak, along the mast) by the foot measurement (tack to clew, along the boom) and divide by two.

Some triangular sails, such as lateens, leg-o'-muttons, and jibs, don't have those convenient right angles. We use a slightly different measurement system for them. Since there is no existing right angle, we add one by drawing a line that is perpendicular to the luff (leading edge) and runs from the luff to the clew (back corner). This is called the luff perpendicular or L.P. We multiply the luff measurement by the L.P. and divide the result by two, which gives us the sail's area.

The standard measurement triangle of this bat-wing ignores the roach, as if it were a normal three-sided sail. With the mast and boom at nearly a right angle, sail area for the triangle is easily calculated—luff times foot, divided by two. Sailmakers label the mainsail luff "dimension P" and the foot length, along the boom, "dimension E." Mainsail area is:

$$\frac{P \times E}{2}$$

As long as the jog around the joint in the mast isn't too big and the upper luff is vertical, we can usually treat it as one continuous edge.

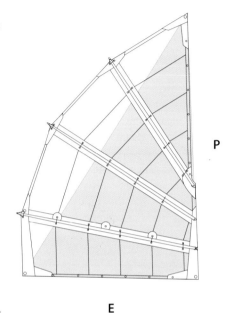

On three-sided sails without convenient right angles, such as lateens and jibs, we draw a line called a "luff perpendicular" from the luff to the clew. Sail area is then calculated as luff times L.P., divided by two. Any hollow in the leech, as shown here, is ignored for measurement.

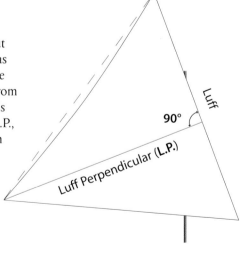

$$\text{Area} = \frac{\text{Luff} \times \text{L.P.}}{2}$$

Calculating Sail Area for Four-Sided Sails

Four-sided sails, such as lugsails, gaff sails, and spritsails, are a little more complex to measure, but use the same basic methods. By drawing a diagonal line from the sail's clew to its throat, we can subdivide the sail into two triangular sections. Each of these is then measured as if it were a three-sided sail, and the results are added together. I like the "L.P. method" for this type of measurement, but usually draw my perpendiculars out from whichever side of the triangle is the longest.

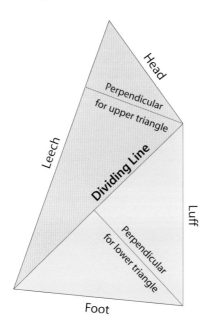

$$\frac{\text{Upper perpendicular x leech length}}{2} = \textbf{area of upper triangle}$$

$$\frac{\text{Lower perpendicular x length of dividing line}}{2} = \textbf{area of lower triangle}$$

$$\text{Upper triangle + lower triangle} = \textbf{total area}$$

Scaling Sail Area Up or Down

What if we have designed a pleasing shape for our sail, calculated its area, and find that it is larger or smaller than we had planned to put on the canoe? What if we also want to have a matching mizzen with the same shape, but smaller? How do we scale the sail up or down?

All we have to do is get out our handy pocket calculator and start multiplying all the sail's dimensions—but, there is a catch. Though the edge measurements of the sail increase in a one-dimensional way (a 6-foot-long luff multiplied by 150 percent is 9 feet long), the sail area is a two-dimensional product. Remember those "luff x L.P. = area" calculations?

If our sail area is 30 square feet and we multiply all the edge measurements by 150 percent, our spars may only need to be 50 percent longer, but our sail area will more than double because the sail is growing in two dimensions. The new sail area will be 67.5 square feet! If our original intention was to boost sail area from 30 to around 45 square feet, we seem to have overshot the mark.

To generate the 67.5-square-foot figure, I multiplied the 30-square-foot sail area by 150 percent—twice, once for each dimension. If you distrust calculators, you can also draw out the sail and measure its shape, but the answer will still be the same. Obviously, if we want to convert our sail to around 45 square feet, we will have to multiply all of our dimensions by a smaller number.

I'm sure there is a formula for this, and I'm sure somebody knows it, but I'm also sure that it's not me. Back to the calculator.

Thirty square feet, multiplied by, say, 125 percent—twice, is 46.87 square feet.... Close, but let's try again. How about 123 percent? This time we end up with 45.38 square feet.

We could start using fractions of percentage points and eventually arrive at precisely 45 square feet, but it's not that critical and I hate multiplying fractions. We will settle for 45.38 square feet and get back to work. We now know that by increasing our sail's edge dimensions by 123 percent we will end up with a sail that is about the size we need.

If we want to shrink our sail because it is too big, or we want a matching mizzen—say, 20 square feet—we could hunt-and-peck percentages (multiplying twice, for area again) and eventually find that reducing the edge dimensions to 82 percent of their original size will yield a 20.17-square-foot sail. Close enough.

Now that we have calculated our sail area, adjusted it as necessary, located the best places in the canoe to step the masts, and drawn the sails accurately on the plan, we are ready to find the center of effort, that theoretical point where the wind's power is focused on the sail plan.

Finding the Center of Effort

This is actually pretty simple, involving no noticeable math or physics. We start by reverting to our basic measurement triangles. For four-sided sails, we will again divide them into the two triangles that we used to measure their area.

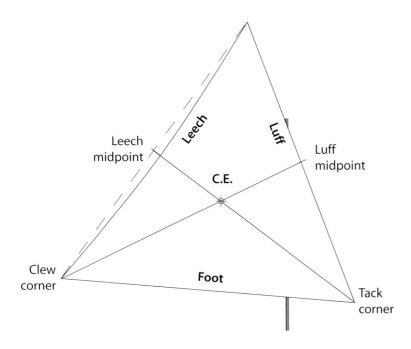

On a three-sided sail, such as a typical mainsail or a lateen, we use the length of the luff and the leech. Put a mark at the midpoint of each of these edges. Now draw two lines: one from the clew to the luff's mid-point, and the other from the tack to the leech's midpoint. The spot where these lines cross is the center of effort of that sail. Here again, for design purposes, we ignore roach and hollow in the leech.

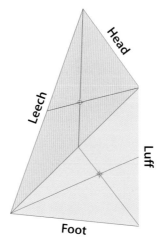

Step 1

On our four-sided sail, we start by finding the C.E. of both triangles. One is upside-down, but that doesn't matter. We use the dividing line as one of our long edges and its midpoint can be used for drawing lines on both the upper and the lower sections. We now have a C.E. for each triangle.

Step 2

Now draw a line connecting the two centers. In order to find the C.E. for the sail as a whole we will need to average these two sections, using their relative sail areas. The "C.E. Total" will lie somewhere along the line between the centers of the sections, but where?

When we calculated the sail's area, we first calculated each individual triangle. Those are the measurements we will use to locate the final position of the sail's center of effort.

When I originally designed this sail, it ended-up being 38.75 sq. ft. total, with 17.3 sq. ft. in the upper triangle and 21.45 sq. ft. in the lower one. Since we already have those figures, we will use them for this exercise.

Connecting the centers

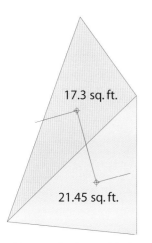

17.3 sq. ft.

21.45 sq. ft.

Perpendiculars added

Step 3

We want to draw two more lines, at right angles to the line connecting the centers. Each line starts at one of the centers, and they head off in opposite directions. It doesn't matter which one goes in which direction. The result should look like Step 3. The length of these lines is important. The length of the upper one is based on the area of the lower triangle; the lower one represents the area of the upper triangle.

You can use inches, feet, astronomical units, or pumpkin diameters, whatever will fit on your page, as long as, in this case, the upper line is 21.45 units long, and the lower one is 17.3 units long.

Step 4

Finally, we connect the outer ends of these lines to each other. The new line crosses the line that connected our individual centers, from Step 2, and the spot where the new line crosses the old line is the actual center of effort for the entire sail. This now becomes the only C.E. that we will use for any future calculations having to do with the sail's C.E.

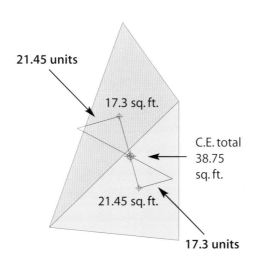

21.45 units

17.3 sq. ft.

C.E. total
38.75
sq. ft.

21.45 sq. ft.

17.3 units

The finished drawing of this four-sided sail, with its C.E. marked, is ready to be inserted into a sail plan. Detail, such as corner patches, grommets, and trim, can be added as desired.

Combined Centers of Effort

For a twin-sailed rig, we place the individual sails in their proper locations on the plan and then use almost the identical technique to find the C.E. for the combined pair. Once we have each sail's area and have marked its C.E., a line is drawn between the two centers and perpendiculars are drawn out from each sail's C.E.; their lengths reflect the size of the opposing sail in some convenient unit of measurement.

The tips of the perpendiculars are connected with a line, and the point where that line crosses the line connecting the centers is the total center of effort for the sail plan.

This same technique can be used to find the C.E. of a big schooner with multiple masts, several jibs, and a combination of three- and four-sided sails. Each sail is measured individually, then the centers are found and combined into sub-groups. These are then combined into larger groups until, finally, only two remain. The combined center of these two groups is the boat's combined C.E.—but that's a lot of work.

Individual and combined centers of effort on a twin lateen rig

Putting It All Together

When we last left our paper sliver cutout of the immersed portion of our canoe's hull, it was a bit tail-heavy because we had added the rudder blade and the sails were not yet definite. We can now draw in the sails. We have placed the mast structure, calculated the sail area, and found the rig's center of effort. Now we can start putting the whole package together and exploring the interaction between the hull and its power source.

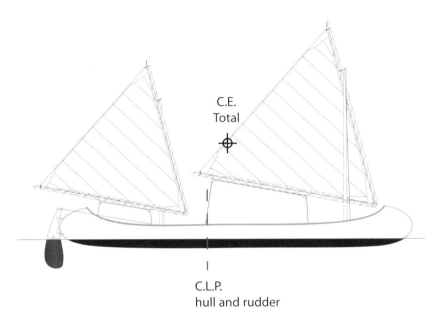

C.E.
Total

C.L.P.
hull and rudder

We can see that, without the leeboards, our sail plan's center of effort is slightly ahead of the center of lateral plane for the hull and the rudder, the focus of the canoe's resistance to sideways drift. If we add some wind, the boat will move forward, probably slipping sideways a bit due to our current lack of leeboards and sufficient underwater area, but it will be sailing.

The C.L.P. of a sailboat's hull acts in some ways as a pivot point. Adding pressure to the sails ahead of the C.L.P. will tend to turn the bow away from the wind; i.e., downwind. Pressure behind the C.L.P. will try to turn the bow up, into the wind. We can see here that with this configuration, with the sail plan's C.E. ahead of the C.L.P., our boat should want to turn downwind.

Unless you do something very peculiar when designing your sail plan, nearly all canoe rigs will end up similar to this, with the C.E. ahead of the C.L.P., although the amount that the C.E. leads the C.L.P. by may vary a bit from plan to plan. This is good. We want the C.E. slightly ahead, and the reason why we want the sails to be trying to turn the bow downwind may surprise you.

We want the C.E. to lead the C.L.P. so that the canoe will hold its course pretty well, with a slight tendency to turn UPWIND.

Wait…didn't he just say that the C.E.-ahead configuration would cause the bow to want to turn downwind?

Yes I did. And it would—on paper. But in real life, as you will see the first time you go canoe sailing, canoes heel over when they sail, sometimes quite a bit! As we heel a sailboat over, its hull shape becomes asymmetrical in the water.

No, the hull isn't bending, but the waterline becomes a diagonal slice of the hull's cross-section, not the horizontal one that we think of for a canoe being paddled.

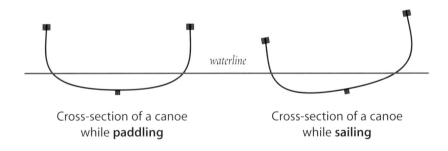

waterline

Cross-section of a canoe
while **paddling**

Cross-section of a canoe
while **sailing**

Waterline Plane, the Curve That Carves

Not only does the canoe's heeled cross-section become asymmetrical, when viewed from the end, but also its waterline plane does as well. Waterline plane might best be described as looking at that same waterline cross-section, but from an aerial view. When the canoe is upright, the waterline plane is normally cigar shaped, but as we heel the canoe the low side gets rounder and fatter and the high side straighter and thinner.

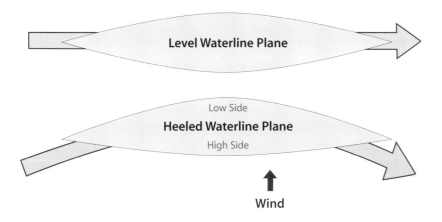

This new asymmetrical hull shape doesn't track in a straight line. Instead, it starts to carve a turn toward the high side. Since sailing craft heel away from the wind as they sail, the hull has a noticeable tendency to turn upwind. The more it heels, the more it wants to turn.

Short, wide canoes are affected more than long, narrow ones, because the fatter shape accentuates the heeled asymmetry. All sailboats will carve upwind to some extent. To get our canoe to sail in a straight line, we will have to find a way to counteract this heel-induced turning force.

We therefore place the sail plan's center of effort ahead of the boat's pivot point, the C.L.P., to counteract the hull's tendency to turn upwind as the boat heels. If the sail's C.E. were even with, or behind the hull's C.L.P., it wouldn't be able to neutralize the steering and we would constantly have to use the rudder to counteract the heeling canoe's tendency to head up. But dragging a rudder through the water at an angle to correct the helm really slows a boat down and is to be avoided.

Once we get our sailing canoe in the water, we want it to have just a slight tendency to turn upwind, which we will correct with subtle rudder use. A sailboat that wants to turn up (or "to weather" in sailor's language) is said to have "weather helm." One that might want to turn downwind (or "to lee") has "lee helm."

We want our canoe to have just a little weather helm. Why? There are several reasons, some of which approach fluid dynamics and I won't bore you to death with them, but the main reason is simple: If you fall out of a boat with weather helm, it will head up and come to a stop, head-to-wind. You might even be able to get back in while it waits patiently for you.

Most paddlers are well aware that a canoe can tip to a point that it sends the occupants into the lake and then it pops right back up, nearly dry. A sailing canoe with a neutral helm or a lee helm might throw you out and keep on going without you. Imagine realizing that you might drown and that, even worse, your 1916 Morris-Veazie is about to sail itself over the dam!

So, it is good to have the C.E. of our sail plan slightly forward of the hull's C.L.P. So good, in fact, that the relationship has a name—it's called "lead," and it rhymes with seed, not Fred. For regular sailboats, the C.E. should lead the C.L.P. by 5 to 15 percent of the boat's waterline length, depending on the type of boat and its rig.

On a canoe, we would probably like to see about a 10 percent lead, but it really doesn't matter because we are about to attach our leeboards. Not only do leeboards contribute the majority of our actual lateral resistance, but also they are infinitely adjustable. What seems like the ultimate add-on contraption is actually a brilliant idea.

Leeboards, the Final Piece of the Puzzle

Though we may want to draw the leeboards on our sail plan, it really isn't necessary from a design standpoint. By far the best way to fit them into the equation is to take the canoe sailing and experiment with the location of the leeboard bracket and the angle of the boards.

Unless the sail plan calculations showed that our C.E.-to-C.L.P. relationship was way out of normal parameters, the best starting position for the leeboard bracket is directly below the sail plan's center of effort—the C.E. on a single-sail rig or the combined C.E. on a twin.

The plan does tell us what part of the boat falls under the C.E., so the bracket should be designed to fit the width of the canoe in that general area. Most brackets have enough adjustability to be moved a foot or two forward or aft of the C.E.'s position, if needed, though such large adjustments are rarely necessary.

On the water, leeboards are used most when reaching across the wind's direction and when sailing close-hauled, going to weather. The more upwind your course, the more important the leeboards are. For sailing off the wind on a broad reach, you can swivel the board(s) most of the way out of the water. The hull shape alone will usually do most of the lateral resisting. On a downwind run, pull the boards all the way up; you won't need them for directional control, and when they're down they contribute drag, costing you speed. Most sailboats also have somewhat more docile handling when they are sailing downwind with the board retracted.

To adjust the position of our leeboard system, we obviously want to be sailing a course where we need leeboards, so that means a beam reach, a close reach, or close-hauled. Usually, only the leeward board—the one away from the wind on the low side of the canoe—is used. The high-side leeboard is swiveled up out of the water to reduce drag. If you happen to be making a series of short tacks, seem to be slipping sideways, or just don't want to have to mess with the boards that day, it's perfectly all right to leave both boards down. You will only lose a little speed. For testing, though, it is better to put your canoe in its optimum sailing mode and pull the windward board.

Trials should begin in winds typical of those you normally expect for most of your sailing and with the active board as close to vertical as you

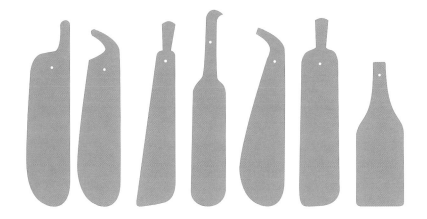

can eyeball. What we're looking for is a bracket location that produces a slight amount of weather helm. If you release the steering rope, tiller, or what-have-you, the canoe should slowly round up and come to a stop with the sails flapping.

If your canoe keeps going straight when the helm is released, or turns downwind, you have too much lead and need to move the leeboard bracket forward. On the other hand, if it seems that you are having to apply massive amounts of rudder to keep the boat from heading up while sailing (too much weather helm), move the leeboard bracket back a bit and try again.

Experiment on both port and starboard tacks, reaching and close-hauled, to find the best all-around position for the boards. It might take a couple of seasons to become a really proficient leeboard handler, getting the best performance with the least amount of drag out of the system.

At certain sailing angles you may find that swiveling the board back a bit improves the handling.

You will also find that since the boat heels more on windy days, it has more tendency to turn upwind. You may need to move the bracket aft a little to reduce weather helm, or hike out to keep the boat more upright. The more symmetrical you can make the waterline plane, the less weather helm it will induce on the canoe.

Gee, we haven't even built the rig yet, and we're already out doing sea trials. Oh well, sometimes a little actual on-the-water experimentation is more valuable than endless pages of text. In this case, I think you will find it so.

One thing that we haven't discussed, and it's worth thinking about, is the size or area of leeboards and rudders. If you look through the available books, magazine articles, and manufacturer's catalogs that mention canoe sailing rigs, you will see a staggering assortment of leeboard shapes and sizes.

I have a reprint of the 1908 Morris Canoes catalog that shows the "best device in a double leeboard on the market." The Morris leeboards looked somewhat like those wooden paddles they use in pizza places to get your pizza out of the oven. I haven't seen any others like them, so perhaps the concept never caught on. The set, with bracket, was only $7.00. What a deal! Of course, back then you could buy a boat to go with the boards for $50 and ship it from Maine to Chicago for $2.80.

Though I have seen at least one chart that prescribed leeboard and rudder dimensions for canoes with various amounts of sail area, there are so many possible hull sizes and shapes that I find it difficult to believe a single chart could cover all of them.

Unless…it doesn't really matter that much.

On regular sailboats, the typical underwater-profile-area-to-sail-area figure is 8 to 10 percent. Most of the canoes that I have measured have more than 10 percent of sail area in the underwater profile if you combine the areas of the leeboard (one board), the rudder, and the sliver of hull that's underwater.

If somebody wanted to find out what the minimum area of the underwater profile should be, they could carve away bits of their rudder and leeboards until they lost steering control or started sideslipping, but the knowledge probably isn't worth the time to get it.

For a standard 15- to 18-foot-long canoe, a leeboard is usually long enough to reach down 25 to 30 inches into the water when the boat is not heeling. This would make it somewhere around 40 inches long overall.

The width is usually 9 or 10 inches and thickness ¾ inch to 1 inch. The rudder blade's immersed section is typically around 8 inches wide, and it extends down into the water 12 to 18 inches.

For small canoes, the boards and rudder could probably be reduced by 25 to 30 percent. If you build a sailing canoe from plans or a kit, the dimensions for these parts should be specified along with the sail area.

Some canoe sailors build only one leeboard. By making it about a foot longer than normal, it will still reach the water even when it's on the high side of the canoe. It's another option that is worth considering.

Congratulations! If you have made it this far, you have survived the most tedious, technical chapter in this book. It was as much fun to write as it is to read. Though I'm sure that some of this material is confusing to read all at once, by working through it step by step, designing a rig on paper is actually not that difficult and can even be…er…uh…interesting.

Spars

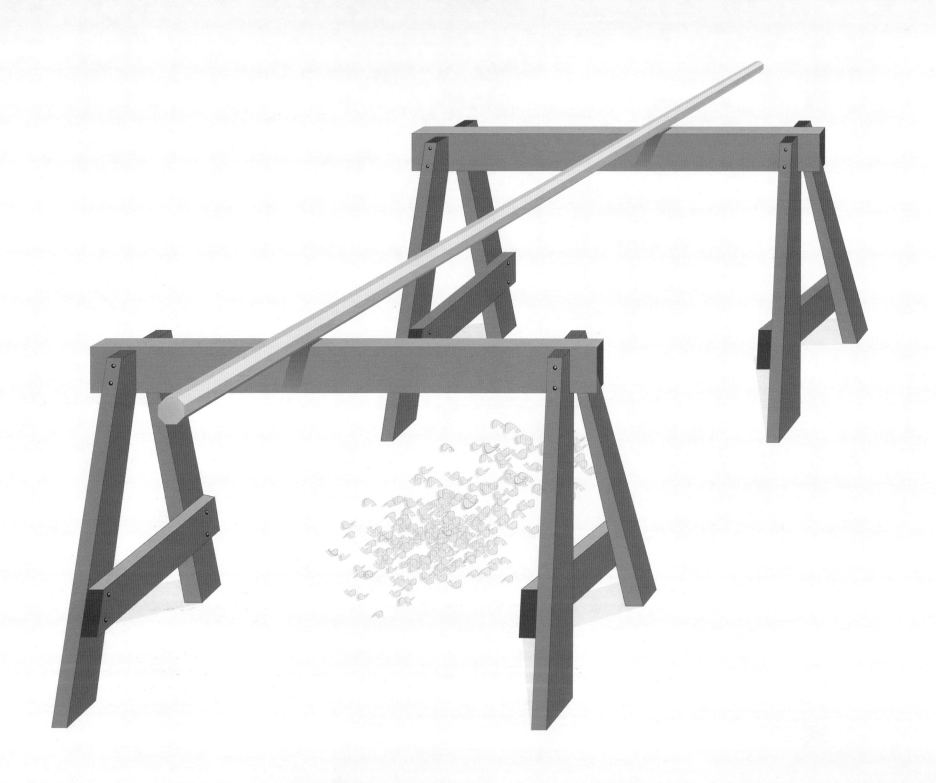

Parameters

The ideal spar—mast, yard, or boom—for a sailing canoe weighs next to nothing, doesn't bend at all, is tremendously strong, requires no hard-to-find hardware, enhances the beauty of the sails and rig, and, unfortunately, doesn't exist. Even so, these are the characteristics that should be kept in mind when designing, buying, or building any spar for a canoe.

Obviously, some compromises will have to be made, and we will probably never approach our ideal, but we must never forget those ideal characteristics. We can use them as a yardstick to help decide when and how to make those inevitable compromises.

If we look at the desired characteristics of a good canoe spar, light weight would have to be at or near the top of the list. Since we have no real keel, no big chunk of lead for ballast, and a narrower-than-usual sailing hull, we don't want anything heavy up there pitching back and forth, exerting its leverage on the entire canoe.

Since our sail area will be relatively small, we also want light spars for performance, especially in light winds. Fitting a 14-pound oversized oak boom, built from the better part of a 2-by-4 and laced to the bottom of a 40-square-foot canoe sail, is a good way to prove that gravity exists, but it is no way to go sailing. In anything but a gale, such a boom will kill our sail shape, and if we accidentally jibe without ducking, it will probably kill us, too.

On racing sailboats, masts are often held up by a number of wires, some of which are quickly adjustable in use. Their primary function is to adjust the amount of fore-and-aft bend in the mast and consequently the amount of draft, or camber, in the mainsail. On a sailing canoe, wires are for the most part unnecessary and generally undesirable, because they make what is already a confined area to work in even more cramped.

Sail-shaping by adjusting mast bend is thus not a real option for most canoe sailors. We usually assume that by using the proper material and diameter for the mast, it will essentially stay straight in use. An unstayed canoe mast that is too flexible has a tendency to allow the entire rig to lean to leeward, which makes rig design difficult and, for what it's worth, looks awful. Many of the production sailing rigs that have been put out by canoe manufacturers over the years have used skinny, aluminum spars which do just that.

As you have probably noticed, many canoe rigs use the mast as little more than a means to hoist a configuration made up of smaller spars and the sail. Since trying to counterbalance a tall, skinny, modern mainsail on a canoe hull is very difficult, the canoe rig often uses width rather than height to spread sail area. Though not necessarily providing the pinnacle of performance, the wider, lower rig makes the sail area more manageable, which is why it's also popular on some types of larger sailing craft, such as schooners.

As we spread out horizontally, these smaller spars (and sometimes even the sail's battens) form the "bones" that support our wings. Rarely do the yards or booms used on canoe sails exceed the diameter of a closet pole. Any kid who ever tried swinging on a closet pole will vouch for its flexibility—at least until it broke.

If we maintain reasonable diameter and weight parameters for booms, yards, and gaffs used on canoe rigs, we are going to have to live with the fact that they will bend in use. We can laminate these spars, which both stiffens them and helps eliminate failure from poor wood grain, but they will still bend.

Just as mast bend on big racing boats influences sail shape, spar bend on a sailing canoe will tend to flatten the sail, removing some of the sail's draft. To perform properly, many canoe sails are actually built to fit bent spars, even though when not under load, the spars are straight as an arrow.

It is not unusual to see 4 or 5 inches of bend on a lateen sail's yard or boom when sailing in moderate winds. As long as the sail is designed and cut to work with that much spar bend, it is not a problem. In heavy air when the mainsheet puts even more tension on the rig, the spars will bend more and will begin to flatten the sail. This, too, is not a problem. A flattened sail is actually desirable, as it depowers the rig, reducing heeling force and weather helm in the process.

The compromise comes in light air when the loads on the rig aren't high enough to bend things much. A flatter sail makes a better light-wind airfoil. Since our sail is cut to allow for moderate bend in the spars, it will be a bit deep in the draft for light loads, and we might lose some speed as a result.

In general, we can live with this. I suppose anyone who can't could build a special light-wind sail, made for straight spars, but the rest of us will simply sail a bit slower and enjoy the fact that light-wind canoe sailing gives one a chance to look around and enjoy the day. The guy with the fast sail will just get done sooner and have to go home and mow his lawn earlier.

When we discuss sail design, measuring and allowing for spar bend will be discussed in more detail. For now, we only need to know that the bending of the spars can affect the shape of the sail and is a good reason to build the spars before cutting any sailcloth.

Shorter spars, like those in some of the bat-wing rigs, don't really bend enough to require sail modifications. They are also more portable, as they break down into smaller stowed packages for tripping and transport. If the short-spar rigs—the gunters, bat-wings, and gaffers—have a serious drawback, it is their complexity. Joining two short spars solidly enough to replace a single mast can involve designing and building connecting hardware. This is, and appears to have always been, a designer's free-for-all. Like most of the spars that they connect, these mechanical fittings use small quantities of materials without requiring a tremendous investment in money or time. Experimentation is encouraged and often rewarded, and rig loads are usually light enough that failure is rare.

A successful piece of spar-connecting hardware should work smoothly, hold up under reasonable strain, and visually complement the rest of the rig. A well-designed fitting, built from a piece of sheet brass or bronze, can be almost like a piece of jewelry—it can be both functional and decorative.

The same is true for laminated or steam-bent jaws for a boom or gaff. They are small parts of the rig, yet they have a great deal of visual impact if their shape, proportions, and construction are carefully planned and executed.

It is entirely possible to build most of the spar systems in this book with almost no metal parts. Since we are dealing with such small components (compared to larger sailboats) and supporting relatively small sails, it is possible to substitute loops and eyes, spliced from chunks of rope, for many of the jaws and hoops that usually join spars and sails to their masts. For example, the halyards, the lines that pull the spars and sails up the mast and into sailing position, normally must pass through a sheave set into the masthead. In a light canoe rig, a hole, with its bearing surface and edges carefully rounded and smoothed, is often all that is needed.

In some ways, canoe sailors are the luckiest sailors of all. Many of the problems common to rigging large sailboats—friction, chafe, stress on the hull and, above all, cost of rigging or re-rigging—are all quite reasonable. After all, how much maintenance does it take to ensure that a halyard hole bored through your masthead still works properly?

The Mast

The word "mast" carries all by itself a connotation of importance—and it is important—yet the mast on a canoe rig can usually be made from a 2-by-2, assuming you can find a good one. It can be carved from a relatively pricey chunk of premium aircraft spruce, laminated from molding stock purchased at a home improvement store, or cut from a carefully selected piece of lumber that may have been originally destined to end up inside somebody's kitchen wall. (If I'm ever reincarnated as a piece of lumber, I'd much rather end up in the hands of a spar builder than as a piece of a soffit over a refrigerator.)

As varied as are the sail plans for canoes, their masts share fairly similar dimensions and construction details. Though some may be only 4 feet tall and others three times that, their diameters usually vary by less than an inch. Granted, a small mizzen stuck on the stern of a yawl-rigged boat may have a mast the size of a broomstick, but most canoe mainmasts are between 1½ and 2½ inches at their maximum diameter (usually at the approximate point where the end of the boom meets the mast) and are tapered below the mast thwart or seat to an inch or so where they fit into the mast step.

The heel of the mast may actually be cut to a square cross-section where it fits into the mast step. This keeps the mast from turning as the boat tacks and jibes. On most canoe sails, however, a round cross-section shouldn't be a problem. Few of the aluminum tubes that are used for masts on popular sailing dinghies have anything other than a round plug in the bottom end, and I've never noticed them turning enough to present any problem. Halyard tension is usually enough to keep the mast from spinning in its socket.

I suppose the determining factor should be what, if any, hardware is attached to the mast. If the boom is joined to the mast by a gooseneck (a mechanical universal joint) or if a gaff sail is rigged with both throat and peak halyards running through blocks (pulleys, in sailor talk) that are shackled to the mast, it might well be worth squaring off the mast at the butt and fitting it to a square mast step to keep the rig from spinning.

Somewhere above the junction of the mast and the boom, we can start tapering the mast to reduce weight aloft. The point at which the taper begins depends on the chosen sail type. At the masthead, most canoe masts are only 1 inch to 1¼ inches in diameter.

The mast for a gaff-rigged sail is a bit different in design from the others. The tapers aren't particularly complex, but it is quite important that they are properly located.

Being a four-sided sail, much of a gaff sail's area is supported by the gaff itself. The throat halyard pulls the gaff up the mast, keeping the luff of the sail tight; the peak halyard, leading from mid-gaff to the masthead and down, adjusts the angle of the gaff. More often than not the peak halyard is set quite tight, pulling the gaff up to its steepest possible angle. This makes the boat point better.

The area where the gaff jaws meet the mast is under a lot of pressure from taut halyards—so much so that most gaffers are fitted with a mast that is actually thickest in the area where the gaff jaws land on it. On normal gaff-rigged sailboats, the mast is often tapered a bit between the gaff and the boom, and usually has a fairly fast taper to the masthead above the gaff's bearing area. For a gaff-rigged canoe, it is usually sufficient for the mast diameter to be uniform from the mast thwart to just above the gaff, and for the top and bottom of the mast to be tapered. If you feel ambitious, you can add a bit more thickness to the mast in the area where the gaff meets it; the mast will look less like a pole and be a bit stiffer.

The masts for lugsails and lateens aren't generally subjected to the focused loads that the masts of gaff-rigged boats endure. Still, it's wise to carry most of the diameter until past the area where the mast and the yard intersect. With some rigs, on one tack the yard will be pushing on the mast and on the other tack the yard will be pulling at about the same place.

The optimal shape for almost any canoe mast (aside from a gaff-rigger), both structurally and cosmetically, is a narrow, tapered heel, nearly maximum diameter where the mast passes through the seat or thwart, and a bit of flare around the point where the end of the boom meets the mast. Above the boom, we want a gradual mast taper along the luff of such sails as the gunter, leg-o'-mutton, and bat-wing. On yard-equipped rigs, we want only a slight taper between the boom area and the yard intersection. Once above the yard, the taper can be accelerated toward the desired diameter at the masthead.

Since the masts of gunter and bat-wing rigs are divided into two pieces, the topmast will support much of the sail area. It may be overkill, but I like to see the diameters of the two spars nearly the same where they overlap. As a sailmaker, I find it difficult to plan for a mast that suddenly changes its flexibility halfway up.

I would put some taper in the lower end of the topmast, both for weight savings and cosmetics. On most bat-wings and small gunters I would taper the topmast to around 1 inch in diameter at the head.

There are a few rigs in this book where I note that stiff masts would be best. The easiest way to gain stiffness is to increase diameter. As we do this, we obviously also gain weight aloft. Laminating may help, as it produces a stiffer spar than a single piece of wood and therefore the mast can be smaller in diameter.

If laminating a mast is being considered, consider also building a hollow mast. While making a hollow spar requires more planning and more work than a solid one, it is the best way to gain maximum stiffness and diameter without just piling on more wood and more weight.

Though there are a few sparmakers who actually build hollow spars by gluing up six or eight wedge-shaped pieces, most hollow spars might be best described as "air channeled." They are built from rectangular stock with rectangular air space inside. Internal blocking is used to fill the void at both ends of the spar and to back up those areas where hardware is attached or where other components of the rig will put concentrated strains.

From the standpoint of weight loss vs. labor expended, it probably isn't worth messing with a hollow spar less than 2 inches in diameter, but for anything larger, especially a long mast, building a hollow spar is definitely worth considering. For a canoe-sized mast, it might add an extra day or two to the construction time, but most of that will be spent planning the project and watching the glue dry. If we can eliminate 20 percent of the wood in a mast, we can eliminate 20 percent of the weight; if a hollow mast is built properly, we won't really lose any strength.

If you can find and afford it, spar-grade spruce is considered the premium raw material for sparmaking. Sitka spruce will generally be clear; Eastern spruce may have a few small knots. A lumber dealer specializing in either aircraft or boat lumber should be able to provide what you need. For stock over 8 feet long, shipping can easily be twice the cost of the wood itself. Air freight is usually cheaper and faster than truck freight, but check with the yard to be sure.

Since canoe spars are so small, their dimensions fall within the sizes available in construction lumber, most of which is either spruce, pine, or fir and all of which can produce a good mast or spar. If you are willing to spend the time, you have a reasonably good chance of finding what you need by sorting through the piles of 2-by-4s at your local lumberyard. This will be especially likely if you are planning to laminate your spars.

Also, check out the moldings used for trimming doors and windows. These are pre-milled and quite smooth, ready to laminate. Since molding stock is usually stored inside, it should be straight and dry—ideal for laminating.

Mast Cross-Sections

There are a lot of possible cross-sections for the block of wood that will become a canoe mast. It can be made from a solid chunk of high-quality spruce, or it can be pieced up, requiring a weekend's work to plan, prepare the pieces, and glue the blank together.

At any place where a fitting will be attached or where a boom or a gaff will eventually meet the mast, a block should be fitted inside to make the mast solid.

Hollow-mast builders must plan carefully for the tapers that will be cut into the ends. For a canoe mast, it is probably unwise to allow the mast walls to drop below half an inch thick anywhere. Blocking can be used to fill any areas where the tapered walls of the mast are too thin.

It is possible to build a tapered, hollow blank from tapered, component pieces, but such a blank is much more difficult to design and to clamp for gluing.

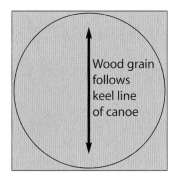

One-piece masts, carved from a good piece of spruce, pine, or fir, are the most common, as well as the easiest to build.

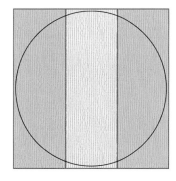

Laminating allows the use of smaller, easier-to-find stock and prevents any grain flaws from affecting the entire mast.

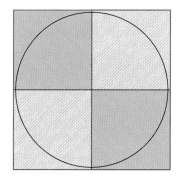

Laminating with quarter-sawn stock gives great strength and best appearance.

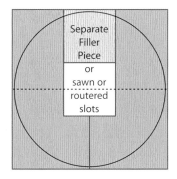

Air-channeled hollow masts save some weight, and some wood, but are more complex to build and require internal blocking or gaps in the cut slots to reinforce stress areas and to seal the ends.

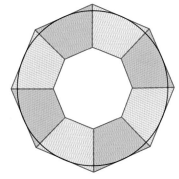

Lightest and most difficult to build and block, using quarter-sawn wood, a mast with a cross-section like this makes the ideal, light, stiff canoe mast—but it is quite a project.

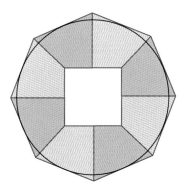

This one is trickier to cut pieces for, but it is easier to block inside. It can even be blocked full length with a combination of spruce for the outside and balsa on the inside, and can be glued up using rubber bands for clamps.

Hardwood Spars

Depending upon where you live and what's locally available, other woods might work for canoe masts and spars. Cedar, hemlock, and redwood, though not as desirable as spruce and fir, are all woods that can produce acceptable spars.

If you happen to be sitting on a pile of straight-grained hardwood, it is possible to build masts and short canoe spars from ash, birch, hickory, cherry, oak, or even walnut. Other than the economy of using something that you already possess, though, I can't see much reason to add the extra weight to your rig, especially at the possible expense of spar stiffness.

Some paddle makers routinely laminate spruce or fir with ash for paddle shafts, especially for whitewater use, where such a combination adds to the strength of the paddle. The same could work for the mast of a sailing canoe, but as long as the diameter is sufficient to do the job, the hardwood isn't necessary. A sailing canoe has a built-in mechanism to prevent the strain on the mast from becoming extreme—it heels over and spills wind.

If you will be laminating with epoxy resin, avoid using it on oak. The two don't seem to be compatible, and the bond will probably fail in time. Ash, on the other hand, works fine with epoxy and would be a better choice. It's also about 10 percent lighter than oak.

Hickory can make a very tough spar. I don't suppose the difference in weight between it and, say, spruce on a mast that's only 5 feet long would be too much of a problem. But, here again, unless you're expecting to be attacked by pirates, where you might have to use your mast to defend yourself, hickory is really overkill.

A good piece of mahogany, if you can find one, would make a very nice canoe spar, but many of the other commonly available hardwoods have enough wandering grain that finding a suitable piece would be difficult.

Planning Your Spars

Becoming a good sparmaker doesn't happen overnight. For those who would prefer to have a professional build their canoe spars, such magazines as *WoodenBoat* and Britain's *Classic Boat* are the best places to find advertisements for wooden spar builders. Those that I have spoken to are quite willing to build canoe-sized spars and at a reasonable price. If you don't already have the glue, planes, spokeshaves, and a pile of clamps, it may actually be cheaper to buy spars than to build them. You will need to provide an accurate plan, showing spar diameters at critical places, such as the mast thwart and the step, though the drawing need not be fancy. Your sparmaker may also be able to make suggestions regarding spar diameter, which is always a guessing game on a canoe rig.

For those who do wish to build their own spars, the first step is obviously to develop a plan. The length of each spar in a rig will come directly from your sail plan. Spars that lie along the edges of the sails, such as booms and yards, should be at least 2, usually 3 or 4 inches longer than the sail's edge. Cutting them shorter than that will make stretching out the sail along the spar difficult.

The length of the mast above the intersection of the yard or gaff will depend on the sail type. On a gaff-rigged boat, the peak halyard runs from the deck up to the masthead and down to the gaff. It pulls up and in on the gaff, dictating the sail's shape and efficiency. If the mast is too short, you won't be able to get enough tension on the peak halyard and the boat's pointing ability will suffer.

On a typical sail plan for a gaffer, the masthead will be below the peak of the gaff but seldom lower than the midpoint of the gaff in its sailing position. This "extra" mast length above the intersection of the mast and the gaff is what will provide the proper leverage to peak up the sail properly.

As we see here, we have more design flexibility when planning masthead height for yard-equipped sails, such as lateens and lugs. The critical factor is to incorporate some means of keeping the yard close to the mast. On one tack, the wind will simply blow the yard up against the mast, but on the other tack, the yard will be blown away from it. If the yard is hanging on a foot or more of halyard, it will be constantly wandering in all directions.

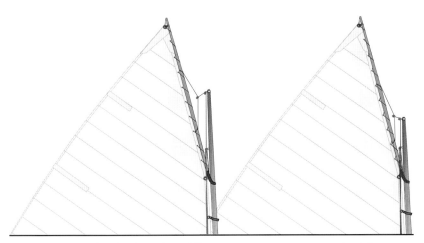

Insufficient mast height above the gaff/mast intersection, as seen on the right, reduces the peak halyard's ability to do its job.

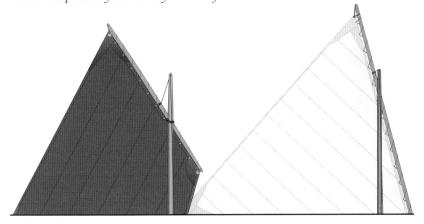

Yard-equipped sails such as this lugsail (left) and lateen (right) can be built either with the masthead extending well above the yard's intersection, or with almost no extra length. Note the string of parrel beads that keep the lugsail's yard close to the mast. The lateen's halyard runs through the mast very close to the masthead, and the yard can be pulled so close that a parrel is not needed. Since lateens are generally not reefable, the sail is raised full height. The exception would be the Jens rig, in which a temporary line, or a part of the halyard, is used for a makeshift parrel, and the yard is fixed at a lower position on the mast to reduce the height of the entire sail.

On the popular small lateen-rigged sailboats the halyard is usually led through a fitting on top of the masthead. The yard can be raised and the halyard cleated with only an inch or two of line between the yard and the masthead, virtually eliminating any play.

Though this method can be used for a lug rig, it is more common to extend the mast a bit above the yard's intersection with the mast. On something the size of a canoe, this might typically be a distance of a foot or so. The extra mast area can be tapered to reduce weight. This little bit of extra wood produces a graceful and somewhat "antique" look—very nice, if that's what you're after.

To keep the yard from wandering away from the mast, a "parrel" is used. In its simplest form, a parrel is just a chunk of line, tied at both ends to the yard, with enough slack to allow the mast to pass through. Round or slightly barrel-shaped wooden beads are often strung on the parrel line to act as ball bearings. Booms and gaffs that attach to the mast with wooden jaws also use parrels, strung between the open ends of the jaws, to keep them in position.

On a reefable sail with a yard, such as a lugsail, the parrel allows the yard to be lowered on the mast, but still keeps it close, even though the masthead-to-yard distance and the amount of hanging halyard between them may double or triple as the reef is put in. Lateens can also use a longer mast and a parrel if desired, instead of a shorter masthead.

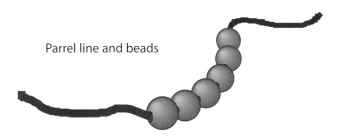

Parrel line and beads

The Topmast

There is some debate about what the upper spar section of a gunter or bat-wing rig should be called. Some see it as a very high-peaked gaff; others call it the gunter. On a canoe rig, it often isn't much more than a fat batten. I usually refer to it as the "topmast" and the lower section of the mast as the "mainmast"—even though this means that on a ketch or a yawl, with two sails, I would have both a main-mainmast and a mizzen-mainmast. I justify this by explaining that I grew up in the cornfields of central Illinois and that there weren't many clipper ships passing through for detailed examination. I'm lucky that I even know what a mast is!

Regardless, like a yard, the topmast should extend a few inches above the peak of the sail for proper luff tension. The overlap between the top and the main masts is the place where some planning is needed. The butt of the topmast will need a parrel, a mechanical fitting, or jaws (with a parrel) to keep it in position, directly behind the mainmast. This can often be accomplished by boring a hole through the topmast's lower end and splicing a loop of rope through the hole. The loop is then dropped over the mainmast, keeping the two spars together.

Since most canoe rigs are so small, the amount of overlap, mainmast to topmast, isn't all that critical as long as the configuration has enough halyard leverage to keep the topmast vertical. I probably would overlap the bottom 25 to 40 percent of the topmast, leading the halyard from deck level through the mainmast (very near its top) and then horizontally to tie off to the topmast.

On bat-wing sails, I like the idea of adding a throat halyard as well, attached to, or near, the topmast butt. We can raise and fix the lower part of the sail with the throat halyard and adjust the topmast angle with the peak halyard, tied mid-topmast. Normally, a nearly vertical topmast is desired for sail shape and pointing ability, but on windy days, easing the peak and letting it fall a bit farther away from vertical will allow the sail to twist off, spilling wind and depowering that big bat-wing roach. The twin halyards and a fairly generous mast/topmast overlap will allow this type of adjustment, even while under sail. More overlap yields more leverage, at the expense of weight aloft.

The overlap between the main and top sections of a gunter or bat-wing sail's mast is commonly one-quarter to one-half of the top section's length. The junction may be accomplished with custom-built metal hardware, curved wooden jaws similar to those found on a gaff, or spliced rope loops. Single or twin halyards can be used to raise the sail. The twin-halyard system allows the sail to be raised into position with the throat halyard and the topmast's angle to be adjusted independently by tensioning the peak halyard.

Mast Diameter

There are a lot of formulas for planning the diameters of wooden masts for sailing ships and boats. Some use a percentage of mast height, others a percentage of the boat's beam. Unfortunately, none of them seem to scale down accurately to canoe size. We are forced to use our own judgment to arrive at the ideal mast for each application. It will have to be a compromise, but a sailing canoe, itself, is a compromise, so we should be getting used to that by now.

Light weight, stiffness, and strength are the desired characteristics for a mast. The mast must fit the supporting structure of the mast step and the mast thwart or seat. The largest diameter that I can possibly imagine

Since most of us have been brainwashed by lumberyards over the years concerning lumber sizing, I have drawn a few cross-sections below—individually, and then superimposed on each other. Notice that a 2-inch-diameter mast is a pretty big stick in comparison to most of the wooden parts of a canoe, and how much wood is gone when its diameter is reduced to 1½ inches. This shows not only how much weight we can eliminate by tapering, but also how much less wood we will have left to resist bending once the taper has been cut.

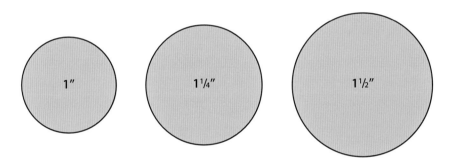

on a "normal" canoe-sized mast would be 2½ inches. Most of the two-piece arrangements on gunters and bat-wings have lower sections with maximum diameters seldom more than 2 inches.

The lateens with medium-length masts seem to vary quite a bit but usually reach 2 to 2¼ inches at the greatest diameter, which is about where the boom crosses the mast. Though it might be nice to have a greater diameter still, on a tall mast for a sail like our leg-o'-mutton, which is approaching 13 feet, we must still keep in mind weight aloft and its potential leverage on the canoe. A hollow mast with a maximum diameter of 2¼ to 2⅜ inches is about as far as we probably want to go.

Masthead diameters of 1¼ to 1½ inches are typical for most one-piece masts and the lower mainmast sections of bat-wings and gunters. The topmasts of these sails may taper to an inch or less at the peak.

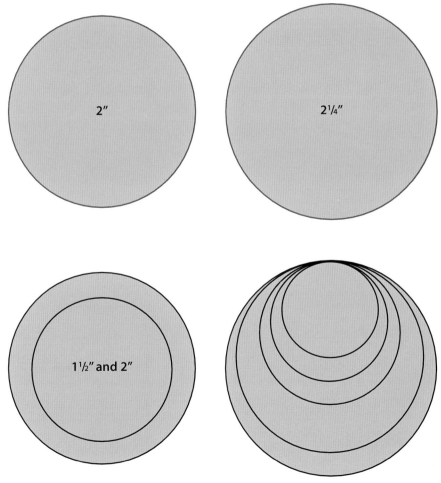

Downsizing Spars for Mizzens

If we are designing a twin-sailed rig, the easiest thing to do is to simply reduce mast and spar diameters proportionally. In some cases, this may result in rather flimsy-looking spars. It is certainly possible to reduce mizzen spar diameters by a smaller percentage. They will end up a bit stockier than the mainsail's spars but may actually look more like spars and less like sticks. The added weight probably won't amount to much.

I can also see the possibility of a ketch rig where it might look better to keep spar diameters the same for both sails, even though the sail area of one is greater than that of the other. The fact that it would eliminate some design work and simplify construction might be enough to make it worth thinking about.

Taper Positioning

As you plan the taper of masts and spars, keep in mind that on booms, yards, and masts where the edge of the sail will be connected to the spar by lacing, hoops, or robands (small, individual ties), the edge of the spar that is against the sail should, theoretically, be straight, with all of the taper being cut into the side of the spar away from the sail. On hollow masts, in particular, this can make the design process a nightmare.

Since canoe masts are so small, most of the time you can safely ignore theory and build for practicality, using a symmetrical cross-section and tapering evenly, all around. The difference, both cosmetically and in use, will be negligible. Since booms, yards, and gaffs are almost always solid, they can be asymmetrically tapered easily if desired.

The Mast-Building Process

A boatbuilder friend once observed, "You could sand the wings off of a fly with a 14-pound disc grinder and watch him walk away, but you're downright dangerous with a hand plane!" I must admit that there is a fair amount of truth in his words. I am not a particularly great spar builder. Perhaps it's lack of patience, or lack of practice. If I take my time and make sure the plane takes small bites, I can turn out a sturdy, functional spar, though I wouldn't recommend checking it with a straightedge for symmetry.

I'll walk you through the sparmaking process here—as long as you promise to do a little research and consult at least one of the many good books and magazine articles that go deeper into the subject.

Once you've completed the planning stages and selected the best stock available, you're ready to start building your mast. For masts with sawn or routed hollow interiors, cutting the grooves, which will become the inner channels, is the first step. A dado blade or a wide router bit is used to cut matching channels on what will become the bonded sides of both the port and starboard halves of the mast. No channels are cut in the ends or in high-stress areas, leaving solid wood for strength.

For hollow masts using smaller filler pieces and internal blocking instead of cut channels, prepare the stock. Bonding surfaces should be as square, flat, and straight as possible, but needn't be silky smooth. Glue will usually bond better to a surface with a bit of "tooth," so there is no reason to polish the gluing areas before assembly. Once the laminates are ready, for hollow or solid lamination, you're ready to start gluing up the blank. Use as many clamps as you can get your hands on and support the assembly along its entire length, every foot or so, to prevent it from developing a curve.

Boatbuilders' epoxy resin is the glue of choice for most spar building. It bonds well, seals out moisture, doesn't require a tremendous amount of clamping pressure, and has pretty good gap-filling capabilities in the event your joints aren't perfect. Epoxy will tend to lubricate the pieces of wood, though, especially as you are trying to get them aligned and clamped tight, so you may want to use small temporary nails or staples to help keep things from sliding as you snug up the clamps. They can be removed after the epoxy hardens and the holes can be filled.

Use plenty of epoxy and wipe up any drips before they harden. You will be drawing the taper on the blank and rough-cutting with a saw, so a drip-free surface will be easier to work with. Once the epoxy has set, the blank can be planed as necessary to yield a reasonably clean, square cross-section. If your blank is made from a solid piece of lumber, rough-cutting and planing, or running it through a jointer, should get you to this point a little faster.

On each end of the blank, draw lines diagonally, corner to corner, crossing at the center. Also, draw centerlines, full length on the blank's sides. This is also a good time to check for straightness. The tapers can now be laid out, either on the port or the starboard side and also either on the forward or after side. Measure up from the butt of the mast to the proper height of one of the significant diameters, measure out from the centerline on both sides, and make a couple of small reference marks.

If need be, a full-sized plan can be drawn on a strip of paper, first to get a preview of your tapered shape and then to transfer the diameter measurements from the plan to the appropriate spots on the blank. What we're after here are enough reference points to draw the taper on the blank using a long batten to connect the points. If you're a strip-canoe builder, that handful of leftover strips from your last boat will work well as battens. Otherwise, a piece of molding stock from a lumberyard or home-improvement store would make a good batten.

Once the shape is carefully penciled on the sides of the blank, the tapers can be cut from the first side with a bandsaw, skillsaw, handsaw, or sabersaw (as long as it's a good one and the blade doesn't wander from side to side as it cuts). Make your cuts slightly outside of the line to allow for planing and smoothing later, and as a cushion to protect against any saw-guiding errors.

Save the excess, as the scrap from one side should have your taper already drawn on it. For example, if you cut the taper on the forward and after sides of the mast, the scrap from one of them should have the port and starboard side tapers drawn on its outside surface.

Temporarily reattach this piece, right back where it came from. You can tack it temporarily with a few small nails or use a few spots of glue from a hot-melt glue gun. If you're using a bandsaw and need a flat bot-tom to run through the saw, or if you just want the blank to be as stable as possible while cutting the other tapers, you can glue or tack both sides back onto the blank. Once you have cut the second set of tapers and removed the scrap material, a plane (hand or power) is used to true up the shape. When done, it should be smooth and square, with a taper according to your plan.

Now we will make the transition from square-sectioned to round in three steps. First the corners will be planed off to turn our four-sided blank into an eight-sided one. Then, the blank will be planed to a sixteen-sided cross-section. Finally, it will be smoothed to a round cross-section.

I firmly believe that the eight- and sixteen-sided layout process is much more complicated than the actual woodworking involved. Once the lines have been drawn on all sides of the blank, the wood is planed down to the lines. The keys are working carefully, using a solid, stable workbench to which you can securely clamp the blank, and doing your best to keep the new faces flat.

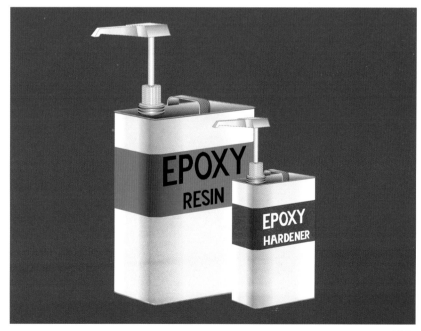

Eight-Siding the Mast Blank

Here is a reasonably accurate way to mark the tapered mast blank for eight-siding. Since we have presumably roughed out the taper on both ends of the blank, the easiest way to start is on paper.

Draw a square the same size as the fattest section of the blank and connect the corners, diagonally, to find the center of the square. Then swing arcs from the square's corners that pass through the center point and terminate at the sides of the square. The dashed lines, shown at center, represent the four new sides that we will add to our square to achieve an eight-sided blank.

Two more holes are drilled to hold a pair of pencils, or scribes, with their points positioned at the arc/side intersections on the drawing. The finished gauge is moved along the spar to mark the cut lines for eight-siding. As the spar tapers, the gauge is twisted slightly to keep the pins tightly against the sides of the blank. The lines drawn by the gauge mimic the taper of the blank. You may need to touch up the lines with a batten and a pencil, but the gauge will give you a good start.

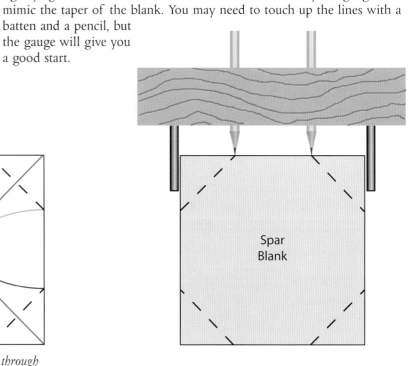

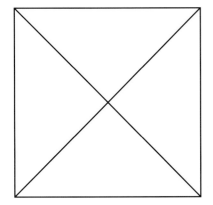

Cross-section of the mast's diameter on paper. Diagonals are drawn to find the center point.

Arcs swung from the corners through the center point will intersect the sides at the reference points for eight-siding.

Next build a spar gauge, which is a simple block of wood with two metal pins (nails will work in a pinch) set into carefully drilled holes. The pins are just far enough apart to allow the largest part of the blank to slide between them.

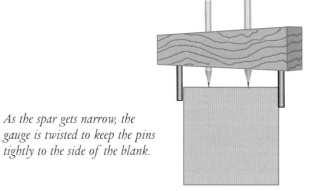

As the spar gets narrow, the gauge is twisted to keep the pins tightly to the side of the blank.

As you can see here, the transition from four-sided to eight-sided involves the removal of a fair amount of wood. It is definitely possible to use a power saw to cut away a good part of the excess before you start with the plane. It is also definitely possible to make a terminal cutting error with the same power saw, thus relegating your mast blank to the scrap pile, so plan and saw very carefully if you use a power saw at all.

It is also possible to use a drawknife, crooked knife, spokeshave, or hatchet to rough cut the mast. Personally, everything that I've ever cut with a hatchet ended up looking as if I cut it with a hatchet, so I I'll stick to my planes and go slowly (though at some point, I will surely start considering getting out the big disc grinder).

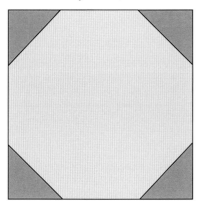

Whatever you use, sooner or later you should have an eight-sided stick. Since you are now finished with the heavy removal but still have flat sides, any necessary holes for halyards should probably be drilled while the blank will lie still. Holes with a diameter of ⅜ inch should handle any canoe halyard. If you are installing sheaves, however, for each you will need to rough-cut a slot through the mast and drill a transverse hole for the axle pin.

Going from eight to sixteen sides entails a lot less removal of wood, as you can see from the illustration. You can certainly draw another diagram and build another spar gauge, dividing the eight-sided drawing into a bunch of 22.5-degree wedges and ending up with the pencils closer together, but it may not be worth the effort. On spars this small, spar gauges aren't really accurate enough to be much help. It is usually easier and more accurate to sixteen-side by eye. Some people skip sixteen-siding altogether and go directly to rounding.

Whatever feels best to you is fine with me. Just go slowly and don't use a hatchet. Seriously consider leaving the tapered section below the mast thwart eight-sided. Sanded smooth, with the corners eased a bit and faired into the upper, rounded section of the rest of the mast, it can look really classy.

The butt of the mast can be cut down to a square about an inch across, left eight sided, or rounded. As long as it fits the mast step that will be anchored to the hull of the canoe, anything goes. Most professional sparmakers sand a spar with an inside-out sanding belt hung around the mast (i.e., the mast is inside the inside-out belt) and spun around by an electric drill with a rubber-faced drum chucked into it as the driving wheel. I have yet to try this method, but it is said to work very well. You work your way up and down the length of the mast, with the drill spinning the belt against the wood and smoothing the surface. Pretty clever.

When varnishing the mast, to avoid runs and drips, consider a trick that I picked up from fishing-rod builders. Drive a small nail into the center of the tip of the mast, allowing it to stick out an inch or so, then drive a screw about ¼ inch in diameter into the butt end, also centered. Now apply a coat of varnish. Lay the nail at the tip end on a block of wood with a small notch cut in it (so that the spar is horizontal), chuck the screw on the other end into a rotisserie motor fixed to anything solid, and plug in the motor. The slow rotation of the mast will keep the varnish from sagging and dripping while it dries.

Turned Masts and Spars

I have talked to people who use a lathe to do most of the rounding and tapering on canoe masts and spars, and with good success. I have tried it myself, and for fairly short stuff it is promising. The trick is finding a lathe that can be extended to take long stock. Delta makes a lathe with a bed that is split in the middle; they sell extension pieces that can be fit in to extend the distance between the head and tail stocks.

I own a Ryobi "mini-lathe" that uses 1-inch-diameter tubes for the rails that the tool rest and tail stock ride on. By substituting long sections of 1-inch pipe for the rails, I can extend the lathe enough to turn spars. I'm sure there are others lathes on the market that might also be modified. Most will need to be secured to a bench or a long beam to keep the assembly from bending and losing pressure on the ends of the blank.

It doesn't take a lot of power to spin a long, skinny stick, so you don't need a high-powered motor for the job, but you do need a really good grip on the ends of the blank. At a certain length, the spar's length-vs.-diameter ratio is likely to make it too flexible to stay put. Obviously, a bit of caution is in order—if your 12-foot lateen boom flies out of the lathe and over the back fence and impales the neighbor's dog, you'll have some explaining to do.

The tricky part of turning a spar is getting an even taper. My first attempts were a bit wavy. Precutting the basic tapers on the square blank, just as we did before, is probably the best way to ensure a uniform shape. The lathe then becomes more of a rounding tool than a shaping one.

A lathe will also allow you turn small knobs and decorations on the top of the mast, or channels for metal bands and fittings. These can be quite attractive when used sparingly; just try to avoid making your mast into something resembling a table leg.

Here are two simple ways to run a halyard through the masthead. On the left, two holes have been drilled and the space between them cut out to make a slot for a sheave, which is held in place by a transverse axle pin.

Masthead Sheaves

Rolling sheave   **"Dumb" sheave**

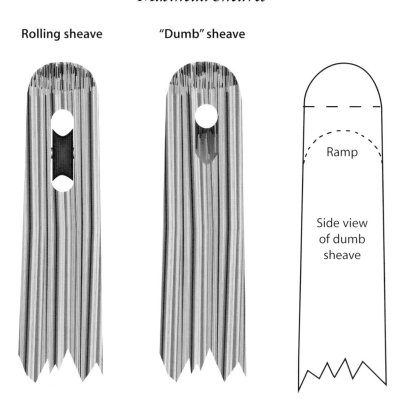

Ramp

Side view of dumb sheave

On most canoe-sized spars the sheave really isn't critical, and a modified hole, called a "dumb sheave," is all that's needed. The hole is bored through the mast, and the lower side of it is carefully curved with a rat-tail file or a dowel wrapped with sandpaper. When finished, the lower portion forms a smooth ramp, up and over, as the line passes through the mast. The ramp part can be protected from rope abrasion by a small metal strip over its bearing surface if desired.

There are occasions when you may need to attach lines to your mast for hanging blocks, shrouds (lines to the side that support the mast), or the lines used for tensioning the sprit and adjusting the sail shape. These lines can be kept from sliding by anchoring them to eye-bolts, or by splicing or seizing an eye in the line and using "thumb cleats," small wooden shoulders fastened to the mast or spar.

Thumb Cleats

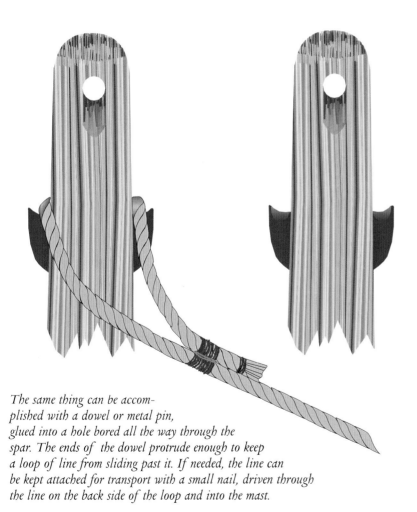

The same thing can be accomplished with a dowel or metal pin, glued into a hole bored all the way through the spar. The ends of the dowel protrude enough to keep a loop of line from sliding past it. If needed, the line can be kept attached for transport with a small nail, driven through the line on the back side of the loop and into the mast.

Yards, Gaffs, and Booms

Though we still must discuss some of the hardware pertinent to masts, let's return to sparmaking and build the rest of the spars first. You will be happy to know that booms, gaffs, and yards are usually somewhat easier to design and build than masts.

Here again, light weight, stiffness, and reasonable strength are the desired characteristics for these spars, yet they are smaller in diameter than a mast and therefore we can expect to have to live with a certain amount of bend. Since the sails are usually laced in position on these spars and left there, nothing has to slide up and down their length. This means that booms, gaffs, and yards needn't be round in cross-section. In fact, a rectangular cross-section is somewhat preferable, as it retains more wood, which makes it stiffer, and it is easier to build. It can still taper a bit toward the ends to keep it from looking like a board, but a nicely finished, rectangular spar, with only the corners rounded off, can look quite good.

If you really enjoy sparmaking and need a challenge, you might emulate the old sailing canoes, which had booms and yards that were round-sectioned at both ends and thickened (vertically) into ovals in the middle. Such a design is beautiful, and the oval center helps resist bend. The real challenge comes when you consider that the side of the spar next to the sail should be straight, with the taper worked into the side away from the sail's edge. We didn't bother with this when designing and building the mast, but as it's easier to produce on yards, booms, and gaffs, it should be the rule. Since there isn't much to be gained by hollowing these smaller spars, we won't do it and therefore won't have to worry about accidentally cutting through the spar's walls with a plane while tapering.

If you decide on rounding your small spars in cross-section, make another, smaller spar gauge for eight-siding. It may still help on a spar blank with an asymmetrical taper. Sixteen-siding is nearly impossible on such small stock. It is easier to go from eight-siding to rounding. Just take your time when doing it.

If I were to oval a spar, I would probably set the spokeshave to take off just a sliver and start with a tapered rectangle, working by eye. Trying to lay out guidelines for a combination of round and oval cross-sections would probably take longer than the actual job.

Rectangular spars can taper in height alone (for example, a boom that is 1 inch by 1 inch at the ends and 1 inch by 1½ inches in the center), or it can change thickness in both directions (1 inch by 1 inch at the ends and 1½ inches by 1¼ inches in the center). Tapering in both directions is more work, but it looks more delicate.

High-peaked gaffs and yards are under a lot of strain. Their shape also has direct bearing upon sail shape. We do not want to "over-taper" them, especially at their outboard ends. The result would be too much flex and not enough tension on the sail's leech, causing the sail to sag and flutter. To prevent this some people go so far as to build gaffs with square cross-sections and no taper at all.

As long as the end is neatly finished and the jaws are nicely done, a square, straight gaff still looks pretty good, and it's easy to make. The same design can be used for a lugsail yard, and even one for a lateen, but it will usually look better with a little taper—just don't cut too much off the tail ends.

Any yard that crosses a mast, such as the yard of a lug or a squaresail, is usually left square or eight-sided for a short distance on either side of the point where it meets the mast and then faired into the round section of the rest of the spar in both directions. This shape makes the yard look less like a pole, strengthens the junction area, and shows respect for tradition—even if it is only a canoe! Some designs even call for a pair of small wooden horns on the yard, forming a yoke, to keep the yard positioned properly; such an arrangement needs a parrel to keep the yard close to the mast.

Here again, like it or not, I am pretty much forced into assigning some kind of guesstimated blanket diameters to canoe booms, yards, and gaffs, even though they're all different. How's that for a noncommittal sentence? You can tell how much I look forward to this part. I'll make my pronouncement sound as official as possible; only you and I will know that I'm guessing:

Henceforth, no boom, yard, or gaff shall have a diameter or minimum dimension of less than ⅞ inch U.S. measure. Said spar may grow to as much as 1½ inches in all directions toward its middle and re-taper on its after end to its former size, if desired. Select, high-quality stock is encouraged, with laminating being acceptable for lesser grades. Mizzen spars may be reduced proportionally or at the builder's discretion. All spars shall be finished with at least three (3) coats of high-quality spar varnish. And yes, lateen spars can be made from a closet pole, as long as the finish applied to said closet pole does not offend the committee.

If you've never had to wade through class racing rules while rebuilding a boat, the above is an example of what they are like and one of the reasons I hate class rules. Anyway, if you are guided by these dimensions, your auxiliary spars should work pretty well.

By the way, you really can build lateen booms and yards from fir closet-pole stock, though you should avoid the type that has been finger-jointed from small pieces. With no taper, a closet-pole spar will tend to sag in the middle quite a bit, but finished carefully it will look pretty good.

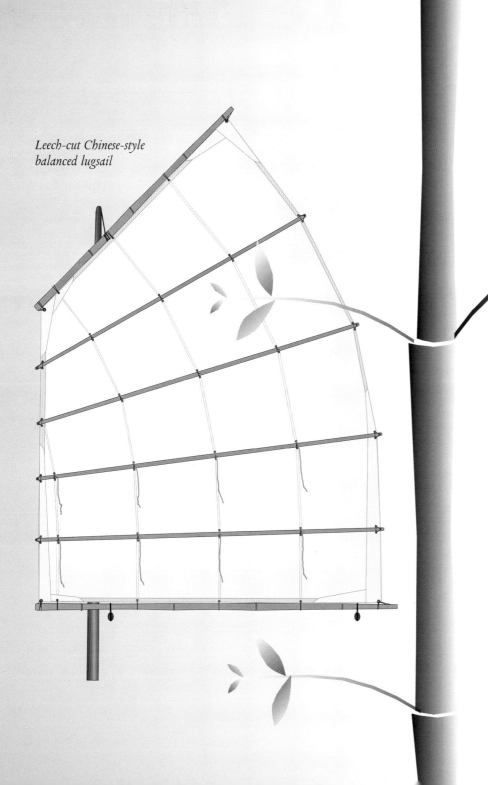

Leech-cut Chinese-style balanced lugsail

Bamboo Spars

Spars That Grow a Foot a Day

I remember seeing a few references to old sailing canoes that used bamboo for spars. I have no firm information on them, but many of the old boats were smaller than the canoes that most of us are used to—much more like a kayak than a canoe.

A 12-foot decked sailing canoe of the Rushton type might have a pair of small balanced lug sails, or lateens, with bamboo yards to reduce weight aloft.

My only non-kabob experience with bamboo as a structural material has been with cross-country ski poles. I skied for several years with a beautiful pair of Liljedahl tonkin-cane poles from Norway. They were strong, reasonably light, and quite stiff—which happen to be the same characteristics we're looking for in a good canoe spar.

Bamboo might also be usable for full-length battens on bat-wings. Batten or spar, the problem is finding big stuff without being arrested for vandalizing the local botanical garden.

I think it might be wise to discreetly fill with epoxy any hollow section where you plan to drill a hole for attaching hardware; brass-banding might also be a good idea. Hangers for blocks could be "wrapped" in place like the guides on a bamboo fly rod.

Spar Tips

Here is a clever way to handle the outhaul on a small spar. The arrangement is simple to build, with no moving parts or difficult-to-find hardware, and it is reasonably quick to adjust. It would work on the end of most booms and the topmasts of gunters and bat-wings.

The same job could be done by a sheave set in a through-spar slot, or by a dumb sheave. Both would need a separate cleat somewhere on the side of the spar. Though either arrangement promises easier adjustment while under sail, it has been my observation that most small-boat sailors, myself included, seldom mess with outhaul adjustment while sailing. The exception would be a loose-footed sail, which is not laced or tied along the boom. Outhaul adjustment is a major sail-draft control on such a sail, and the means for making it should be within reach of the sailor's normal position in the canoe.

I have also seen spars with small eye-bolts or screw-eyes protruding from their ends to tie off to, and spars with just a hole. The outhaul pennant is run through the hole and knotted. It looks a bit crude, but it works. Brass eyes have a tendency to break off in use. If you use them, they should be the heavy-duty type.

By now, you can probably see how clever the method illustrated here is. I picked it up from a boat design by Phil Bolger in a book by Dynamite Payson—two very clever fellows.

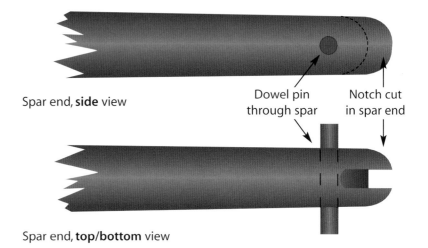

Spar end, **side** view

Dowel pin through spar

Notch cut in spar end

Spar end, **top/bottom** view

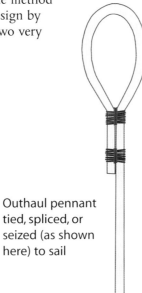

Outhaul pennant tied, spliced, or seized (as shown here) to sail

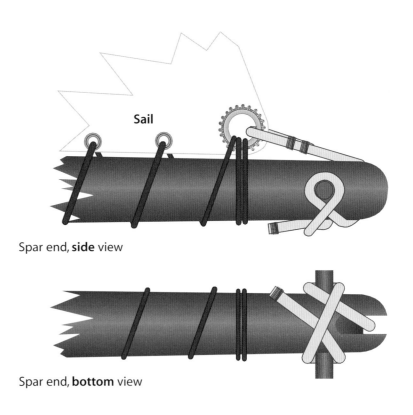

Sail

Spar end, **side** view

Spar end, **bottom** view

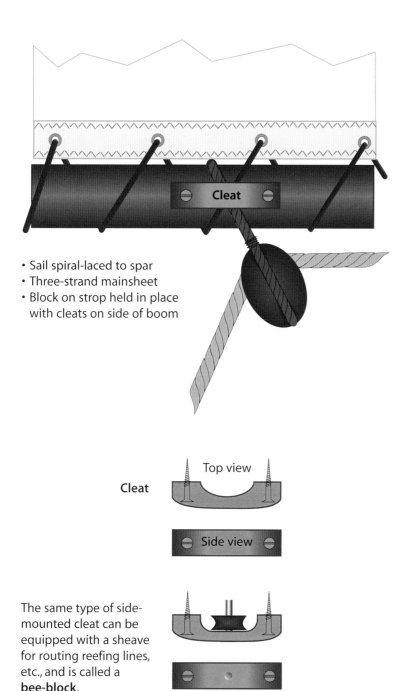

- Sail spiral-laced to spar
- Three-strand mainsheet
- Block on strop held in place with cleats on side of boom

Cleat

Top view

Side view

The same type of side-mounted cleat can be equipped with a sheave for routing reefing lines, etc., and is called a **bee-block**.

Block Hangers

Here is a simple cleat that can serve multiple purposes on booms, in particular, and is more secure than a thumb cleat. In this case it is used to keep the mainsheet block (pulley) from sliding up or down the boom.

Sometimes this type of cleat can be several feet long, with multiple passages used for adjusting the fore-and-aft position of blocks and fittings. In the process, it can help stiffen the boom. Adding an axle-pin and an internal sheave can turn it into a low-friction turning block, often used for routing reef lines.

Some of the old decked racing canoes had reefing systems using multi-sheaved bee-blocks. The lines ran back and forth from the boom, up the sail, through a reef point, back down the other side of the sail to the boom—then forward to the next block on the boom, back up, through the sail, and so on.

Once everything was set up like this, easing the halyard and pulling the appropriate end of the reefing line would pull a whole section of the sail down and bundle it against the boom. The line was cleated, the halyard snugged up, and the sailor set off with a reefed sail. If the wind let up, easing the reefing line and tightening the halyard would pull the sail back up for maximum area.

Fully battened sails, such as balanced lugs and bat-wings, are relatively easy to set up this way. The reef points are usually set just above the bottom battens and use the batten's stiffness to help pull the sail down and control the reefed area.

Mast Tip

The top of the mast on some traditional vessels is sometimes painted white. Normally, on a gaff- or lug-rigged boat, the white would start just above the intersection of the mast and the gaff or yard. Painting this area white was originally done to seal the end-grain of the wood against moisture. These days, we have transparent resins, varnishes, and sealers available for the job, so the white is more a matter of appearance and tradition than function, especially on a boat that won't see much weathering. Even so, on a small boat or canoe, it can sometimes add a nice touch.

Mainsheet Block Placement

When designing a boom, it is important to consider how—and even more important, where—you will attach the blocks that will route the mainsheet along, under the boom. It is quite possible to sail with no blocks and no routing—with just a rope tied to the boom—but we can make it do more.

The first rule of thumb is to avoid hanging mainsheet blocks at the midpoint of the boom to prevent tension on the sheet from adding even more bend to our already bendy spar. By moving the blocks toward the ends of the boom, we gain in several ways:

A boom block, set fairly far aft and pulling down on the end of the boom, will help keep the sail's leech tight for better sail shape. Moving the other block up, close to the mast, gets it out of our way and is less prone to cause boom bend, because the sail's luff and/or the gooseneck fitting, joining the mast and the boom, will help support the boom.

For booms equipped with jaws and capable of sliding up and down on the mast, there is an important added bonus to keeping the forward mainsheet block fairly far forward. So rigged, the mainsheet system becomes a self-adjusting luff-tensioning device. When sailing upwind, with the sail trimmed in tightly, the strong downward pull on the forward mainsheet block will help flatten the sail and move its draft forward, exactly what we need for close-hauled work.

As the sail is eased out for reaching or running downwind, less downward tension is exerted and the boom comes up a bit. There is less luff tension and more draft in the sail—again, just what we need.

Most iceboats use this type of sliding-gooseneck system, because it is simple, almost immune to problems, and works very well. Since most canoes can easily be set up this way, and because the use of boom jaws eliminates building or finding mechanical gooseneck fittings, this arrangement merits serious consideration for any canoe rig.

Spar Hardware

Over the years, there has been a wide variety of hardware used to fasten the parts of canoe sailing rigs together. Most of it is brass, or bronze, consisting of combinations of pieces formed from sheet metal, rod, eye-bolts, and a few screws or rivets. Seldom is there a need for the heavy, and usually expensive, cast or welded fittings that can contribute heavily to the high price of modern sailboats.

A round-sectioned mast, a halyard tied with a clove hitch to a yard that slides on a string of wooden beads, a few wooden hoops or loops of line to hold the sail to the spars, and a boom with curved wooden jaws hugging the mast—that's the real hardware of the sailing canoe. The small bits of metal that form hinges and slides are often there more out of convenience than necessity.

It is possible to build a canoe rig in which the grommets and corner rings on the sail are the only metal components anywhere above the mast thwart. The "hardware" on such a rig consists only of a few pieces of line and some holes bored through the spars. Yet another builder might join the same spars together with elaborate brass fittings, engraved with grand canoeing scenes from the last century. Both are correct, both work well, and both can be quite elegant. Neither really takes much money to produce; one just takes more time.

I thought long and hard about this section. What would be the best way to show all the small joints and pieces that fit the various spars together, from rig to rig? How would I organize them?

I finally decided that the best organization was to pretend that they were all rolled up in a blanket. I would simply unroll the blanket on the ground, let them find their own order, and let the reader sort through those that might be pertinent to his or her own sailing rig. Labeled as needed, here are some, but by no means all, of the possible ways to connect a pile of sticks together in order to spread a sail and catch the wind.

Lateen Rig Fittings

The most common fitting for joining the boom of a lateen to its mast is a single hardwood jaw, screwed or riveted to one side of the boom. It can be laminated, or cut from a piece of wood with favorable grain. A small parrel or keeper line can be added from the jaw's tip to the boom if desired, though it usually isn't necessary. Interlocking loops of line (one secured around the boom, one slid over the mast) or a parrel lashed to the boom could also work. The popular Sunfish sailboat uses a nice bronze swiveling gooseneck with a big ring that slides over the mast. It would be possible to buy one and use it on a canoe, but you might need to thicken your boom to around 1½ inches in diameter to clamp it on.

Wooden-Jaw Gooseneck

Sunfish-Style Bronze Gooseneck

Brass or copper bands, cut from tubing and fit over, or let into, the ends of the spars add a nice touch and help prevent fittings from splitting the boom under load.

Eyes used to join yard and boom at tack corner.

Leather hinge tacked or screwed to the yard and boom.

It's a good idea to lash the tack ring of the sail to the yard-boom joint if possible. I have omitted this on some drawings for clarity.

Piece of line let into holes in the ends of the yard and boom, glued with epoxy. Nails through the spars, into the line, might be a good safety measure.

This **sheet-brass hinge** sandwiches both spars with metal plates screwed to flat spots milled on the ends of the spars. A rivet is used for a hinge pin.

Meeting of the yard and boom with **no joint fitting.** I am convinced that a ⅞-inch (#6) sewn ring in the sail corner is strong enough to hold the spar ends together without failure, as there isn't a significant strain on the joint.

Goosenecks and Jaws

Gaff Jaws

Jaws for gaff, gunter, and some bat-wing sails are very similar to boom jaws, except they curve up at about a 45-degree angle and may need longer "horns" to reach around the mast. The parrel must be loose enough to allow the gaff to lie horizontal when the sail is dropped.

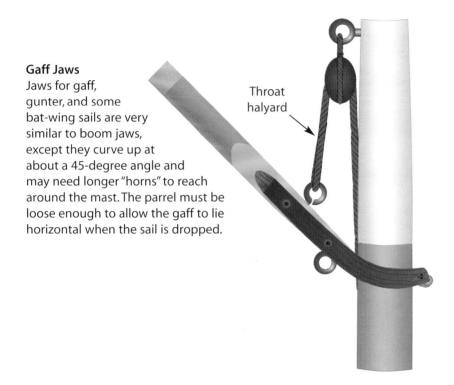

Throat halyard

Top View

Boom

Mast

Parrel

Wooden-Jaw Boom Gooseneck

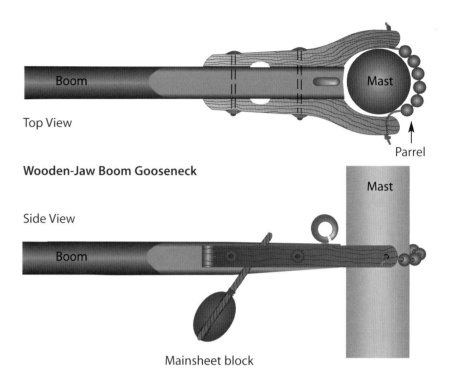

Side View

Mast

Boom

Mainsheet block

It is also possible to build boom and gaff jaws from brass or bronze. Since they are small on a canoe rig, they won't add all that much weight. Boom jaws could be bent from bar stock. Gaff and gunter jaws might have to be custom cast due to their compound bend.

Eyebolt Gooseneck

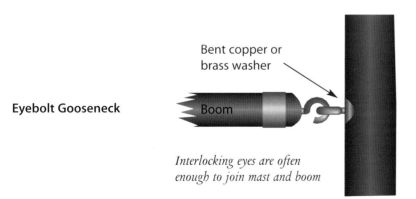

Bent copper or brass washer

Boom

Interlocking eyes are often enough to join mast and boom

Mechanical Gooseneck

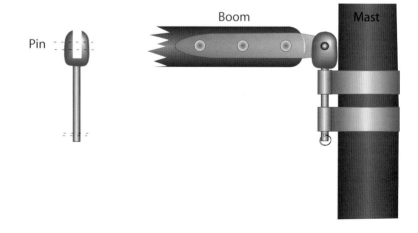

Boom

Mast

Pin

A Patina of… Rust?

Browning Steel Hardware

Sometimes the hunt for materials for boatbuilding can seem to take as long as the actual building process. If you're building some of your own sailing hardware, trying to find just the right piece of brass or bronze can be maddening.

Aluminum-framed dirigibles were crashing regularly in the 1920s, so I guess you could consider aluminum to be a traditional metal, though it doesn't look like one until you prime and paint it to look like wrought iron.

Stainless steel is great stuff for boat hardware. It's strong, corrosion-resistant, and reasonably available. It wears out drill bits quickly, unless you use the really good ones, but you can do most of your work with a drill, hacksaw, and files, or a stationary belt-sander.

The only problem with stainless is that it looks so…so…STAINLESS. It's too clean and shiny to look as if it belongs on an antique canoe, and there isn't much you can do to make it blend in. It's too bad we can't just use plain old steel—the kind you get at the hardware store—and steel screws, too. No hunting for expensive marine metals.

I have a habit of buying old, beat-up, neglected sailboats and bringing them back to life. As long as they are interesting boats with a pleasing shape, they're worth working on. Invariably, I will find fittings and accessories that have been added at some point by someone who thought they could get away with plain steel screws or bolts. They didn't. Even when these items are painted over, the rust will eventually come through.

But…you can use plain steel to fabricate very nice, durable fittings that look great on an antique canoe. You just need to know a trick or two. The key to this scheme is rust.

Back in the days of flintlock rifles and before gun-bluing was used to treat metal, the barrels, locks, and other metal parts of guns and rifles were "browned." Most of the so-called "replicas" that you see in sporting goods and gun shops have ornate, polished brass trim all over them. In reality, the working woodsman's rifle usually didn't have any

brass on it at all. In those days, sunlight reflecting off a fancy fitting on your rifle could get you killed. All the metal parts were a dark, satin brown that blended in, shed water, and had an understated, simple elegance. Though "browning" isn't what most people would consider a "marine" finish, on a day-sailed boat such as a sailing canoe, it will work—and look pretty good.

The process is simple. First, you build the steel part and finish the surface and edges as you would any metal component that you wanted to be proud of. Any zinc plating, etc., should be removed. Next the bare steel piece is degreased.

You will need to find a gun dealer that knows a bit about muzzle-loaders. Have him sell you a bottle of "browning solution." Not much is required, and it isn't very expensive. Follow the directions. It's been awhile, but as I remember, you brush the solution on the steel once or twice a day over a period of a few days. The piece begins to rust; eventually it will build up a very smooth, even coat of the nastiest orange rust you've ever seen. After the prescribed number of coats and days, the piece is dipped in boiling water, which stops the process. Then it is dried off and oiled with linseed oil. In a matter of minutes, it will have a dark, satin-brown, water-resistant finish—a patina of rust. Even screws and bolts can be browned to match the rest of the hardware.

I think browning would work great for canoe hardware, though I wouldn't leave the boat out in the weather all the time. It's definitely worth trying. Periodic oiling will keep the parts looking good and keep your rusty parts from…well…rusting.

Mast Hoops

Mast hoops are a common way to attach the luff of a sail to a round mast. They are usually made from a thin strip of oak, steam bent and wrapped, two or three layers thick, around a form. The ends of the overlapping layers are then bolted or riveted together. Hoops should be about 25 percent larger in diameter than the mast. On a boat the size of a canoe, the hoops would usually be spaced 12 to 18 inches apart and attached to sewn rings or grommets set in the sail's luff.

When the sail is lowered, the hoops stay attached and stack up on top of the mast/boom intersection. The sail's luff folds "accordion-style." On a gaff sail, the gaff jaws stack on top of the hoops, with the gaff lying on top of the boom. On a bat-wing with hoops, the sail is laced to the topmast and the hoops are used on the luff between the boom and topmast. Two or three hoops are usually plenty.

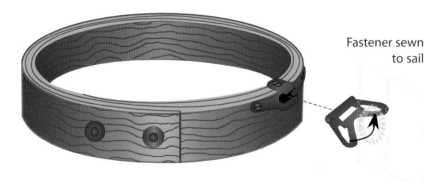

Fastener sewn to sail

Some people use bronze hoop/sail fasteners, rather than sew the hoops directly to the sail. One part of the fastener is sewn through a ring or grommet to the sail, and the other part is screwed to the hoop. Hoop fasteners allow you to remove the sail, leaving the hoops stacked on the mast. For a canoe, where it's usually possible to stand next to the boat on land and slide the hoops right over the top of the mast, they are not really necessary, but some people like them. Hoops are generally available from sailmakers and supply shops for traditional boats.

Bat-Wing Hardware Options

There can be a lot going on in the throat area of a bat-wing sail. The connection between the mast and the topmast, the inner ends of two or three battens, hoops, lacing, and halyards can all be trying to occupy a relatively small space. Meanwhile, the sail must set properly and then be able to fold down into a reasonably neat, horizontal pile along the boom.

In the simplest form of the bat-wing rig, the tack ring is attached to a fixed gooseneck (at the mast/boom junction) and the halyard is tied about halfway up the topmast. The luff between the tack and the bottom of the topmast is not connected to anything, but the upper section is laced to the topmast. The sail is raised by pulling the halyard until the topmast tie-off point is tight against the masthead. As long as there is enough halyard tension, the luff stays tight and the topmast vertical.

Adding jaws or a sliding mechanical hinge to the butt of the topmast and luff lacing or hoops to the lower luff makes everything more solid and makes partially lowering the sail for reefing easier. There seem to be as many different ways to rig bat-wings as there are bat-wing sails, so the drawings on the opposite page are as much for inspiration as explanation. Feel free to experiment; you might come up with something even better.

A good system should go up smoothly; keep the peak high, the topmast in line with the main mast, and the luff tight; and fold down into something that is manageable. Twin halyards are more trouble than single, but they allow you to ease the topmast out a bit to put more twist in the sail, spilling wind on days when you're being overpowered.

Since bat-wings are essentially gunter sails with oversized fully battened roaches, a bat-wing system will work on a normal gunter rig as well. It will actually be easier to engineer, since most gunters don't have full-length battens. They use jaws on the heel of the topmast, lacing or hoops on the lower luff, and lacing on the upper luff to the topmast. Gunters generally use only one halyard.

Bat-Wing Throat Construction Options

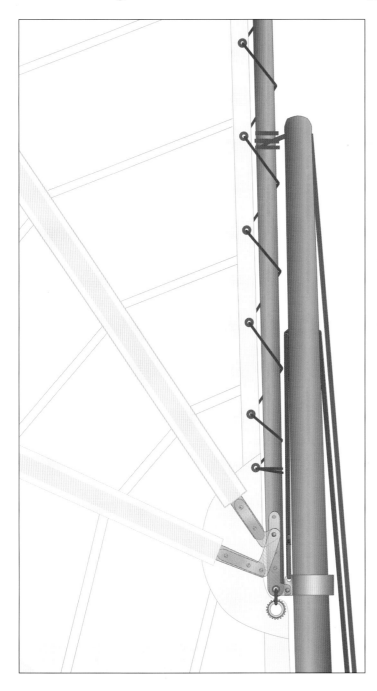

The rig at the **left** has both throat and peak halyards, sleeves for battens, and a mechanical fitting joining the topmast and battens to a sliding ring around the mast. The rig at the **right** uses wooden jaws with a parrel, wooden mast hoops, and battens that lace to both sides of the sail. It is rigged with a single halyard, but could also be rigged with two, which would allow more adjustment of the topmast angle and the sail twist.

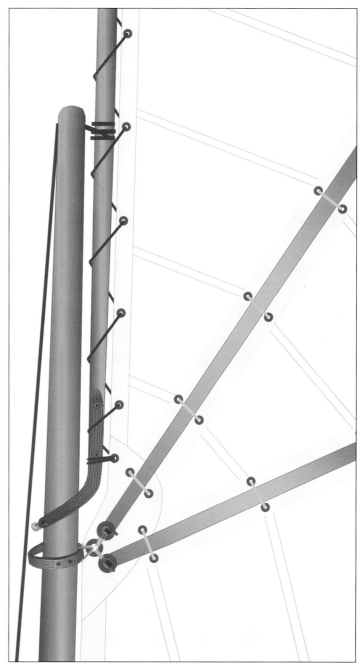

Rope Grommets

The rope grommet has many uses aboard a sailing canoe, or any other traditional boat. It can substitute for a wooden mast hoop or it can be made penny-sized and oversewn onto a sail to replace a brass ring for a flexible reinforced opening. Grommets are common on bags, stitched around the top as a heavy-duty edging; I've even seen a big grommet ringing the brim of a hat or two.

Grommets are also often seized into a figure-eight and used for hanging blocks, for pulling the corners of sails out on the yards, and for any other purpose where a strong flexible loop is needed. All traditional sailors should learn how to make grommets; they are cheap compared to most marine hardware, and the work is relatively easy and fun.

To make a grommet, you will need a chunk of three-strand line that's approximately ten times the desired diameter of your grommet (60 inches for a 6-inch grommet). Carefully unlay the strands. You now have the materials for making three grommets. Form a loop in the center of a strand, about the size of your finished grommet, as seen on the opposite page. Maintaining the strand's natural, tight twist (we don't want mushy strands—the sign of a sloppy sailor), pass one end over the other and start to re-lay the strands.

Work around the ring in both directions, laying the strands into the hollows and twisting them into the ring. Keep the lay tight, but don't overtension or overtwist the strand, or your finished grommet will have a tendency to work into a figure-eight all by itself (another sign of a bad seaman—"Would ya' look at 'im—'is grommet's all twisted!").

If you started your work at the top, as in the drawing, each loose end will be passed all the way around the ring and back to the top. As the two pass each other, moving in opposite directions, you will see that the combination leaves behind something looking just like three-stranded rope. Continue with both strands until you reach the starting point, then check your diameter, just to be sure.

To finish the grommet, tie the strands in a single overhand knot and snug them into the last remaining hollow where they meet. If you tie the knot in the wrong direction, it won't want to lay into the hollow properly. Done right, it's almost seamless. Before cutting off the excess, tuck each strand once under its nearest, outboard neighbor. If you untwist it a bit while doing this, it will lay smoother. Pull the ends tight, cut off the excess at a slight angle, and blend in the end.

If you were successful, you should have a good-looking, and untwisted, rope grommet. A grommet is normally a bit fatter in the area around the knot, but it should look pretty smooth. If it is not, wiggle the sides around or stretch the grommet over a fid (or anything pointed) to even it out as needed.

Now make a second grommet, identical in size to the first. You will soon discover that the trick in making multiple grommets is getting them to come out to the same diameter.

Once you have learned to make multiple grommets of the same size, try making penny grommets.

I prefer manila rope for grommets that will be used as mast hoops. It's a little stiffer than Dacron and holds its shape better. Something in the range of $5/16$ to $3/8$ inch would be a good size. The grommets can be laid up right through the sail's ring, as seen on the opposite page, or hand-sewn to it with sail twine. Make the grommets large enough in diameter to slide easily on the mast. Like wooden hoops, a size that is 20 to 25 percent larger than the mast's diameter should be fine.

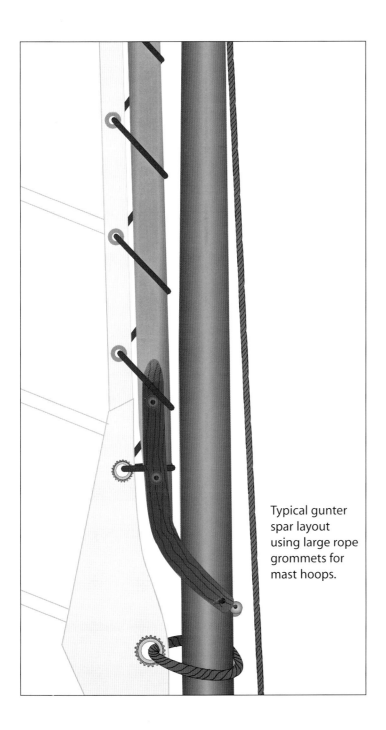

Typical gunter spar layout using large rope grommets for mast hoops.

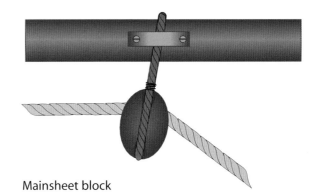

Mainsheet block with becket made from a rope grommet and seized into a figure-eight to capture the block and fit over the boom.

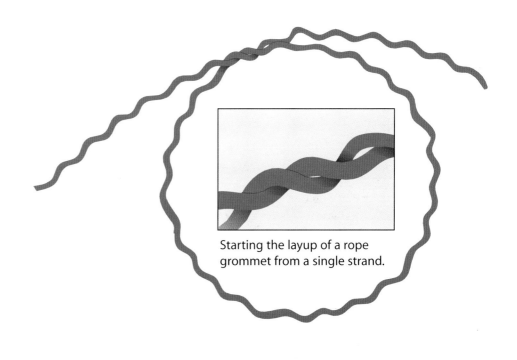

Starting the layup of a rope grommet from a single strand.

A Riveting Discussion

At times, I have mentioned riveting various parts together. Riveting is a good way to attach boom jaws, metal hinges, and other pieces of hardware to spars and other components of the rig.

It is important to note that I am not talking about "pop-rivets," those little aluminum expansion rivets that keep the gunwales from falling off most of the fiberglass and plastic canoes on the market. Pop-rivets fall into the "rather crude—but reasonably effective" category; they don't belong on a classic boat.

When I say rivet, I'm talking about a real boatbuilder's rivet, the type that held together Viking ships and is still used today for fastening lapstrake boats.

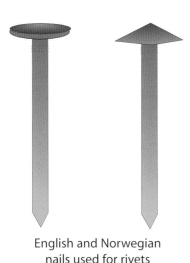

English and Norwegian nails used for rivets

Actually, a completed rivet is a combination of two pieces, and these days both are made of copper. The first part is a square-shanked nail. English rivets have a disc-shaped head, like that of a common nail; Norwegian rivets have a pyramid-shaped head. Each type is available in various lengths and sizes. The second part is called the "rove." It is a small dome-shaped washer, with a small, round hole in the center.

Rove

A rivet is stronger than a screw because it passes all the way through the pieces to be joined, locking them together. The hole for the shank of the nail is necessarily less than that for a countersunk screw, leaving more wood for strength. A finished rivet looks good and is fairly easy to remove if necessary.

Riveting is fun, as long as you're not building a 75-foot Viking ship. Here's how it is done:

A hole is drilled through both pieces of wood (or wood and metal if that is what you are joining), and the nail is driven through until it just emerges through the other side. Here is one of the few instances in life where you are actually supposed to drive a square peg into a round hole. The square shaft's corners dig into the wood and keep the rivet from spinning.

Next, the rove is positioned over the point of the nail and backed-up with a "rove-set," available from the same traditional boat chandleries that sell riveting supplies. The rove-set is a metal tool with a concave end that matches the shape of the rove; it also has a hole drilled in it to clear the exposed shank of the nail as you drive it the rest of the way through the stock and into the rove.

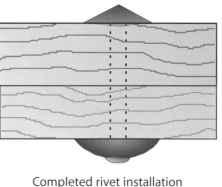

Completed rivet installation

Once the rivet's head is firmly against one side of the work and the rove tightly against the other side, the excess nail is cut off with a big pair of nippers, leaving just a bit sticking out past the rove. The other end of the rove-set is then used as a backing iron against the head of the rivet while you mushroom the cut-off end with multiple taps of a small ball-peen hammer to lock the rove in place. You now have a rivet.

Traditionally, the head of the nail is against the outside of the boat and the rove is against the inside. A finished rivet is strong and could even be considered decorative.

I am amazed that I have never seen rivets used to fasten the gunwales on a wooden canoe. They would be stronger than the typical brass or bronze screws that are traditionally used. More importantly, the gunwale would be stronger, as the small holes required for rivets means there will be less weakness induced by drilling.

The Forked Mast

The idea of using a forked stick for a mast, throwing the halyard over the fork and tying it off on one of the after thwarts as a makeshift backstay, "voyageur-style," has much merit. I can't help thinking that the arrangement would work well for some of the more modern downwind sails, such as spinnakers, just as it did for the squaresails used by the fur traders.

A real stick, cut on the spot as required, would certainly save weight when tripping, but I like the idea of building a small forked mast made to fit the mast thwart and step and having it on hand all the time. It might even double as a walking stick. I can think of several good ways to build one.

The easiest would be to make a single wooden piece with jaws and glue, rivet, or screw it to the top of the mast. If you use a type of wood that steam-bends well, such as ash, you could laminate the mast from two pieces, the ends of which could be pre-bent back to make the fork.

If the mast were to be of spruce or fir, I would adopt a different technique:

After cutting or laminating the blank for the mast into a long, skinny, square section, I would draw my mast taper, leaving the last 8 inches or so full-sized and square. Next, I would make multiple rip cuts down from the end, creating a comb-like section at the end with "teeth" that are about ⅛ inch thick. I would divide the strips into two batches, slather them with epoxy resin thickened with microspheres or a similar filler, and bend and clamp them to make the forked shape. Once the glue has cured I would clean up the fork, shape it as necessary, and glue in a small hardwood block that can be shaped as a bearing surface to prevent wear from the halyard. The rest of the mast could then be tapered and rounded. A metal band or lashing for a collar, fitted to the mast just below the fork, would help prevent the mast from splitting in use. I would also tie a stopper knot in my halyard/backstay line, just above the yard or sail, to bear on the fork and keep backstay tension from trying to pull the sail through the fork.

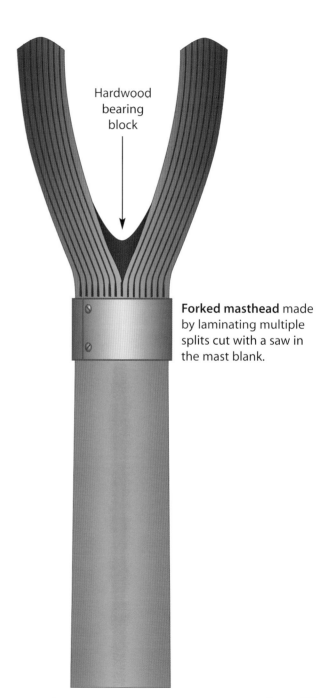

Hardwood bearing block

Forked masthead made by laminating multiple splits cut with a saw in the mast blank.

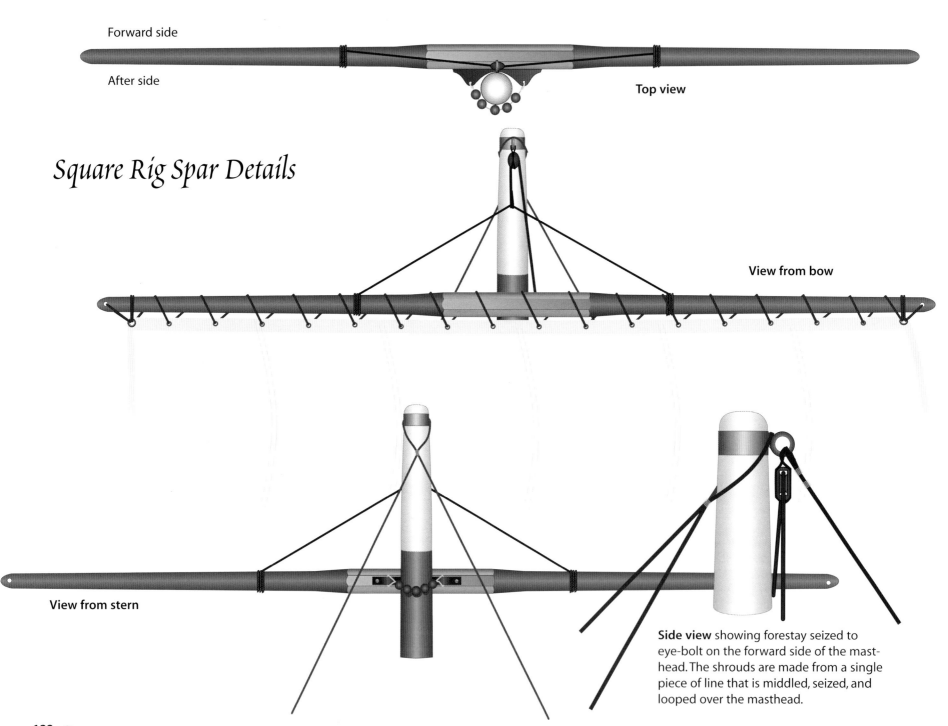

Forward side

After side

Top view

Square Rig Spar Details

View from bow

View from stern

Side view showing forestay seized to eye-bolt on the forward side of the masthead. The shrouds are made from a single piece of line that is middled, seized, and looped over the masthead.

The Squaresail Yard

Though the yard for a squaresail could just be a pole, there's no reason not to make a properly proportioned one. A proper yard adds elegance and credibility to the whole rig. Let's face it, if you show up in many places with a squaresail these days, people are going to see you as a curiosity. You might as well look like a sailor, instead of a guy who hung a tarp on his mast!

The yard shown here is left eight-sided in the center, tapered toward the ends, and fitted with a small yoke and parrel system on its after (mast) side to keep it in place. The halyard is run through a block suspended from an eyebolt on the forward side of the masthead. A simple lashed-on bridle connects the halyard to the yard. The shroud lines are actually made from one piece of line that has been middled with a loop, seized at its center. This is dropped over the masthead and kept from sliding down by the eye-bolt.

A forestay would normally be secured to this eye and the bow, but it may not always be needed. If the mast is stiff enough, even the shrouds can be eliminated in most conditions. I haven't added any braces—control lines attached to the outboard ends of the yard—because they won't be critical for running downwind. But if you want to see how high your squaresail can reach, the braces will help control the yard's angle to the wind.

The outhauls are tied through holes bored in the ends of the yard. There are many possible ways to make this connection, some of them quite complex. For our purposes, this is simple and will work fine. The slot, pin, and hitch method from page 110 would also be good.

The yard illustrated here is rather fat, mostly because I was limited in drawing space and didn't want to lose too much detail by making it thinner. In real life, I think I would build most canoe yards around 1½ to 1¾ inches in diameter at the center, tapering to 1 to 1¼ inches on both ends.

Lubricating Spar Connections

If you have just waded through this entire chapter in one sitting or have even gone so far as to build all your spars, you may feel as if a bit of lubrication of the alcoholic sort is in order. But wait, we're not quite done yet. The yoke on a squaresail yard, the jaws of a gaff or boom, and the junction of a lugsail's yard and mast may first need a little lubrication of their own.

Two freshly varnished wooden surfaces, under tension, rubbing against each other, won't stay varnished for long. And before the varnish is gone, the surfaces seem to generate a sticky friction that inhibits the motion of the parts. Something has to be done to at least one of the surfaces to help break friction's grip and help prevent the varnish from being rubbed off.

Traditionally, the bearing surfaces of spar-to-spar junctions were leathered and liberally coated with tallow. Most of us don't keep much tallow around these days, and even if we did, on a rig that's likely to be bundled up whole and stuck in a bag, the stuff would soon be all over the sail, no doubt leaving permanent stains.

After I pondered the predicament for quite a while, the best alternative to leather and tallow that I could think of was felt. A thin strip of felt, glued (or possibly tacked) to the bearing surface of a gaff, boom, or spar, would both protect the mast's varnish and reduce friction as the spar rotated on the mast when sailing.

The heavy felt used for pack-boot liners is very tough stuff, though you might not need that much thickness. Sometimes you can find insoles of the same material, ⅛ inch thick; this would be ideal.

I suppose the felt strips could be lubricated with dry silicone, but as someone who spends a fair amount of time refinishing and painting old boats, I hesitate to recommend it. Residual silicone from polishes and such is a boat painter's nightmare and really tough to remove. If you ever want to re-varnish a mast or spar that has been tainted with silicone, you might have a lot of trouble. Spending an afternoon watching freshly applied varnish bead and fisheye will drive anybody to lubrication of another sort.

Sprit Rig Spar Details

Here is a common method for tensioning and adjusting a sprit. The line involved is called a "snotter." (No, I don't know why, and yes, if it were up to me, I would choose a nicer name.) One part of our snotter is made from a rope grommet seized to hold a brass thimble, or a small block, and dropped over the masthead where it comes to rest on a thumb cleat. The adjusting part is spliced to the end of the sprit, runs up through the hanging thimble for a two-to-one purchase, and comes back down to a cleat mounted low on the mast.

We actually want to encourage this mast to spin as we tack, as it will keep the tension on the snotter even from tack to tack. (This is why we cleat the snotter on the mast, rather than on the thwart.) A round-sectioned mast, possibly with a small Teflon chip stuck on the bottom or laid in the mast step, is in order.

The sprit for a typical canoe rig should be about 1¼ inches in diameter at the center and taper to around 1 inch at the bottom and ¾ to 1 inch at the peak. A metal band fitted to the sprit just above the hole for the snotter will help prevent the sprit from splitting under tension.

Since the sail should have a brail—the line that collapses the sprit and the sail against the mast for furling—there really is no need for a halyard. The sail can be left laced to the mast, and the whole rig dropped into place.

Another, smaller, seized rope grommet is fitted to the peak ring of the sail and the sprit stuck through it. The sprit has a small shoulder cut into it to keep it seated in the grommet.

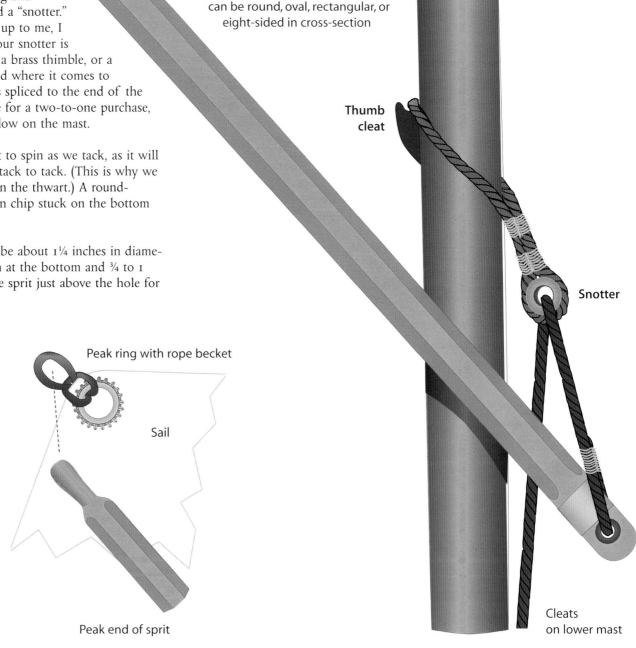

Sprit
can be round, oval, rectangular, or eight-sided in cross-section

Thumb cleat

Snotter

Cleats on lower mast

Peak ring with rope becket

Sail

Peak end of sprit

Finishing Your Spars

A carefully applied finish will not only protect your spars, but go a long way toward turning a pile of slightly tapered sticks into integral parts of a sailing craft. Whether you choose glossy varnish or the more subtle look of an oiled finish, it is well worth the money to buy a high-quality product developed for the marine market and follow the directions on the can carefully.

Years ago, I learned that hardware store wood finishes just don't make the grade for boatwork. Though you may pay twice as much for a can of marine spar varnish, it will have a smoother, more durable finish with longer-lasting gloss than a comparable hardware store polyurethane.

If your boat is old and your spars are new, you may want to tone down the color of your spars to get a closer match. Wood stain is generally not the answer because it ends up looking more like stained wood than old wood. Some of the people who refinish antiques artificially age replaced wooden components by applying a base coat, or two, of orange shellac, before they varnish.

The shellac's golden tone helps make the newly varnished sections blend into the older, yellowed varnish and darkened wood on the rest of the piece. Though it might compromise the weatherability and adhesion of the subsequent coats of marine varnish a bit, I doubt that you will have any problems on something that gets as little weather as a canoe spar.

Oil finishing is less tedious than varnishing and some people like the more natural, satin finish that oil produces. Building up a nice looking, durable surface and protecting the wood requires frequently smoothing the spar with steel wool or fine sandpaper, followed by a rubbed-on coat of oil. Over time, and with work, you can achieve a silky, "gunstock" finish.

This is a brush built for varnishing cylindrical objects, like spars and oars. Its bristles are packed into an oval shape to provide more uniform coverage on non-flat surfaces. Though you can do a first-class job with any good varnish brush, these pricey beauties are great if you want to treat yourself to the best.

Chapter Eight

Mast Support

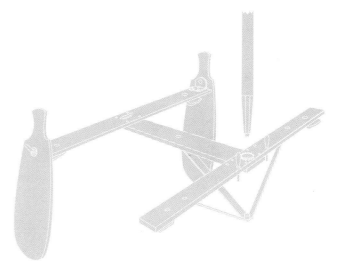

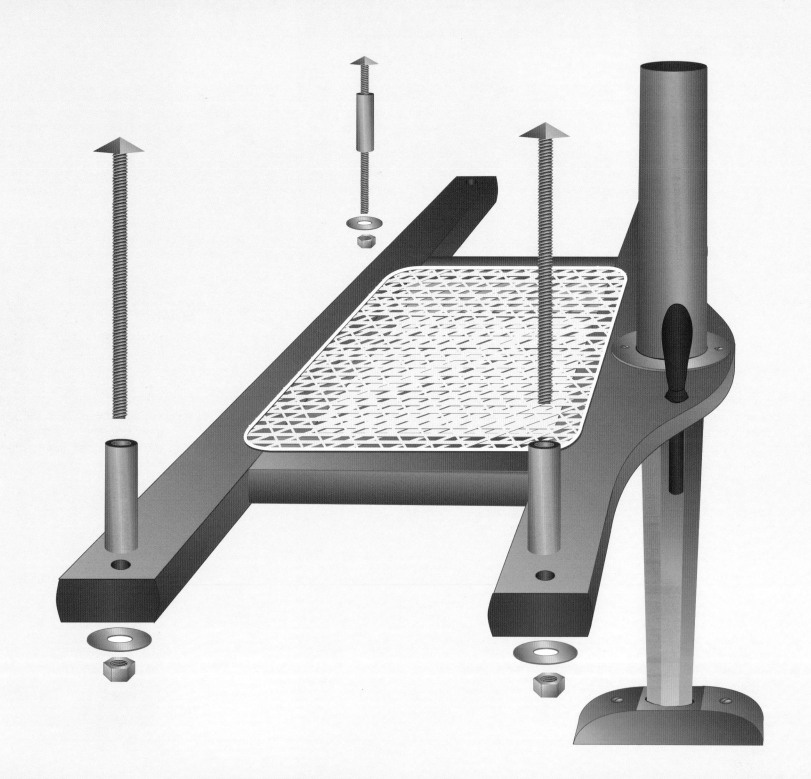

Stepping the Mast

While some canoe rigs, with their hinges, battens, and folding masts, are quite complex, attaching the rig, however complex, to the boat couldn't be easier: Drop it through a hole in a thwart, make sure the heel fits into the mast step, and raise the sail. Occasionally, a pair of rope shrouds are used as backstays, but even they are quite simple and quickly tied off.

When we were discussing rig design, using the existing structure of the canoe for supporting the mast(s) was one of the design criteria. Though we might replace a seat or a thwart with one that has a mast socket bored through it, we want to drill as few new holes in the gunwale as possible. This is important for both cosmetic and structural reasons. There really isn't very much wood in the gunwale of a canoe. Drill a ¼-inch hole in a ¾-inch-wide inwale, and you have lost one-third of its strength. This is particularly true when it is an empty hole, which it will be when the boat is being paddled and a mast thwart isn't necessary.

The one instance where I would be tempted to live with extra holes just for a mast thwart would be when fitting a twin rig with a rudder. Some of these rigs, as we saw in Chapter Six, require replacing both the bow and the stern seats with mast seats and running the boat backward to get the mainmast as far forward as possible. Such an arrangement involves permanently bolting the rudder gudgeons to what is, in reality, the bow of the boat (at least when the boat is paddled). When you return to the paddling mode, you have these "things" that look very much like they don't belong there bolted to the bow stem of your beautiful canoe.

I don't build or buy ugly boats, and I try hard to make sure that I don't alter them in any way that would make them ugly. In my mind, bow-mounted rudder gudgeons aren't acceptable. I would much rather take my chances drilling extra holes in the gunwale for a removable forward thwart and mounting the gudgeons on the stern where they belong and where they are less of an eyesore.

Most single-sail rigs replace either the bow seat or the thwart just behind it with one made to take a mast. The seat is caned as the original, but it has a wider after cross-bar with a hole bored through it for the mast to drop through (see page 130). A mast thwart (page 131) is just a wide thwart—sometimes shaped, sometimes parallel sided—like those in the old Chestnut freight canoes. It is typically about 5 inches wide and has a hole in its center.

Usually leather is tacked around the inside of the mast hole or around the mast itself to prevent varnish-to-varnish contact and the abrasion that it can cause. I have also seen at least one mast thwart with a bronze collar lining the hole. It was pretty classy but probably had to be custom made.

These days, most thwarts are made from flat lumber with the edges rounded off with a router. If you build your own, you might consider thinning the ends and thickening the middle, as the canoe makers used to do. A 5-inch-wide thwart that is 1⅛ inches thick at the center and tapered to ⅝ to ¾ inch thick at the ends looks much more graceful than a plank of uniform thickness, especially if it will be straight-sided rather than hourglass-shaped in plan view.

The mast step (page 131 and 132) is glued and/or screwed to the inside bottom of the boat and has a hole bored in it to take the heel of the mast. The step can be as fancy as you want to make it, but most are nicely finished blocks of hardwood 1¼ to 1½ inches thick. In a wood-and-canvas canoe, the step can span two ribs, with the hole, open at the bottom for drainage, between the ribs; or the step can run crosswise, atop a rib, with the underside carefully shaped to match the curve of the rib. Which arrangement you choose may depend on where the ribs lie in relation to the position of the mast socket in the seat or the thwart. If necessary, the step can be made to span two ribs and the hole for the heel of the mast positioned forward or aft in the step as necessary.

The Mast Seat

Many of the small shops that build canoe seats will build mast seats on a custom basis. If you have the tools and the time, building one yourself isn't particularly difficult. The crosspiece with the mast hole is usually positioned toward the stern of the canoe. The primary reason for this is to get the mast step, which will be in the bottom of the canoe directly under the mast hole, out from underfoot.

Belaying Pins

Cleating a halyard to the seat or to a thwart, instead of to the side of the mast, helps keep the rig from falling out should you ever capsize. I turned a bunch of little belaying pins on a lathe while building prototype parts for a mini-schooner that I've been designing for years. I used walnut and finished them with oil. It struck me that they would be neat for tieing off canoe halyards as well.

The holes for belaying pins must be fairly close to the edge of the seat frame. To use a removable pin, the halyard is brought down and passed behind the lower section of the pin, below the seat. It is brought up and wrapped around the head of the pin and then back down. The excess is coiled and hung on the pin. Several figure-eights can be used instead of a hitch, if desired.

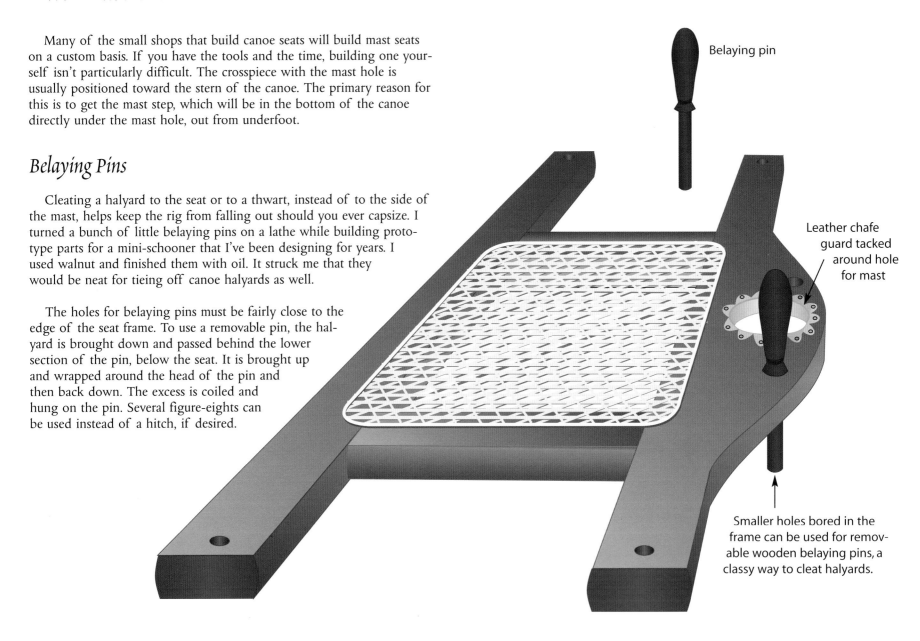

Belaying pin

Leather chafe guard tacked around hole for mast

Smaller holes bored in the frame can be used for removable wooden belaying pins, a classy way to cleat halyards.

The Mast Thwart

A mast thwart is, obviously, a little easier to build than a mast seat. It can replace any thwart in the canoe, or be a temporary bolt-on addition, used only for sailing. This is sometimes the case for twin rigs, where the position of the main mast falls between the bow seat and the deck. For canoes with large sails, a mast thwart is also stronger than a mast seat.

Custom-cast or machined bronze liner for socket in the mast step—a nice alternative to leather

Mast step, glued and/or screwed to the bottom of the canoe to take the heel of the mast

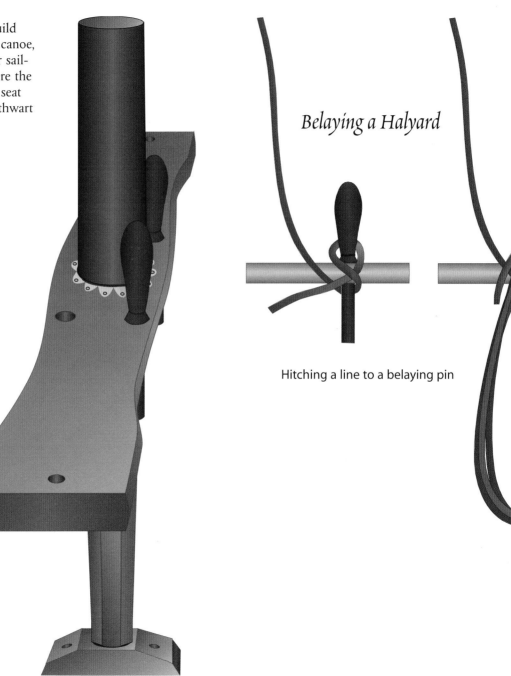

Belaying a Halyard

Hitching a line to a belaying pin

The Mast Step

Transverse Mast Step—viewed from the bow or the stern of the canoe

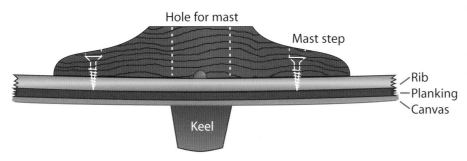

The bottom of the mast step has been shaped to fit the curve of the top of the rib. Notice that there isn't much wood for the screws to grab. The bulk of the attachment's strength comes from the glue bond. Epoxy will actually exceed the grain strength of the cedar rib, making screws unnecessary, though screws will help hold the step in place while the epoxy hardens. All varnish should be removed from the rib where the step will be glued for a good bond and a watertight seal. A small limber hole, or drain, has been cut in the side of the mast hole to help prevent rot. The inside of the hole should be well sealed with epoxy or varnish.

Fore-and-Aft Mast Step—viewed from the side

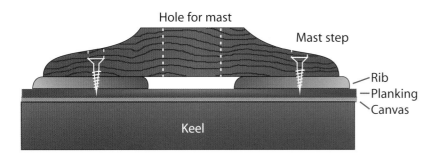

This is the ideal position for a fore-and-aft step. The mast hole lies between two ribs. You may have to adjust the shape of the step and the placement of the hole to conform to the structure of your boat and the position of the mast hole in the thwart or seat. The latter is a good reason to plan the position of the step before that of a mast thwart when designing a rig.

The drawings at left show two options for mounting the mast step in a wood-and-canvas canoe. Of course, not all sailable canoes are built of wood/canvas construction. You wouldn't be able to use screws to help attach a mast step to a fiberglass, plastic, or stripper canoe. Fear not, epoxy will do the job on 'glass boats and strippers, and most plastic boat manufacturers can provide a special glue and instructions for using it. Since most of these glues are permanent, the step should probably be sealed with epoxy, even on the bottom, before installation to prevent rot.

Fitting a mast step to an aluminum canoe is more difficult. Aluminum tends to oxidize so quickly that even during the short time between preparing the surface and mixing the epoxy the quality of the bonding surface will deteriorate somewhat. If you plan to glue the step in place, check with the epoxy's manufacturer for an "aluminum etching kit," which will help you get the best possible bond.

Welding an aluminum step into an aluminum canoe can weaken the hull; riveting can lead to leaks.

Rigging Decks

The only other way to fit a step in an aluminum canoe that I am aware of is to suspend it from a rigging deck. A rigging deck is a framework of cross-bars, clamped to the gunwale. Three or four diagonal struts, fixed to the cross-bars and converging at a "cup-shaped" step, just above the bottom of the canoe, secure the heel of the mast. Up top, one of the cross-bars can have a mast socket, replacing the mast thwart or seat used in wooden boats.

The same concept can be used for any canoe. Since the rig is clamped in place, no holes have to be drilled and nothing has to be glued to the boat. If you have a boat that you don't wish to modify in any way, and you're willing to steer with a paddle, this may be the way to go.

Lost in the Woods Boatworks, in Nobel, Ontario, builds such a frame for sailing canoes. It has the mast thwart, mast step, leeboard bracket, and halyard cleats all built into a single clamp-on unit. It should work on almost any open canoe and on some kayaks.

I don't know who came up with the idea of the rigging deck, but it's a good one. With a single clamp-on structure, we can step the mast, attach the leeboards, cleat the halyards, and attach fairleads, blocks, and cleats for steering and sail-control lines—without drilling a single hole in the canoe or gluing anything on.

Most of the parts that I show here in metal can also be made from wood, which might look nicer than aluminum, though bronze would be pretty classy. If there are any drawbacks to the system, they would be its bulk, a bit more obstruction of interior space, and the potential that the gunwale clamps could slip if they are not very secure. We will take a closer look at similar clamps in the next chapter, when we look at leeboard brackets.

Notice how the heel of the mast has been tapered below the mast socket and ends with a peg sized to fit the mast step. If you are concerned about the mast spinning while sailing, the peg can be square in cross-section.

This mast has been left eight-sided, below the "partners"—the level at which the mast meets the rigging deck. This shape looks good and requires less work for the sparmaker.

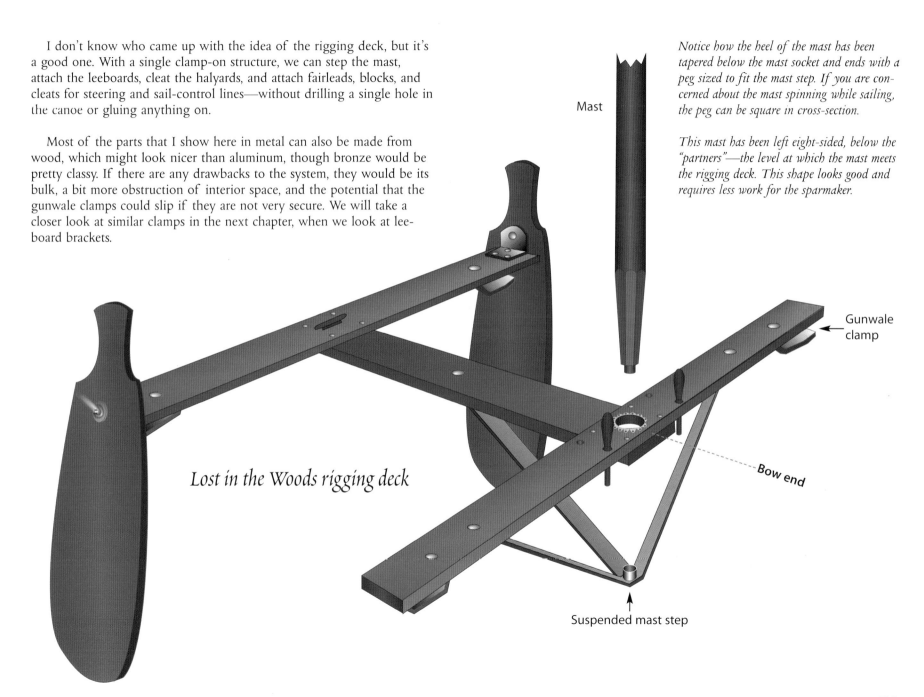

Mast

Gunwale clamp

Bow end

Lost in the Woods rigging deck

Suspended mast step

Standing Rigging

The word "rigging" is used to describe rope or wire used to support or control a sailboat's spars and sails. "Running rigging" denotes rigging that moves, such as the halyard, the line that pulls a sail into position on the mast. "Standing rigging" is rigging that is static, consisting of lines and/or wires that help to hold the mast up and in position. Though adjustable, standing rigging is not constantly in motion, tuning or trimming the sails.

Most canoe rigs have no standing rigging at all. The stiffness of the mast and the support of the mast thwart, or seat, and the mast step are all that is needed to hold the rig in place. Ropes and wires tend to be in the way, eating up space, which is already at a premium in a sailing canoe. In general, standing rigging should be avoided. The possible exception is for downwind sails, such as squaresails and spinnakers.

Downwind sails are clearly "auxiliary propulsion." They are only usable when your desired course happens to be pretty close to the direction the wind is blowing. You should be able to sail a reach, so your sailing course won't just be limited to straight downwind, but you won't have the ability to sail upwind as you would with a more general-purpose rig.

To make a downwind sail worth bringing along on a trip, it must make up into a pretty small package, something that you aren't tempted to toss into the bushes by the third portage. Using a mast that has a smaller diameter and less weight and propping it up with a couple of simple rope shrouds (lines leading from the upper mast, down and back to the gunwales) is well worth considering.

Since a downwind sail is suspended from the mast rather than laced to it, it doesn't exert the type of bending forces on the mast that most general-purpose canoe sails will. Most of the bending power will simply be trying to pull the masthead forward and to some extent, depending upon heading, off to the side.

Adding shrouds, and in some cases a rope forestay leading to the bow, will help prevent both the chances of a gust breaking the mast and the unsightly appearance of a mast that is too limber to stand up to the breeze. In some cases, such standing rigging will improve performance as well. A mast that leans over, spilling wind every time a puff comes along, isn't taking maximum advantage of the free power source that's providing your ride.

For a canoe-sized boat, standing rigging can be either rope or very light steel cable. Cable has most of the advantages—low windage, low stretch, high strength, and low cost. On the other hand, it's one of the world's most obnoxious materials to work with and isn't very attractive.

Some of the new wonder ropes, such as Kevlar, Vectran, and Technora-cored lines, have strength and stretch characteristics similar to cable, but in a softer, friendlier (and more expensive) form. They have reasonably small diameters and would work well, though there is generally nothing traditional about their appearance. Somehow, something about holding up a squaresail with Kevlar shrouds bugs me, if you know what I mean.

My choice for standing rigging is regular Dacron rope, but a specific type that is acceptable in physical characteristics and far superior in cosmetic characteristics. Dacron will definitely stretch in use, but for our purposes, since it is only there to help the mast hold its shape, we can live with some stretch.

For mast support I prefer "three-strand filament Dacron" in $\frac{3}{16}$ to $\frac{1}{4}$ inch diameter. Made by New England Ropes, it is available through some of the marine mail-order suppliers, but you probably won't find it at your local boatshop due to lack of demand. The line is fairly hard and stiff, splices well, and is pretty cheap in these sizes. The entire cost of the standing rigging for a canoe is about the same as a decent lunch.

White Line: Elegantly Incorrect

When it's new, filament Dacron is white — too white to look antique, or natural in origin, so you may want to tone it down a bit. I use diluted wood stain for changing the color of rope used on sails, and the technique works equally well for standing rigging. I'll go through the entire process in the upcoming chapter on sailmaking, but for now, just keep in mind that although clean, bright-white, three-strand rope is very handsome and nautical-looking on a wooden boat, in most cases it isn't historically accurate. The decision to use it or not is yours.

For a squaresail, I think I would have a rope forestay available when needed. It will only cost a couple of dollars for a line long enough to reach from the masthead to the bow deck; the combination of the shrouds leading aft and the forestay forward will really stabilize the mast in all directions. For running downwind, you probably won't need a forestay, but it's good to have one ready to go in case the masthead starts wandering around.

For spinnaker sailing, a forestay just gets in the way and makes jibing more tedious, so I would recommend deleting it. Small spinnakers can be run without shrouds, as well. Just watch the mast. If you're getting a lot of bend, hang the shrouds. They could even be permanently connected to the masthead and secured to the gunwales only when needed. The rest of the time they could be wrapped around the lower part of the mast to keep them out of the way.

Shrouds are easiest to make from one piece of rope, folded in half. A loop is formed at the fold, just big enough to slide over the masthead and down until it hits a thumb cleat, eye-bolt, or some other fitting that stops it. If you install an eye-bolt for the halyard block and/or the forestay (near the masthead, forward side), that fitting will also fix the position of the shrouds, as we saw on page 122. The loop itself can be seized with sail twine or formed by just tying an overhand knot in the folded line. I'm sure there must be a splice that would work as well. (My splicing skills are pretty basic, so I stick to seizing.)

Shroud Adjusters

Though the lower end of the shrouds can simply be tied to the gunwales, port and starboard, or to either end of a thwart, there are slightly more sophisticated ways to connect their lower ends to the canoe. Here, a brass thimble is seized to the shroud, about 8 inches short of the gunwale. An adjusting line is dead-ended with a stopper knot passed through an eye-strap. It then runs up, through the thimble, and down to a small cleat for a two-to-one purchase with quick adjustment.

The eye-straps and cleats are mounted on the sides of the canoe's inwales. To get them out of the way, it might also be possible to mount them on the underside of the inwales.

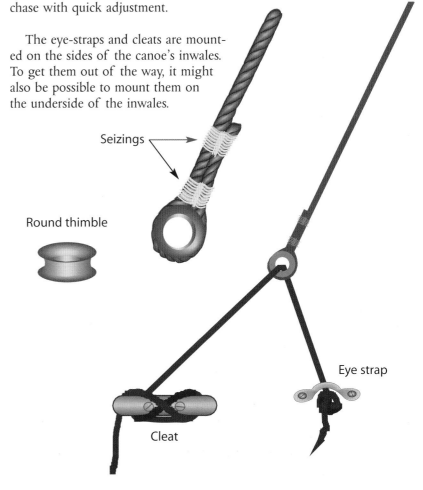

Seizings

Round thimble

Eye strap

Cleat

Gaff-Rig Forestays

The tip of the mast on a gaff-rigged boat may have a tendency to bend backwards while sailing. As it does, it pushes the middle of the mast forward. This is caused by pull of the mainsheet on the sail and that of the peak halyard on the gaff. To get the boat to sail best, the peak halyard is usually set quite taut; the halyard tension that is pulling the gaff up and in is also pulling the masthead backward. This mast bend can cause poor sail shape and performance.

The obvious fix is to make the mast as stiff as possible, but to do that, we pay a weight penalty. More wood for stiffness equals more weight aloft. We can often do better by rigging a light forestay as a bend preventer.

Since we probably won't need shrouds, the forestay shouldn't be under a lot of tension. We don't want to pull the masthead forward; we just want to stop it from being pulled aft. Wire is a better choice here than rope, because we want something that has minimal stretch. It will also be more aesthetically correct. A rope forestay on a fore-and-aft rigged boat would be an oddity.

We should be able to get by with $\frac{1}{16}$-inch steel cable. On a big sail, $\frac{3}{32}$-inch might be wiser. A small turnbuckle could be used at deck level to adjust forestay tension, though with careful measurement it might not be needed.

The stay can be looped over the masthead or attached to an eye-bolt on the forward side of the mast. Don't loop bare wire over the mast, as it will tear up your varnish. To protect the mast from chafe, a strip of leather, sewn into a tube about the diameter of a drinking straw, can be slid over the wire before the top loop is swaged.

A small forward-facing strut is sometimes added just above the gaff/mast intersection to help stiffen that section of the mast as well. A small metal saddle with a socket for the strut is a relatively simple fitting for attaching the strut to the mast.

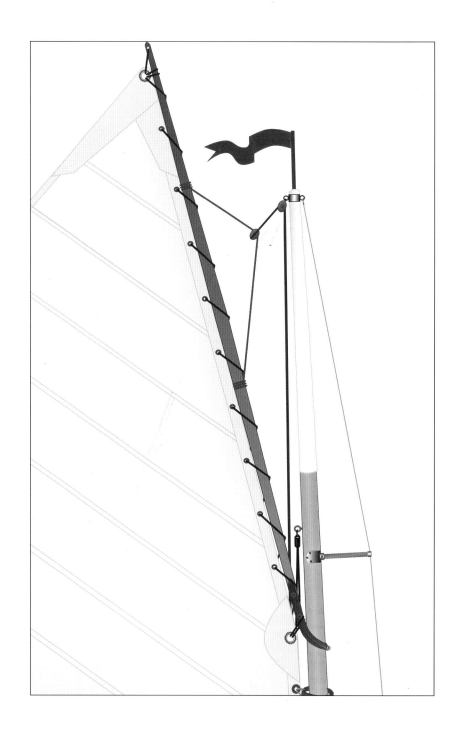

Large outrigger canoes were often rigged with many lines supporting and stiffening their masts

Chapter Nine

Leeboards

Resistance

One of the characteristics that makes a canoe such a good general-purpose boat is its ability to slip sideways. Good paddlers are as adept at moving their boats sideways as they are at moving them forward. This movement isn't necessarily done consciously; it's just part of positioning the canoe, whether to avoid a boulder on a river run, or just to pull alongside a dock to load a passenger. To get that same canoe to function as a sailing craft, we need to limit its sideslipping ability, preferably without making any permanent modifications that will inhibit the boat's paddling performance.

Since the shallow-draft canoe hull provides very little resistance to motion in any direction, we add leeboards to increase the hull's lateral resistance. Leeboards are really nothing more than wooden fins that stick down into the water; their primary function is to keep the power of the sail from blowing the canoe sideways.

If the only sailing we were ever planning to do was traveling downwind, with a squaresail or spinnaker, we wouldn't even need leeboards. Any canoe will sail downwind, even without a sail—or a skipper! Ask anyone who has ever failed to pull their boat far enough up on shore at night and awakened after a storm. Downwind sails are just a more effective way to capture the wind than the windage provided by the hull.

It's when we also want to sail across the wind, or upwind, that we need to increase the canoe's lateral plane, forcing the hull to use sail-captured energy to move it against the wind, rather than downwind. On a canoe designed specifically as a sailing model, it is possible to build lateral resistance into the hull by adding a daggerboard or centerboard and possibly a small tail-fin called a "skeg".

A daggerboard drops vertically through a narrow trunk, or walled-off opening, in the boat's bottom. Centerboards either swing down or unfold from a narrow box-shaped housing inside the canoe. Though these arrangements are excellent for sailing, they are not always desirable in a canoe that will spend much of its life being paddled.

Aside from their extra weight, and the fact that a daggerboard or centerboard trunk takes up valuable space, the addition of a rigid structure to a canoe hull's bottom creates a potential weakness called a "stress riser."

The easiest way to understand a stress riser is to imagine running over a rock on a river trip. Any canoe hull has a certain amount of flexibility, which is part of what makes it durable and allows it to occasionally hit a rock without tearing out the bottom. Adding a rigid structure to the bottom of the boat would make a stiff spot there. Should that part of the bottom hit a rock, something's going to give—and it probably won't be the rock.

By adding removable brackets and leeboards to a general-purpose canoe, we can create good lateral resistance for sailing and still maintain the original flexibility and weight of the hull for other forms of adventure. We can also gain the ability to move the leeboards as needed, to effectively "adjust" the hull shape in relation to the sail plan for best performance. This can't be done on a boat with a centerboard or a daggerboard in a fixed trunk.

Leeboards are usually mounted on both sides of the canoe; the windward board, however, is often swiveled up, out of the water. Just before tacking it is swiveled back down; after a tack, the opposite board becomes the board to windward and is retracted. Some canoes use only one leeboard, made long enough to reach the water on either tack.

The leeboard bracket is a cross-bar clamped on top of the gunwales. "Shoulders" or "chocks" are fitted to the ends and form a flat surface, against which the leeboard is pinned with a single bolt and a large wing-nut, or a variation on the theme.

There are many possible ways to build and attach a leeboard bracket to a canoe. The following pages show a few typical examples of brackets and their connecting hardware.

Wooden Leeboard Bracket

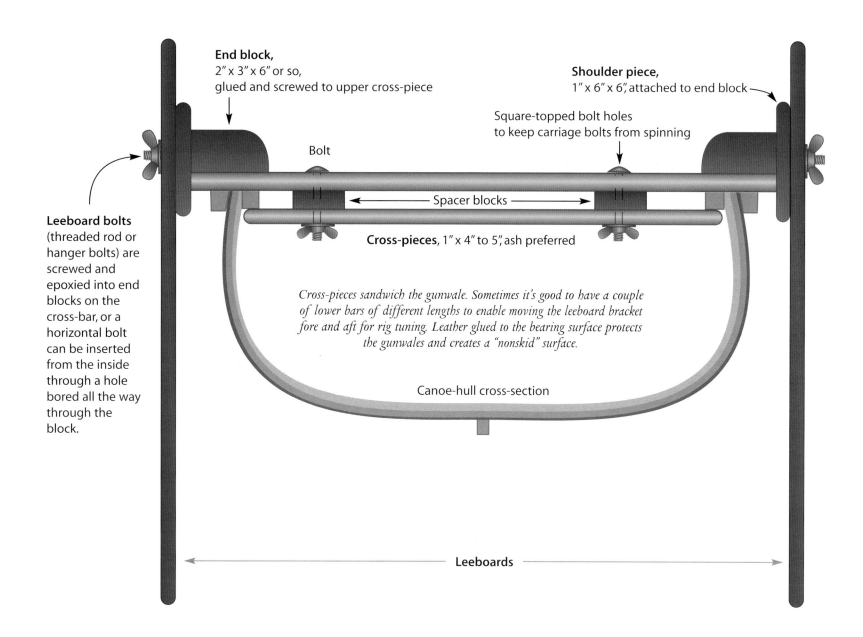

End block,
2" x 3" x 6" or so,
glued and screwed to upper cross-piece

Shoulder piece,
1" x 6" x 6", attached to end block

Square-topped bolt holes
to keep carriage bolts from spinning

Bolt

Leeboard bolts
(threaded rod or
hanger bolts) are
screwed and
epoxied into end
blocks on the
cross-bar, or a
horizontal bolt
can be inserted
from the inside
through a hole
bored all the way
through the
block.

Spacer blocks

Cross-pieces, 1" x 4" to 5", ash preferred

*Cross-pieces sandwich the gunwale. Sometimes it's good to have a couple
of lower bars of different lengths to enable moving the leeboard bracket
fore and aft for rig tuning. Leather glued to the bearing surface protects
the gunwales and creates a "nonskid" surface.*

Canoe-hull cross-section

Leeboards

Leeboard Bracket with Aluminum Chocks and Clamps

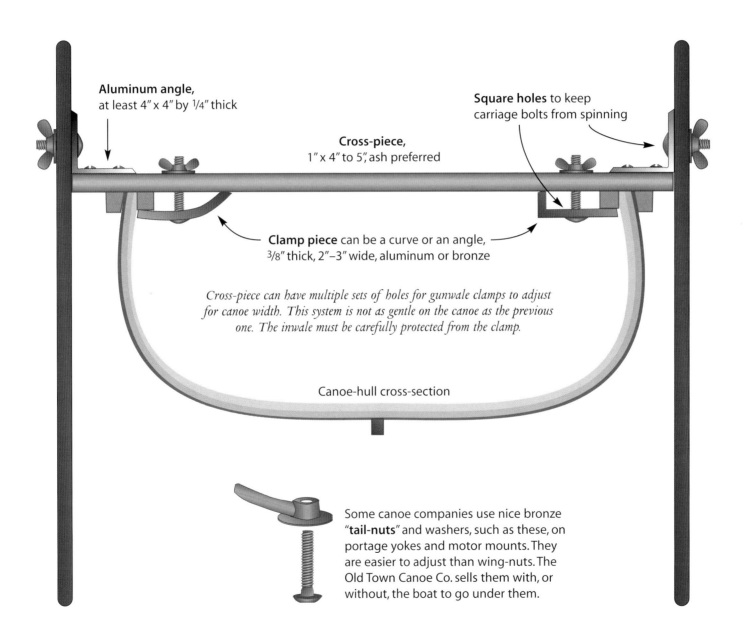

Aluminum angle,
at least 4" x 4" by ¼" thick

Cross-piece,
1" x 4" to 5", ash preferred

Square holes to keep
carriage bolts from spinning

Clamp piece can be a curve or an angle,
³/8" thick, 2"–3" wide, aluminum or bronze

Cross-piece can have multiple sets of holes for gunwale clamps to adjust for canoe width. This system is not as gentle on the canoe as the previous one. The inwale must be carefully protected from the clamp.

Canoe-hull cross-section

Some canoe companies use nice bronze **"tail-nuts"** and washers, such as these, on portage yokes and motor mounts. They are easier to adjust than wing-nuts. The Old Town Canoe Co. sells them with, or without, the boat to go under them.

Morris-Style Leeboards and Bracket

Here is a nicely designed leeboard bracket that wouldn't be difficult to build. The side rails are ¾-inch-by-1½-inch mahogany. The bracket is 4½ to 5 inches by about 38 inches wide. Since there are no handles on the board tops, the thin leeboards were probably just left down. Some other versions show more board above the bracket, which would make them easier to swivel up, out of the water.

This bracket is connected to the gunwale with a pair of brass hooks, which might not be very kind to the wood or its varnish. A small plate or block might be worth attaching to the underside of the gunwale to protect it. A bolt and block, or a bolt and curved metal plate, such as the previous brackets used, would also work.

This leeboard shape from a Morris catalog also shows up in some early Old Town Canoe Co. catalogs. (Morris eventually went to work for Old Town, so perhaps that is the reason.) From the available photographs, the boards look very thin—only ½ to ⅝ inch thick. I have drawn them 35 inches long and 11¾ inches wide. Though it would be tempting to make them out of plywood, it really isn't a good choice. Plywood is all end-grain, which is difficult to seal, and it isn't as stiff as solid lumber. Ash would be a good choice, or maybe maple. The blank could be made from several pieces, glued side-by-side and doweled or splined together.

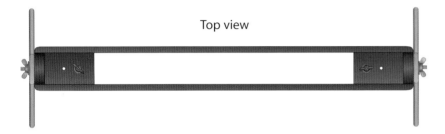

Top view

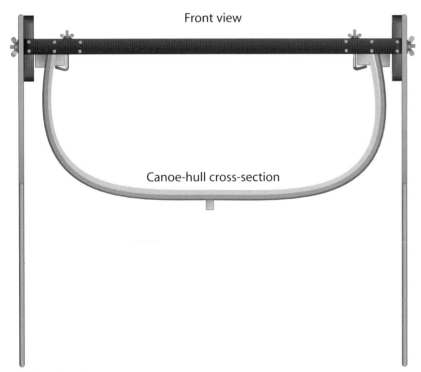

Front view

Canoe-hull cross-section

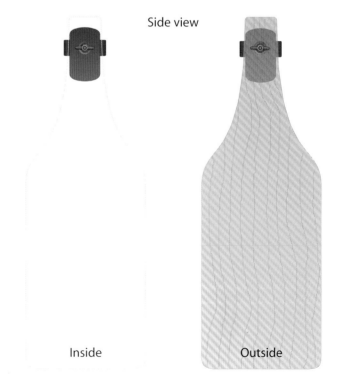

Side view

Inside

Outside

Simplified Leeboard Systems for Small Canoes

Small wooden canoes, many of them built from kits, are enjoying a comeback. Glued plywood lapstrake boats and stitch-and-glue sheet-ply constructions are allowing people to explore new facets of the sport, canoe sailing being one of them. Leeboard attachment is often simplified on these smaller canoes. The illustration on the left, below, shows a pair of metal brackets that can be attached to the flat side of some of these boats and a leeboard dropped straight down through them. Usually only one leeboard is used, becoming, in reality, an externally mounted daggerboard.

The same boat might be equipped instead with one, or a pair of, pivoting leeboards, bolted right through a reinforced portion of the hull. The side panel of the hull acts as the shoulder to support the board, and no leeboard cross-bar is needed.

The simplest method uses a line anchored to the bottom of the boat to hang a single leeboard over the leeward side. The pressure of the wind, trying to push the boat sideways, keeps the leeboard against the hull. When tacking, the leeboard is pulled out and hung over the other gunwale. This method isn't particularly sophisticated, but on a small canoe it may be all that's necessary.

Side-mounted drop-in
daggerboard-type
leeboard

Pivoting Leeboard System
using hull for bracket

Is this what canoeists mean when they talk about having a **hangover**?

Stopper knot

← Rope

Leeboard

Leeboard

Bracket Basics

Assuming that the shoulders or chocks are securely attached to the leeboard bracket cross-bar, most of the in-use forces on the bracket are trying to move it, not to break it. All points where the cross-bar touches the canoe should be faced with leather or rubber, both to work as non-skid surface and a varnish protector. Using a fairly wide cross-bar will also spread the clamping pressure over more of the gunwale, avoid making dents, and keep the bracket from twisting.

If your sail plan happens to put the sail's center of effort (which should be the approximate location for the leeboards) over a thwart, you might be able to clamp the bracket to the thwart. A pair of large U-bolts, or a system with bolts ahead of and behind the thwart, pulling a plate up against the bottom of the thwart, might also be good. It is possible to drill holes in the gunwale and bolt the bracket to the gunwale, but you already know my feelings about drilling extraneous holes in the boat.

I've shown regular bronze wing-nuts on bronze carriage bolts in these drawings. Don't expect to find either at your local hardware store. There are companies advertising in boating magazines that specialize in bronze marine fasteners; you should be able to order bolts, washers, and nuts from them at a reasonable price. So-called "tail-nuts" are easier to adjust than wing nuts, especially for the bolt holding the board to the shoulder.

The area where the leeboard and the chock, or shoulder, meet deserves protection and nonskid treatment, too. Leather, rubber, or, perhaps, a bronze or nylon washer will help create friction to keep the board up or down, and to protect the finish. We want the board to kick up if it hits something, but we don't want it to wander up while we are sailing and have other things to concentrate on.

Leeboard Clamp

It seems to me that some sort of cam-lever, like the device shown here, would be great for quickly adjusting leeboard angle. It wouldn't have to move much, just enough to free the board for swiveling and then to lock it down again. If the lever worked, adjusting the leeboard would be quicker.

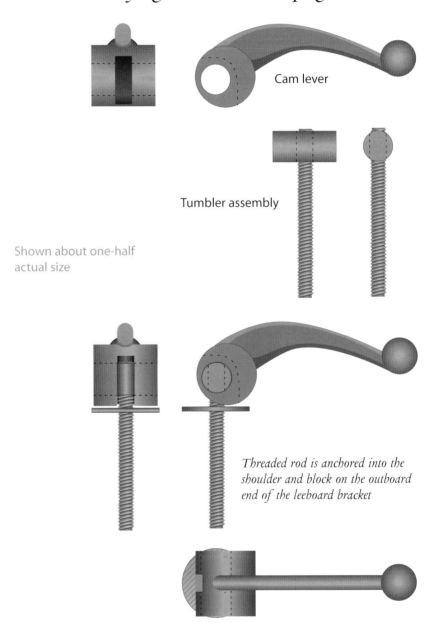

Bradshaw's Newfangled Leeboard Clamping Device

Cam lever

Tumbler assembly

Shown about one-half actual size

Threaded rod is anchored into the shoulder and block on the outboard end of the leeboard bracket

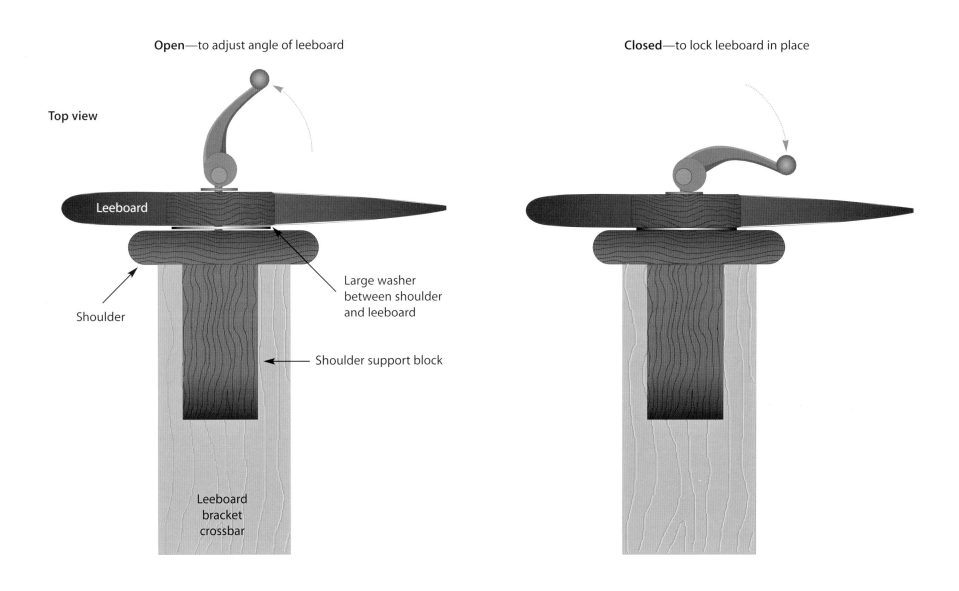

Open—to adjust angle of leeboard

Top view

Leeboard

Shoulder

Large washer between shoulder and leeboard

Shoulder support block

Leeboard bracket crossbar

Closed—to lock leeboard in place

Bradshaw's newfangled leeboard clamping device in action

Leeboard Shapes

I doubt anyone has ever made a comparison study of the efficiency of various leeboards. Shapes seem to vary by manufacturer or by region. Here are a few of the boards used in the various drawings in this book. Some are based on photographs, mostly from sailing rigs once offered by canoe makers; others are my creations. A leeboard that has parallel leading and trailing edges is usually easier to shape into an airfoil than one that doesn't, because it has a consistent cross-section. A board with lots of taper toward the top may have to be thicker to resist bending. A straight handle is generally stronger than a curved handle, since it avoids the possibility of cross-grain failure on the curve. All in all, however, I think it's pretty safe to simply pick a board shape that you like.

Leeboard Construction

Just as there are many possible leeboard shapes, there are many choices when building them. Of the woods, mahogany is the most common, followed by ash. If you can't find a large enough piece of wood to make an entire board, edge-gluing smaller stock will work fine. In many cases, a glued-up board may be less prone to warping than one made of a single piece. A thin leeboard, such as the Morris type shown on page 144, could even be made with wood strips sheathed with clear epoxy and fiberglass, just as a wood-strip canoe or a Sawyer paddle is.

Rolling five or six coats of epoxy over the 'glassed surface will provide enough thickness for sanding the surface smooth without cutting into the glass fibers. A final coat of varnish will protect the epoxy from ultraviolet light deterioration and make a clear, smooth leeboard. With a finished thickness of about ½ inch, a strip-built board can be quite light in weight yet reasonably strong.

More typically, leeboards are between ¾ and 1¼ inch thick and tapered on their leading and trailing edges. It would be possible to edge-glue pieces of lumber of varying thickness to rough-out the taper, but it is both easier and more common to build a blank of uniform thickness and remove wood from it to arrive at the desired taper.

Leeboard making is actually very similar to making laminated canoe paddles. A variety of woods can be used, and they can be mixed or matched. Softwoods, such as spruce and cedar, can be used as middle pieces for lightness; harder woods, such as maple, birch, and mahogany, can be used as the leading or trailing edges for durability.

To build an edge-glued blank for a thicker leeboard, the grain of the wood should be taken into account. If the blank is built with the all of the grain running in the same direction, it may warp in time, creating a board that will try to steer the boat. Even epoxy and fiberglass reinforcement probably will not stabilize a thick board, so it's best to consider the problem before you begin gluing up the pieces (see page 150).

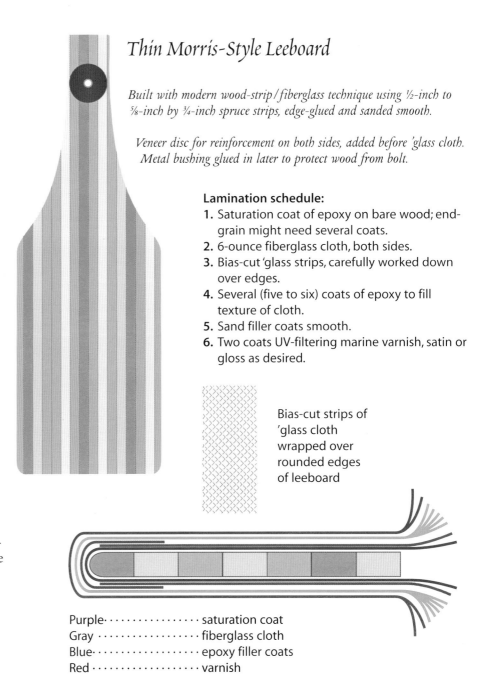

Thin Morris-Style Leeboard

Built with modern wood-strip/fiberglass technique using ½-inch to ⅝-inch by ¾-inch spruce strips, edge-glued and sanded smooth.

Veneer disc for reinforcement on both sides, added before 'glass cloth. Metal bushing glued in later to protect wood from bolt.

Lamination schedule:
1. Saturation coat of epoxy on bare wood; end-grain might need several coats.
2. 6-ounce fiberglass cloth, both sides.
3. Bias-cut 'glass strips, carefully worked down over edges.
4. Several (five to six) coats of epoxy to fill texture of cloth.
5. Sand filler coats smooth.
6. Two coats UV-filtering marine varnish, satin or gloss as desired.

Bias-cut strips of 'glass cloth wrapped over rounded edges of leeboard

Purple	saturation coat
Gray	fiberglass cloth
Blue	epoxy filler coats
Red	varnish

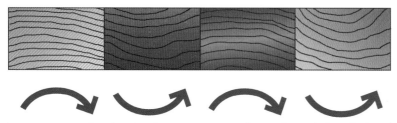

Above, a cross-section showing the proper way to glue up the stock for a leeboard blank to minimize warping. If the board ever does warp, at least it will be in a subtle S-curve.

Below, a board glued up with all the grain going in the same direction. And below that is the warp that the board is likely to take over time.

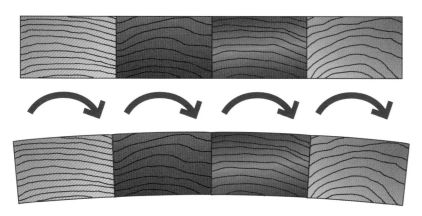

Obviously, reading the grain isn't always this easy, but always keep the grain in mind whenever you are gluing several pieces of wood together to make a blank for a leeboard, a rudder, or any other part.

If desired, joints can be reinforced in several ways. Plan your tapers carefully before gluing up the blank, because you don't want internal reinforcement to become exposed while you are shaping the board. Some areas might be too thin to be reinforced, and only butt joints will work.

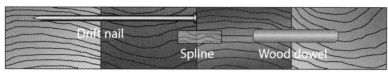

Drift nail

Spline   Wood dowel

Leeboard Size

Yacht designers use formulas to compare sail area with the lateral plane of the hull, keel, and rudder to arrive at a sailboat design that will hold its course without slipping sideways. Depending on the type of boat and structure of the keel, the underwater profile should have a total area of between 7 and 15 percent of the sail area. A larger lateral plane will add drag; insufficient underwater profile will allow the boat to blow sideways.

For canoe sailing, we can use such a formula as a very rough guideline, but there are many unknown factors that work their way into our equation, making it more of an educated guess. For example, a canoe is much more susceptible to change in its lateral plane due to crew movement than most sailboats.

Throughout this book, we have been working with the premise that the canoe will ride level, fore-and-aft, while sailing. It is nearly impossible to design a sail plan for any other situation. A sailor, moving as little as 2 or 3 feet forward or aft in the boat, can drastically change the entire lateral plane of a canoe, making all previous design work moot.

Back in the days when most canoe manufacturers offered sailing rigs for their boats, most had only one leeboard style available. The same boards and bracket were often used on canoes from 13 to 20 feet long, with or without a rudder. The lateral plane for each possible configuration would be different, as would the ratio of the lateral plane to the sail area. In spite of this, there aren't many reports of canoeists being blown out to sea and ending up in Africa or Australia due to insufficient lateral plane, so we might do best not to make too much out of the ratios.

I think we can safely adopt a standard size range for leeboards and downsize them a bit for smaller-than-average boats. For those that demand a mathematical guideline, the canoes that I have measured, though all over the board individually, would suggest that a lateral-plane to sail-area ratio of about 10 to 12 percent is "normal."

Example: A 17-foot-long canoe with a traditional round end profile and drawing 3 inches will have a waterline length of about 15½ feet. Multiplying 15.5 feet by .25 foot (for the 3-inch draft) gives the hull portion a lateral plane of 3.875 square feet. If we add a typical leeboard (one only, for design purposes, since leeboards are often used one at a time) with 24 inches submerged and a 9-inch width, it comes to 2 feet x .75 feet = 1.5 square feet added to our lateral plane.

Steering can be accomplished with a rudder or paddle; let's estimate the underwater portion to be 7 inches wide and 16 inches long. That will add another .77 square foot (7 x 16 = 112 square inches, or .77 square foot). Now, adding the hull figure to those for the leeboard and the paddle or rudder, we have a total lateral plane of 6.145 square feet.

If we purchased or built a 55-square-foot lateen sail for the canoe, 10 to 12 percent of 55 square feet would be a range from 5.5 to 6.6 square feet. Our 6.145-square-foot (11.17 percent) lateral plane fits right in.

On the other hand, we know from experience that the same leeboard and rudder were also sold for 14- and 20-foot canoes. These two boats would calculate out at 5.45 square feet (just under 10 percent) and 6.82 square feet (12.4 percent), respectively.

We also know that some manufacturers sold rigs with larger sails, for high performance, having as much as 75 square feet of sail area. The leeboards and rudders used with these sails were usually the same, and only, models offered by the company. Having more sail area will decrease the lateral-plane to sail-area ratio. On our 17-footer, the ratio would decrease to about 8 percent, but the boat would still sail quite well.

This seems to tell us that too much math is bad for you. Though the formula might be handy as a guideline for design work, or downsizing a plan for a small canoe, it is not written in stone. For an average-sized canoe, we should be able to build "average-sized" leeboards and expect reasonable performance, which is what most of us are after anyway. But running the numbers has its advantage: if anyone asks you about your leeboard size, you can baffle them with mumbo-jumbo and maybe they'll go away.

So what's average size for a leeboard? As far as I have been able to determine, each board in a pair should have 1 to 1½ square feet of surface area below the waterline when the boat is level. Above the waterline, the board must obviously be large enough to reach the leeboard bracket and extend far enough above it to provide a handle if you intend to be able to retract one board while sailing.

For systems using only one leeboard, adding more length, rather than just area, is the key. The board has to be long enough to maintain lateral resistance even when the boat is heeling with the leeboard on the high side. This means adding 10 to 15 inches to its length.

A 9-inch-wide, straight-sided blade with 18 to 20 inches of its length immersed (1.12 to 1.25 square feet), another 12 inches above the water to reach the leeboard bracket, and an 8-inch-tall handle at the top would be 38 to 40 inches long. This is quite typical of most of the pairs of leeboards sold by canoe makers over the years. For a single, longer board, the added length necessary to do the job would make the board 48 to 55 inches long.

If the blade of the board isn't straight sided, you may need to add a bit of length to keep the area within parameters. The calculations for figuring the area of a weird four-sided shape are hauntingly similar to those used for figuring sail area in Chapter Six.

Tapering Off

The ideal underwater cross-section for a leeboard is a perfect airfoil shape. Building such a shape is challenging and, to my mind, a complete waste of time. (Such a statement should raise some eyebrows among sailors.) My point is that most small boats are fitted with daggerboards, leeboards, centerboards, and rudders that fall into the "modified slabs of wood" category, not airfoils, and most of them sail just fine.

If you are seriously racing, maybe it's worth the effort to painstakingly plane the board to perfection, but my response is the same one that I give my sailmaking customers when they are contemplating spending a lot of money on "go-fast" modifications: "Yes, it may make your boat faster— but—a five-second lapse of concentration anywhere on the race course will probably wipe out any gain that you achieve with it. Now, can you honestly tell me that your concentration is that good?" I try to convince them to use the money instead to buy the crew an extra round at the post-race party, so at least somebody will like me.

In the many hours that I have sailed small boats, I can't think of one occasion when it occurred to me that the cross-section of my daggerboard was holding me back. So make your own call, based on your skills, desires, and time, but don't expect to lose much on-water performance with a pair of tapered leeboards that may not be aerodynamically perfect.

Thin Morris-style leeboards really don't have enough wood for tapering. Cutting a nice radius on all the edges is about all that can be done. On thicker boards, both the leading and trailing edges will benefit from some time spent with a plane.

There really is no easy way to mechanically taper a leeboard blank with simple power tools. I once cut a 4-foot-by-1-foot airfoil sailboat rudder with a dado blade in a radial-arm saw by making nearly full-length stair-stepped rip cuts, but it was tedious work.

The top section of the board (everything higher than about 3 inches above the water) needs no taper at all. In fact, the areas that bear against the shoulder of the leeboard bracket and the washers on the bracket bolts should be flat and full thickness. The handle can be shaped and rounded as desired; just be careful concerning the grain of the wood. You don't want to create a handle that will break because it was cut across the grain.

The leading edge of the leeboard can be thinned, but we don't want a knife edge. A rounded edge will have better performance than one that has been "sharpened." The trailing edge can be reduced more, and for a longer section of the chord (cross-section). If you taper the edge to less than 3/16 inch, though, it becomes quite fragile. The little bit that you might lose in performance by keeping some wood on the edge will be made up in durability. Once you get a few inches above the waterline, the taper can be blended out and the board can be left rectangular in cross-section.

Leeboard Cross-Sections

9" x 1 1/8"

Nice airfoil, but the sharp trailing edge won't last long

9" x 1/8"

A good shape; trailing edge less prone to damage

9" x 3/4"

More common shape; easier to build

A Plan for the Plane

Shaping the Leeboard Blank

After the leeboard blank has been selected or constructed, the profile shape can be cut and the tapers drawn on both sides. It's also a good idea to draw a centerline down both the leading and trailing edges. Mark the minimum desired thickness on the trailing edge by measuring out in both directions from the centerline. This will give you a line to plane to. Also, for boards such as the one shown here, a "begin rounding here" line on each side, near the leading edge, will help you keep the rounding consistent.

If I had to build 500 leeboards, I would definitely find some kind of machine to cut the bevels. For two boards, even making a simple router jig would probably take longer than just getting out the hand plane and doing the job. If desired, a saw, router, or—my favorite—the big disc grinder, can be used for some of the heavy removal on the trailing edge. Just don't try to cut all the way down to the line with a power tool.

If your skills with a hand plane aren't great, a Stanley Surform is a pretty fast yet controllable wood remover. When I was building a lot of strip boats, I used the tool when I had to cut long tapers on strips. I was building spruce boats with dark cedar or redwood accent stripes, and it was occasionally necessary to cut tapers as long as 10 feet on a ¾-inch-wide strip to level the edge where the dark strip was to be added. The Surform is quite controllable, but leave room to sand, as it can leave a fairly rough surface.

I really think it is worth gluing a bushing into the bolt hole. Use epoxy, which will help seal the end-grain around the hole and protect the wood from the bolt's threads. You can buy bronze bushings at most hardware stores. Clean the bushing, rough it up with sandpaper, and glue it into the hole. Epoxy-wood-bronze may not be the best bond in the world, but even if the bushing comes loose, the epoxy will still help to protect the wood.

Just because a leeboard is fairly simple doesn't mean it can't be reasonably nice to look at. This board would be about 9 inches wide, 39 inches long, and ¾ inch thick.

Most of it is flat. The tapers are those of the bottom board on the previous page. The leading edge is rounded off starting ¾ inch back from the edge. The trailing edge has a 2-inch-wide bevel, tapered from ¾ inch down to ³⁄₁₆ inch.

On the bottom, the round of the front edge is blended into the taper of the back edge, but some thickness is left on the tip for durability.

A brass or bronze bushing lines the bolt hole to keep the threads of the leeboard bolt from chewing-up the wood and varnish. Some leeboard builders even attach a circular metal plate (large washer) to the board around the bolt hole for protection.

The straight handle is practical, strong, easy to make, and good-looking. All upper edges can be rounded or beveled slightly for cosmetics and durability. Varnish does not last long on perfectly square corners.

Shallow-Draft Leeboards

Running aground in knee-deep water isn't something that most canoeists are familiar with, yet when we add a sailing rig to a canoe it becomes a reality. The fact that shallow water is sometimes the most interesting to explore inspired me to start pondering a shallow-draft leeboard system.

Long, narrow underwater foils are the most efficient. To maintain sufficient lateral plane, a shallow-draft leeboard will have to be shorter and wider than the ideal. When the alternative to a short board is running aground, the potential loss of performance is something we can live with.

After considering several leeboard styles, I finally decided that the teardrop-shaped leeboards, common on Dutch sailboats for hundreds of years, were the best choice. They are also quite elegant.

The chore at hand was to blend Dutch leeboards with the Native American canoe hull. I grabbed a canoe from another drawing that just happened to be planked with a technique that dates back at least to the Vikings and stuck a rig on it that I had been meaning to measure out for a possible canoe rig. The rig is probably British in origin, but its basic shape came from a 1900 Hudson River ice yacht. Could such a cultural grab-bag ever look anything but peculiar?

The results are on the next page. Unusual? Yes. Unconventional? Maybe. But peculiar? I don't know, I kinda like it. And it should sail pretty well, especially when the bottom's not far below the keel.

Construction of this radial fan of lumber is a bit tricky because each piece is a wedge, but a little planning before cutting any wood will help eliminate any problems. The leeboard is designed for ¾-inch-thick stock, mahogany and ash with splined or doweled joints.

There is no taper, and all edges are rounded. Since the board is short, I didn't worry much about adding a handle for retraction; just grab an edge and pull. A hand hole or rope loop could be added near the top if desired.

As the boat heels under sail, most of the windward leeboard will come out of the water fairly quickly just because of its short length, so swiveling it up may not really be needed.

A bushing lines the bolt hole, and a brass plate or large washer surrounds it to protect the wood from abrasion.

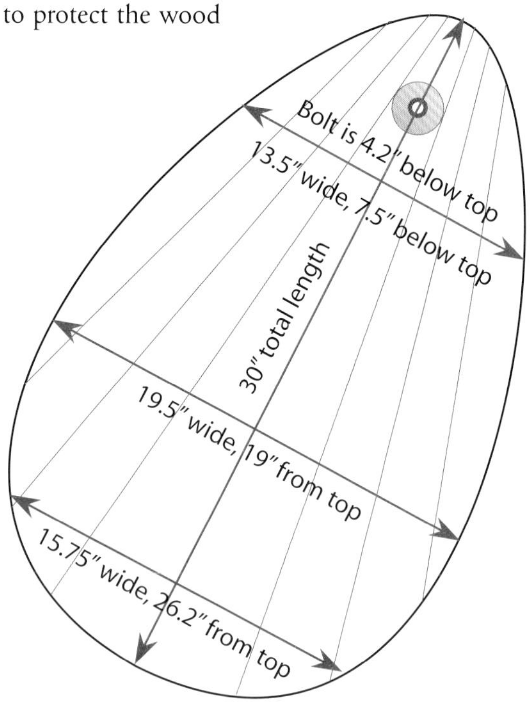

Bolt is 4.2" below top

13.5" wide, 7.5" below top

30" total length

19.5" wide, 19" from top

15.75" wide, 26.2" from top

Gaff Sloop with Shallow-Draft Leeboards

Here is our Shallow-Water Special, and though it's truly a cultural "mutt," it's a pretty good-looking one. The leeboard is 2½ feet long and 19½ inches wide, with a draft of about 14 inches at this angle. Even so, it gives us about 1.25 square feet of immersed area for each leeboard, which is similar to the underwater area of most regular leeboards. The rudder blade is bronze. In shallow water, it can be allowed to swing free, as needed, to clear obstructions. Its weight will keep it down in most winds.

The rig is a gaff sloop of moderate proportions and was inspired by old iceboat rigs.

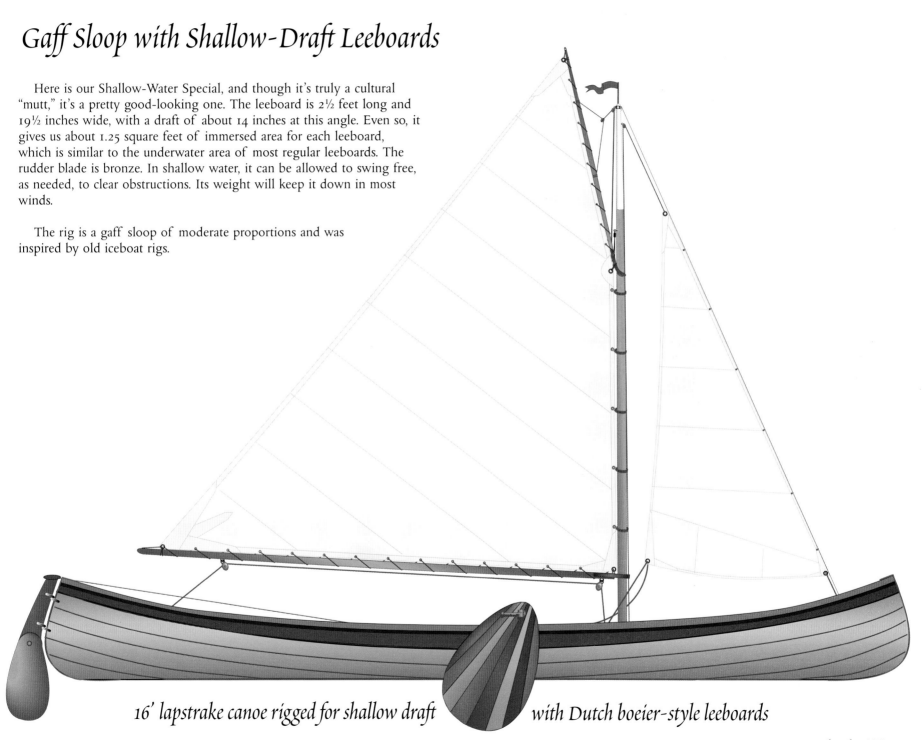

16' lapstrake canoe rigged for shallow draft   *with Dutch boeier-style leeboards*

Daggerboards

Though not common, it is possible to build a daggerboard well into some canoes. A single board is then dropped straight down through the keel, replacing the leeboards. Putting in a well is not the type of modification that you want to try on a general-purpose boat, or on your wood-and-canvas classic, but it could be done on small plywood canoes designed for sailing and flatwater work.

The well is a tall, narrow box built around a slot in the boat's bottom. The height of the box helps stabilize the daggerboard and, since it is open on top, keeps the rim well above the waterline to prevent water from coming in.

On a small sailing canoe, in which the sailor sits on the bottom, kayak-style, the well could be straddled without being too big a problem. I suppose it could also be shifted off to one side, where it would work like the single-leeboard systems.

Back about 1970, Old Town built a sailing version of their model FG fiberglass canoe called the Wahoo. It had daggerboard wells molded into both sides of the hull and used twin boards, like internally mounted leeboards. Moving the daggerboard wells out to the sides allowed the bottom to flex more in the event you hit something (though FGs weren't very flexible) and opened up the center of the canoe. With a 75-square-foot lateen sail on a 16-foot canoe, I doubt the name Wahoo had anything to do with fish.

A daggerboard is straight sided, or tapered toward the bottom in profile, and has some form of blocking or transverse pin near its top to keep it from falling through the well. Using a piece of shock cord to pull forward on the top of the board will jam it against the forward end of the well, allowing the sailor to adjust how far down into the water the board goes. All that's needed is enough board down to prevent sideslipping. Any more just adds drag and slows the boat.

Here is a typical daggerboard. Its underwater profile and tapers are cut exactly like the leeboard that we saw on page 153. The handle has been replaced with a grab hole, and a strip about 1 inch by 1 inch by 10 inches has been added on both sides as a stop, to keep the board from falling through the well.

The daggerboard well is just large enough to accommodate the board and is nearly gunwale-high. It is carefully fitted and sealed around a slot in the canoe's bottom.

In a decked canoe, the well would go all the way through the deck, using the deck structure to support the top of the well. A daggerboard well in an open boat must be supported on at least one end with a thwart or brace to keep it from twisting from side to side. A well standing alone wouldn't be very strong.

Daggerboard

Daggerboard well

Centerboards

Sailboat-style centerboards swing down from an internal box called a centerboard trunk. It is similar to the daggerboard well, but it is closed at the top and is as long as the board, which pivots on a bolt. This requires both a long box and a long slot in the hull, two elements that make the arrangement undesirable for a canoe. The box takes up too much interior space, and the slot both weakens the hull and causes a lot of drag, especially on a long, narrow hull such as a canoe.

I suppose the trunk could be mounted off to one side to get it out of the way, but there is no getting around the drag. The only advantage that I can see for a big swing-centerboard on a canoe would be its ability to kick up if you hit something. On impact a daggerboard either stops the boat dead or breaks something. If swinging up is the only advantage to a centerboard, we would be better off with leeboards. They swing up, too, and require no holes or slots in the boat.

The only type of centerboard that is at all common on sailing canoes is the fan centerboard (page 158), a very clever example of engineering with elegance. I have never had the opportunity to use one, but they are said to work well. Though I wouldn't necessarily recommend cutting a slot in the bottom of your existing canoe to mount one, if you're planning to build a sailing canoe, just the fact that the fan is a really interesting gizmo might make it worth adding.

The Fan Centerboard

The trunk for a fan is much shorter than a trunk for a sailboat-style swing centerboard, because the fan is divided into individual, hollow sleeves and a blade. A lever mounted on the trunk fans out the parts and also retracts and telescopes them into the trunk when the board is not needed.

Fan centerboards were sometimes used on decked sailing canoes, where they could be designed into the structure of the boat without adding a weak spot, as they might in a retrofit. Today they are the specialty of the house at Robert Lavertue's Springfield Fan Centerboard Company (20 Treetop Ave., Springfield, MA 01118). Robert says he got tired of hunting for parts for sailing canoes, so he started building them. Whether you are looking for a fan centerboard, a pair of rudder gud-geons that were actually designed to be used on a canoe, or other, hard-to-find canoe hardware, his shop is a good place to start any search.

The Springfield Fan Centerboard uses a bronze blade and a couple of hollow sleeves, and is available in lengths of 3 and 4 feet. The trunk is only 7 inches tall, and the extended centerboard is 18 inches deep. The board requires a ⅝-inch-wide slot in the keel that is the length of the centerboard. The assembly weighs over 20 pounds, so it isn't the type of add-on that you would really want to permanently attach to your paddling/portaging canoe. But for a sailing canoe it adds ballast for stability.

I have seen drawings of fan centerboards having as many as seven hollow sleeves. Rushton's Nomad model had such a fan, and the trunk was only 34 inches long and 2⅝ inches square. This would put the pivot pin and control system very close to the waterline of the canoe, so any holes in the trunk for them would need to be carefully packed or sealed to prevent leaks.

It is important to note that the "keel" on most of the sailing canoes suitable for fan installation is much more like the keel on a wooden sailboat than the strip of mahogany screwed to the bottom of a typical wood-and-canvas canoe. The sailing keel may be as wide as 4 inches and 1 inch thick, and is rabbeted to take the thinner planks on either side of it. To cut the necessary slot and attach the trunk for a fan centerboard, you must have such a structure as a base.

Though scratch-building a fan centerboard yourself would be quite an engineering challenge, it would be an interesting project.

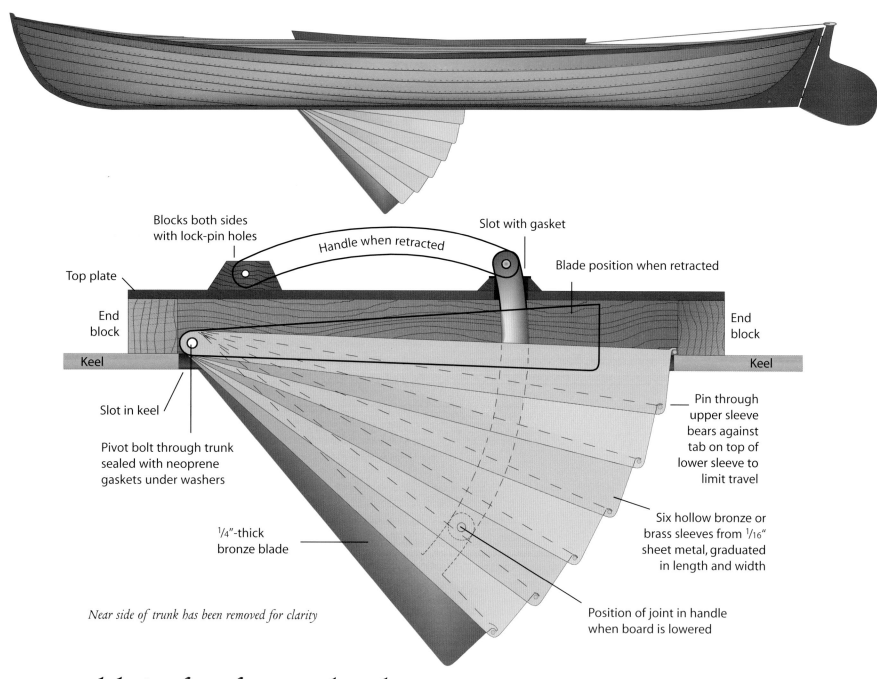

Blocks both sides
with lock-pin holes

Handle when retracted

Slot with gasket

Blade position when retracted

Top plate

End
block

End
block

Keel

Keel

Slot in keel

Pivot bolt through trunk
sealed with neoprene
gaskets under washers

Pin through
upper sleeve
bears against
tab on top of
lower sleeve to
limit travel

Six hollow bronze or
brass sleeves from 1/16"
sheet metal, graduated
in length and width

1/4"-thick
bronze blade

Near side of trunk has been removed for clarity

Position of joint in handle
when board is lowered

Proposed design for a fan centerboard

Adding the design of a fan centerboard to this chapter meant working from the only two drawings that I possess which even hint at the fan's construction. I borrowed what details I could make out and filled in the blanks with my own ideas to produce the study plan shown here. I believe it to be sound in design, but there are probably a few elements that the old masters included that I have yet to discover. I'm certain that there are other ways to handle some of the construction and deployment details, but I wanted to at least give you some idea of how the fan works.

I haven't worried much about exact dimensions, but we can assume that this board would be between 30 and 40 inches long, depending on the size of the boat. The slot in the keel would be about 1 inch wide and would be as long as the longest sleeve.

I guess the sleeves could be folded at either the forward or after ends. I folded them aft because I thought it would add more stiffness to the unit. It also might cause more drag, since the after end of each sleeve is closed. Folding the sleeves at the pivot-pin end would leave their after

ends open and could reduce drag, but getting them all to pivot together might be a bit more difficult. It would also be possible to close both ends of each sleeve.

The handle and the blade are both ¼ inch thick. Where the handle meets the stub atop the blade, their thicknesses are reduced so that the riveted joint is still flush and ¼ inch thick. This allows the joint to pass through the gasket for lowering and raising the board.

The stopper tabs and pins or rivets at the after ends of each sleeve are there to keep the sleeves from descending too far. The job might also be done with an internal line or cable through them.

This is one of those design projects where you draw a full-sized plan and spend a lot of time trying to visualize all the details at work. It's only after an extensive "bug hunt" that the actual construction can begin. Hopefully, this will give anyone contemplating building a fan centerboard a start. If the building project seems too uncertain, keep in mind that you can always buy a ready-made and proven unit.

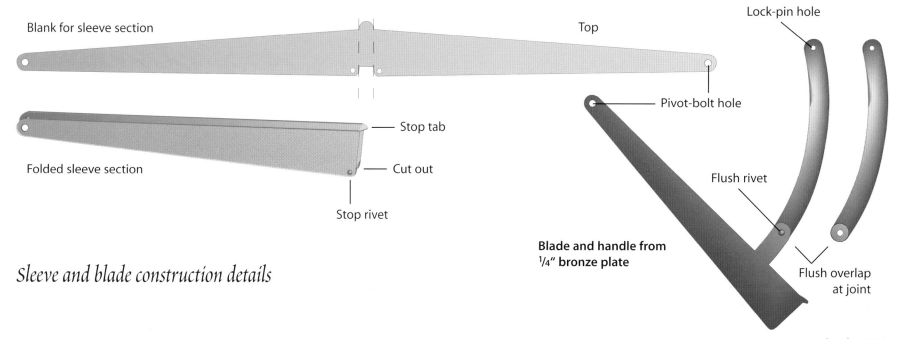

Blank for sleeve section

Top

Lock-pin hole

Folded sleeve section

Stop tab

Cut out

Stop rivet

Pivot-bolt hole

Flush rivet

Blade and handle from ¼″ bronze plate

Flush overlap at joint

Sleeve and blade construction details

Chapter Ten

Steering

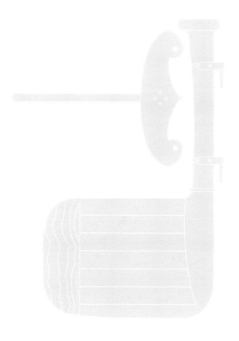

The Rudder in Your Closet

There are several obvious advantages to steering a sailing canoe with a paddle. First of all, you probably already own one. That's pretty difficult to beat for an economical solution. Although it's possible to use almost any paddle for a steering oar, a fairly long traditional model is probably the first choice. Since you won't always sail from the same position or the same location that you paddle from, a little extra length may come in handy.

The other major advantage to paddle steering is that it does not require drilling any holes through your canoe. Unless the boat was designed and built with a sternpost to support a rudder, mounting a rudder can be a bit traumatic. Perhaps I'm more sensitive than most canoeists, but I can't imagine attaching rudder fittings to a beautiful canoe without spending a couple of days mentally debating the pros and cons of even having a rudder and a couple more days double-checking my plan prior to getting out the drill.

Paddle steerers are spared this boat-driller's anguish. In addition, they are allowed to use all the subtleties of paddle angle and pitch, just as a good paddler does, to help steer the boat. Should worse come to worse, they have a fairly effective bracing and braking device right in their hand.

I say hand—singular—because if you're sailing alone and are built like most folks, that's about all you will be able to commit to steering the canoe. Your second and third hands will be busy trimming the sail(s) and adjusting the leeboards.

Though it isn't always that bad, there will be times when that third hand would be quite helpful. Much of this is because cleating the mainsheet, the line that controls the sail, can be risky in a boat that is as "tender" (a polite way of saying "tippy") as a sailing canoe. Even with the best quick-release cleats, there is always the risk that a puff of wind will knock you over before you can release the sheet and ease out the sail.

With two people aboard, things may get a bit cramped, but those extra hands are a major benefit. The duties can be divided into helmsman and trimmer/leeboard-manager, and you can sail by committee. On a nice day, this can be a lot of fun and often makes learning to sail a canoe easier. Strategies and decisions can be discussed, and no matter what, at least you're not stuck out there "alone against the sea." Those extra hundred-odd pounds of ballast won't hurt either.

With two sailors in the canoe, you may be able to steer from the normal paddling position in the stern. The mast, however, will probably prevent the crew from using the bow seat, forcing the trimmer to sit on the bottom, either forward of or, more often, aft of the mast. Paddle-steering from the stern seat, seated or kneeling, offers a lot of steering leverage, since the paddle is so close to the stern. If you need more stability, sitting on the bottom just forward of the stern seat will lower the canoe's center of gravity dramatically yet still allow the paddle to reach the stern.

Solo sailing with paddle steering is sometimes tricky; if your rig sports twin sails, you may want to start growing a fourth hand, as well. Sitting in the stern generally changes the boat's center of lateral plane enough to unbalance all of your design work, so you will be forced to move forward to keep the boat reasonably level. This will mean that your paddle will no longer reach the stern. You will lose some leverage, and paddle pitch will become more important for steering.

If you sit on the bottom, just aft of the leeboard bracket or center thwart, stability will be good, the leeboards will be conveniently close, and the sheets controlling the sails will be handy, but steering will be more of a challenge. In light winds, once you learn the routine, you shouldn't have any serious problems. It is when the wind picks up and the speed at which things happen increases that one-handed paddle-steering starts to get hairy.

A Fool and His Paddle… *are soon parted*

On my first venture as a canoe sailor, or any kind of sailor for that matter, I had masts made from sticks forming a very primitive bipod, a tarp for a sail, and a paddle for steering. It was strictly downwind sailing and in a fairly good breeze. At some point something let go. I lunged for it and, without thinking, let go of the paddle.

Of course there was no spare, so there I was, heading for the rocks, powered by a flapping square spinnaker/tarp/thing, with no steering control. I had to "go forward," as we sailors put it, douse the "rig," and stand in cold water for about twenty minutes to keep the boat off the rocks while waiting for my paddle to float in.

At least I learned a lesson that day. A light line, tied to your steering paddle, is not a bad idea, especially if you don't carry a spare. I heartily recommend it to all beginning sailors. I had paddled for years without ever dropping a paddle, but in this case, I just let go of it as if there would be no problem in doing so. I was distracted by the newness of powering the boat with something other than muscle and trying to learn how to maintain control.

Simple Steering Options

Your decision about whether a paddle will suffice as steering gear will depend, largely, on what you want to get from the sport. For leisurely cruising on beautiful days with fairly light winds, paddle steering should be just fine; it is much simpler than trying to mount a rudder on a boat that wasn't built for one.

Those interested in high performance in stronger winds and in large sail plans will quickly begin to push the limits of paddle steering, finding it lacking in boat control. Also lacking will be your ability to perform other needed tasks, not the least of which is hiking out to keep things upright. In these conditions a fixed rudder system starts to make more and more sense, both in convenience and control. When sailing a high-powered open boat, control and safety go hand-in-hand.

Before getting out the drill to add gudgeons for a rudder, there are a couple of other options for steering that might be worth considering. They involve some hardware, but it is usually clamped to the gunwales rather than screwed to the stern. In short, these systems create a captured steering oar or paddle, hung from the gunwale on one side at the stern.

Using a cross-bar similar to that for an outboard motor side-mount, it's possible to position an oarlock, or some sort of paddle-holding chock far enough outboard that the oar will steer the canoe without hitting the stern as you try to tack. This means that the oarlock or chock will have to be about a foot out from the side of the canoe.

The system prevents losing the steering gear overboard if you let go of it but has some fairly serious limitations. Since it hangs the oar off one side of the boat, the system will probably be less effective on the opposite tack as the canoe heels. You may eventually lose control altogether. It also may be inconvenient at times, requiring you to be in uncomfortable positions or locations just to be able to reach the steering oar.

In light winds, with limited heeling, the system should work reasonably well. A paddle used with a side-mounted keeper should have a sturdy shaft, as you are creating a fulcrum and focusing the strain on the shaft where it meets the bracket. It would be quite possible to break a light paddle shaft with such a system.

When using an oar, I would be tempted to use an oarlock with a pin through it and the oar, which will allow you to keep the oar vertical in the water. The oar will always be in position, even if the sailor, sitting on the bottom of the boat, can't see the blade. In fact, the oar's handle will probably be higher than the sailor's head, another reason why the system may turn out to be less than perfect.

Paddle and Oar Brackets

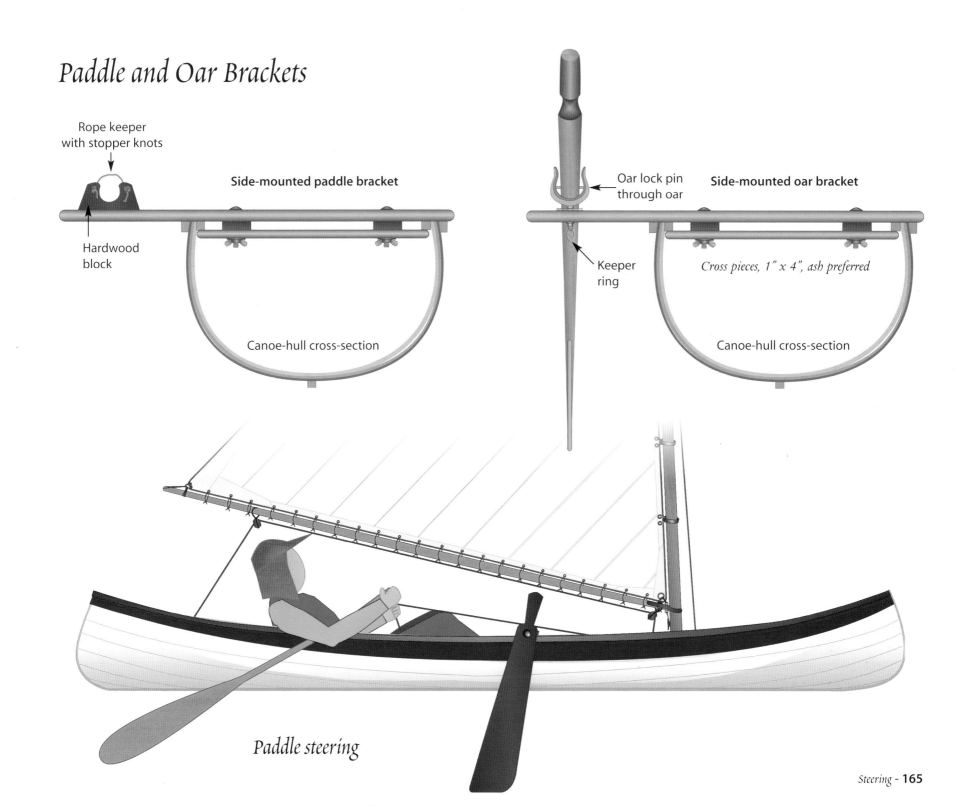

Rope keeper with stopper knots

Side-mounted paddle bracket

Hardwood block

Canoe-hull cross-section

Oar lock pin through oar

Side-mounted oar bracket

Keeper ring

Cross pieces, 1" x 4", ash preferred

Canoe-hull cross-section

Paddle steering

Rudder Basics

The installation of a rudder on a sailing canoe, though not absolutely necessary, has some major benefits. Since the rudder blade hangs off the stern of the boat, it has more leverage than a paddle hung from the side. The sailor is now able to move about, hiking to balance the canoe, moving forward for proper trim, and steering efficiently with one hand from any position or location.

This mobility greatly expands the canoe's ability to handle higher winds. Yes, it's still a tender, open boat, but the sailor can now participate in balancing it, rather than having to sit on the bottom as ballast. Since one hand will always be free of steering duties, adjusting leeboards and trimming sails is easier, especially while tacking when several tasks must be accomplished within a very short period of time.

A rudder is held to the stern of the canoe with small hinges, one part with a pin and the other with a hole to receive it. The piece containing the pin is usually attached to the rudder assembly and is called a "pintle." The receiving piece is permanently mounted to the canoe and is called a "gudgeon." Two sets of these hinges are used, so the canoe will have two gudgeons attached to the stern—an upper and a lower gudgeon—and the rudder will have two corresponding pintles.

The only drawbacks to mounting a rudder on a sailing canoe involve making permanent modifications to the boat. Most of the available rudder gudgeons are built to be screwed or bolted to the flat transom of a dinghy. They won't fit the narrow stern stem of a canoe. Task #1 will be finding or making gudgeons that will work. Luckily, there are a reasonable number of other canoe sailors who found themselves in the same predicament and are now making and selling proper canoe gudgeons.

Some of us have a problem with disturbing the lines of a beautiful canoe by screwing hinges to its stern, even if they are nice hinges. When you're not sailing, the actual rudder assembly can be removed (unless you want to use it to steer while paddling), but the gudgeons stay attached. Luckily, this has been taken into account by most of the people building canoe gudgeons, and they do their best to make them as small and as elegant as possible.

I look at it this way: I would rather not have rudder gudgeons bolted to the stern of my paddling canoe, but I'll live with them as long as my sailing rig is as classy-looking as any ever built and the gudgeons allow me to sail the canoe efficiently and with control.

The final, and most critical, gudgeon-related obstacle is the actual attachment of them. Most canoe sterns weren't designed for rudder fittings. Above the waterline, the sides of a canoe are not heavily built and may have inadequate strength to support bolted-on rudder gudgeons without internal reinforcement.

As anyone who has ever built or assembled a canoe has seen, a canoe is a cooperative structure. Its parts, individually, are lightweight, bordering upon flimsy. Not until the boat is nearly complete does it gain any real strength or rigidity. Perforating thin wood planking, fiberglass, plastic, or even aluminum for bolt holes and the attachment of fittings relies on the strength of that particular plank or skin, rather than the combined structure. In most cases, something more must be added to spread the load.

Since many modern boats have sealed flotation tanks in their ends, you may also need to open the tank, reinforce the skin, and then rebuild the tank, in order to mount rudder gudgeons. Blind mechanical fasteners may be possible, though they aren't very strong; if they are used with modern marine super-adhesives and bonded to the boat's skin, you may be able to escape the ordeal of opening the tank.

Simple Gudgeons and Pintles

This is a typical **pintle**, built from solid rod and sheet metal about ⅛ inch thick. The hole in the pin's lower end is for a keeper-ring or cotter pin. The straps are to be bent to fit the rudder.

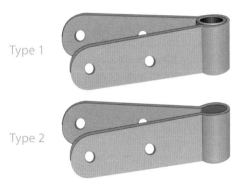

Type 1

Type 2

The **gudgeon** is bent to fit the stern stem of the canoe and attached with screws or bolts and sealant. When the rudder is mounted, the pin of the pintle drops through the tubular part of the gudgeon, which is welded to the strap section. If the metal used is stiff enough and carefully bent to shape, the tube can sometimes be eliminated.

Canoe side at the left, rudder side at the right, the rudder assembly is joined to the canoe with two sets of these fittings.

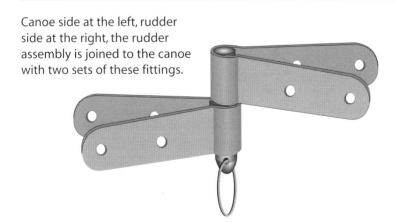

Brass vs. Bronze

To the majority of the boatbuilding industry, brass is not considered a "marine metal." Yes, it gets used for lamps, compass housings, and other decorative items, but it has neither the strength nor the corrosion-resistance that would qualify it for any serious structural use.

The canoe industry, on the other hand, uses brass for much of its hardware; even the clench nails that hold many wooden canoes together are brass. Sailing canoes are often loaded with small pieces mostly built from brass sheet metal, and even though some of these boats are nearly a century old, the hardware still works fine. What, then, is this discrepancy between the two branches of the boatbuilding industry?

To start with, there is size. Canoes are small and tender sailboats. The sail area just isn't large enough to put much strain on fittings, and even if it did, the boat would heel over and spill wind, relieving much of the pressure. Remember the previous discussion about flimsy parts being united to make a reasonably solid unit? There is a good chance that a brass fitting is much stronger than the portion of the boat that it is attached to and is also stronger than the method used to attach the fitting to the canoe.

Secondly, canoes aren't left all summer on a mooring or expected to cross oceans. Most aren't even stored outside, so the corrosive effects of weather or salt water are only very temporary problems for canoe hardware.

Bronze is, without a doubt, far superior to brass. A good bronze fitting will last a century without being pampered. It is more difficult to find than brass, it may cost a bit more, and its toughness can make it a bit more challenging to machine, but if you can find it, use it. When your grandchildren inherit your canoe, they will appreciate that you used bronze instead of brass for fittings.

Other Materials for Rudder Parts

Most modern rudder gudgeons are built from stainless steel. Just as we found with boom and spar hardware, stainless is a good marine metal but not very antique in appearance. It can be worked by hand tools, but with difficulty, and brushed to knock down some of its modern look, but it will never have the warmth that bronze and brass have.

Aluminum, in a high-quality alloy such as 6061 T-6, is also a possibility, but again, its appearance doesn't do much for a traditional boat. If you can find a company specializing in anodizing and willing to take small orders, you might be able to have parts treated. Most annodizing doesn't look any more antique than bare aluminum, but if you can get the parts "hard-coated," they will have a dark gray satin finish (similar to those expensive cookware sets) that is quite durable. At least the dark color will be a little more subtle than standard aluminum.

Here again, I think common steel that has been "power-rusted" and oiled by the browning treatment described in Chapter Seven might be a possibility. Since most canoe hardware gets only limited exposure to weather, the treatment might be worth trying if bronze or brass aren't available.

You might consider the plastic rudder fittings available for dinghies. They are probably Delrin and should be strong enough for a canoe. Usually black, they are decent looking, but it's pretty obvious that they are modern plastic, not antique bronze.

The pintles and gudgeons shown on the previous page are very simple in terms of shape. If you purchase canoe fittings from one of the shops specializing in sailing canoes, there is a good chance that their pintles and gudgeons will be a bit more ornate. Most of them are reproductions of originals made in the days when canoes were crafted, not just molded and pop-riveted, as many are today.

Custom Cast Hardware

I had a long conversation with Roger Winiarski, president of Bristol Bronze (P.O. Box 101, Tiverton, RI 02878), a company that specializes in the reproduction of old marine fittings. Roger is a true hardware fanatic and obviously enjoys his work. His catalog lists pages of cleats, blocks, and various fittings from antique boats. In addition, he can replicate multiples of old parts and fittings from an existing original.

Much of his business is custom work. A customer, restoring an old boat, will have one remaining cleat, oarlock, or other antique treasure and a hole where its mate used to be. At Bristol Bronze the original is cleaned up a bit and a rubber mold is vulcanized around it at about 300 degrees Fahrenheit. The finished mold is then used to cast wax copies of the piece, and the original is returned to its owner unharmed.

The wax copies are invested (surrounded by a plaster mixture) and put in a kiln. The heat is cranked up, and the wax is burned out completely, leaving a block of investment with a hole inside—exactly the shape of the original piece of hardware. Molten bronze is then cast into this new mold under vacuum pressure or by centrifuge. Once it cools, the investment and any sprues (small tunnels leading through the investment to get the bronze to the cavity) are removed, and the piece is ready to be cleaned and buffed.

Custom hardware can also be built by using a mock-up if an original can't be found. It can be made of the same casting wax and invested directly, or from plaster, metal, or other substances that will withstand the heat of vulcanizing a rubber mold around it to produce multiple copies. Wood is not good for mock-up construction because it contains moisture, which isn't compatible with 300-degree rubber.

There are several companies doing custom casting, both reproductive work and new designs. Some are also doing fancy, decorative, yet still functional hardware. If you need a fitting, and it has to be just right, these folks can help.

The Willits Brothers Rudder Gudgeon

I saw this style of rudder gudgeon in a photograph of an old Willits Brothers canoe featured in *WoodenBoat* magazine (issue No. 55, November/December 1983) and was struck by its design. If you were ever to have bronze gudgeons custom cast, this would have to be one of the best designs to copy.

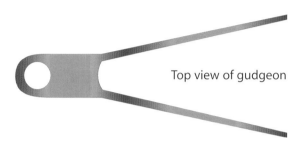

Top view of gudgeon

Aside from their pleasing shape, these gudgeons are also very well engineered. The broad flanges spread the strain over a wide area of the stem, and the fairly long distance between the stem band and the hole to receive the pintle gives good clearance for the rudder. The Willits rudder was straight and plumb on its leading edge, and spaced far enough from the stem that it didn't have to mimic the curve of the stem.

Willits canoes had exposed hardwood stems, brass stem bands, and multiple layers of planking. Of particular interest is the screw pattern used to fasten the gudgeons, the asymmetry of which puts two screws into the exposed part of the stem on different lines of grain to prevent splits. I assume the inner screw went into the plank rabbet area of the stem, on the inside. Notice how the screw patterns of the two gudgeons are flip-flopped to follow the curve of the stem and to position as much wood as possible under the screw holes.

This type of gudgeon would work well on almost any canoe. It is strong and as nice-looking as any that I have seen. Though I am not aware of anyone currently producing the Willits type, perhaps an original will eventually find its way to one of the bronze-hardware companies where they can pull a mold from it. If not, I'll eventually get around to making a pattern and send it in myself, because I want a pair of my own.

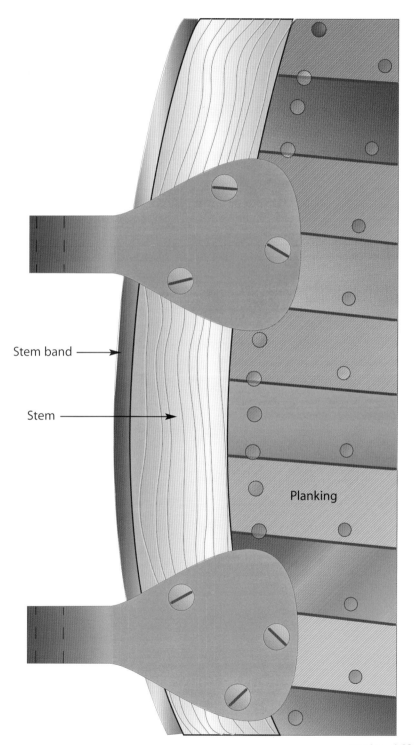

Stem band

Stem

Planking

Other Rudder Gudgeon Possibilities

There are countless ways to hinge the rudder to the canoe's stern. Here are a few more to consider. System #1, at right, uses four strap gudgeons and a single pin, instead of pintles on the rudder and gudgeons on the boat. System #2's gudgeons have been replaced with one long tube inside a flange that has been shaped to fit the canoe's stern stem. In system #3 short pins, instead of pintles, pass through double-strap gudgeons on the rudder which sandwich those attached to the boat. The same principle is used in system #4, but the castings for the rudder blade are slotted to take the gudgeons.

Small boats with fairly thick wooden skeg/sternposts, like many of the decked sailing canoes, might be able to use system #5, shown below right, which consists of simple eye-bolts set into the rudder and the stern stem with a single pin. This is not a fancy or particularly heavy-duty system, but it might be all that is needed to do the job.

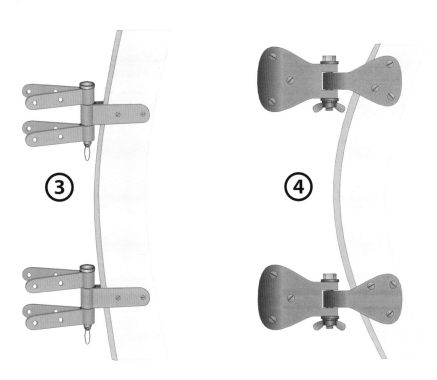

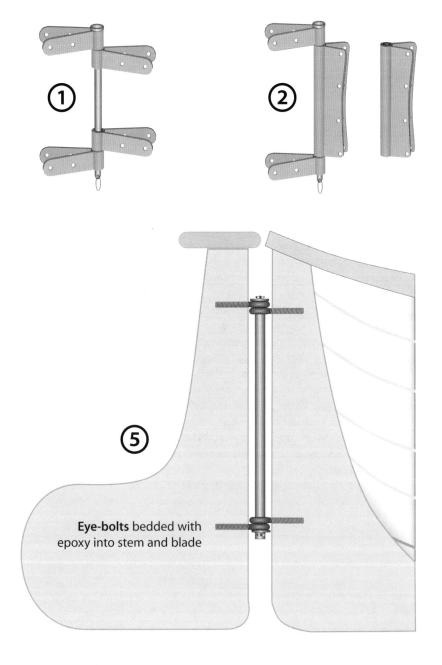

Eye-bolts bedded with epoxy into stem and blade

Planning Rudder Installation

In some ways, the next few pages are the most important in this book. We are approaching the moment when you start drilling holes in your prized canoe. The positioning of these holes has to be right. There is little margin for error, and plugging your mistakes and redrilling will be quite difficult. I don't mean to scare anybody, but installing a rudder is a serious step, so before you drill, you must develop a plan for your rudder and its fittings. Check and double-check your plan; the most important tool for rudder installation is definitely a pencil.

Your plan will need to address the relationship in shape between the stem profile of the canoe and the corresponding profile of the rudder assembly, the location and attachment of the rudder gudgeons, and the internal structure's ability to support them. If necessary, the stem profile can be duplicated or traced on cardboard for a mock-up or full-scale drawing.

A canoe with a long, tightly curved stern stem may need a rudder that mimics that shape; another, when equipped with the right gudgeons, may be able to use a rudder assembly with a straight leading edge, which is somewhat easier to build. Stem shape may also limit the separation between the upper and lower rudder gudgeons. Since much of the strain on a rudder is lateral, more separation will make the installation stronger, yet 5 or 6 inches may be as much as is possible on a tightly curved stem.

The lower gudgeon should not be in the water when sailing or paddling the canoe, unless it can be let into a sternpost to be flush. On a normal recreational canoe, this will mean that the lower gudgeon will have to be 3 or 4 inches above the bottom of the hull. The upper gudgeon should then be positioned as high above lower one as the stem shape, rudder shape, and gudgeon/pintle clearance will allow. Before we can mount the gudgeons though, we need to plan the rudder assembly itself, in order to establish its relationship to the stem of the canoe.

A Simple Rudder Assembly

As you can see from the drawing below, a rudder for a canoe doesn't have to be very complex or fancy to do the job. As simple as this one is, it's still reasonably good-looking and should work well. The assembly can be all wood, all metal, or a combination of the two. Metal construction allows the builder to use thinner, smaller parts, though finished weight is probably pretty close to wood. Metal construction, however, will cost more than wood.

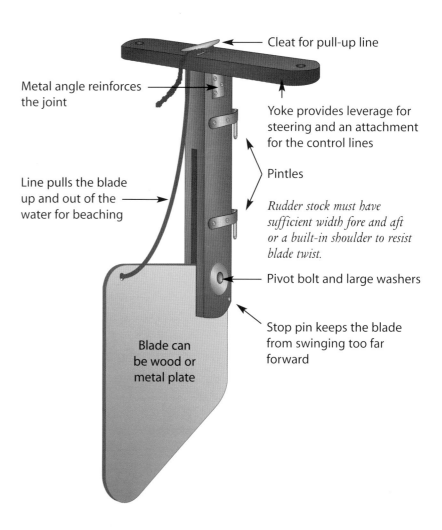

Cleat for pull-up line

Metal angle reinforces the joint

Yoke provides leverage for steering and an attachment for the control lines

Pintles

Line pulls the blade up and out of the water for beaching

Rudder stock must have sufficient width fore and aft or a built-in shoulder to resist blade twist.

Pivot bolt and large washers

Stop pin keeps the blade from swinging too far forward

Blade can be wood or metal plate

The rudder blade can be either metal plate or wood. Metal tends to hold up better when dragged over rocks, and it doesn't float, so it will usually stay down without having to use a pull-down line. Wood can be tapered into a more efficient airfoil; furthermore, finding a chunk of mahogany is often easier than hunting up a piece of suitable brass or bronze plate.

Since sailing canoes have a fairly long history, much of it rooted in the days when "average" craftsmanship was equivalent to modern custom work, there are a myriad of different rudder designs in use today, some plain, some quite fancy. Simplest of all would be a vertical slab of wood with two pintles attached and a yoke stuck on top. It would be quite functional—until you encountered a rock at speed, which would probably tear the gudgeons out of the canoe.

Shortening the slab and bolting a free-swinging metal blade to one side would be a definite safety improvement. From there, it's possible to further refine the assembly, with the pinnacle being a custom-cast, bronze stock and yoke with filigree decorations and a 3-D likeness of J. Henry Rushton himself, the legendary canoe builder, on both sides— possibly a bit excessive, but you get my meaning.

As was noted in the simple-rudder drawing, and as we saw with lee-board brackets, a flat slab that will feel lateral pressure needs to bear against a fairly large surface to keep from twisting. For a leeboard, the shoulder piece, perpendicular to the cross-bar, does the job. For a rudder, the base of the rudder housing needs to be wide enough in profile to keep the blade on course. On wooden assemblies, the entire housing may be as wide as the blade. Metal assemblies may have a very narrow shaft-like upper section coming down from the yoke and flaring near the bottom to support the blade.

Blades themselves vary from rectangular, to oval, to a variety of odd-shaped fins. Theoretically, a tall, narrow blade will be most efficient, but as long as the blade has enough length to stay submerged as the canoe heels, it would seem that almost anything goes and has been tried over the years.

Yoke Vs. Tiller Steering

Canoe rudders are fairly unique among sailing craft. Most canoes use a yoke on the rudderhead, while few sailboats do, instead using a tiller. On a sailing canoe, a tiller seldom works well. The sailboat skipper is usually seated, on one side of the boat or the other, alongside the tiller. A canoe sailor would usually be sitting directly in front of a tiller, where it would be quite hard to reach. In situations where the canoeist could sit off to the side, hiking out to balance the canoe, he or she would be near the center of the boat (fore-and-aft) and too far forward to reach a normal tiller.

The other drawback to a standard tiller system is that the rudderhead must be tall enough to clear the stern stem of the boat. On a canoe, with its up-turned ends, this would require a pretty tall rudder. Push-pull control ropes attached to a yoke in a loop, or a Norwegian-style "steer-stick" (a simple, push-pull stick attached to a single-sided yoke), are much more common. More on these systems later. For now, we just need to know that our rudder assembly will probably have a yoke on the rudderhead.

Pull Up, Pull Down

Raising and Lowering the Rudder Blade

Since wood floats, a wooden rudder blade will need something to keep it down. At high speeds, even a metal blade can have a tendency to rise, causing loss of steering control. The easiest—though far from most practical—way to prevent this is to squeeze the blade between the sides of its housing with a big wing-nut on the pivot bolt. This method works, but you have to hang over the end of the canoe to adjust the wing-nut, and if it loosens while sailing, you have a serious problem.

A pull-down line made of rope can be used, but when cleated, it's almost as dangerous as a blade that doesn't kick up at all should you hit something. Most of the systems using lines to pull and keep the rudder down actually do it by pulling up on the forward side of the blade. Substituting shock cord for rope is a good way to allow for the occasional blade-meets-rock encounter while still keeping the blade down at high speeds. Various other methods, most employing springs, have also been used over the years.

A pull-up line, usually attached to the top or back of the rudder blade, is used for launching and landing in shallow water. Though sometimes handy, it really isn't necessary as long as the rudder blade can kick up on impact. The line's ability to pull up the blade will vary with blade design and the routing of the line itself. If you have a wooden blade that floats up when released, it will probably assume a horizontal position in the water, and the pull-up line can do the rest.

A metal blade, which must be lifted by the line, may be more difficult to get started. Often the pull-up line is attached to a bump, or tab, on the trailing edge of the blade, which gives the system a little more lifting leverage. The line is usually routed over the top of the yoke and is cleated there, or might be made long enough to reach a cleat near the sailor for remote raising and lowering.

On a sailboat, a tiller works well. The skipper sits on one side or the other and comfortably steers the boat.

On a canoe, a tiller is generally as uncomfortable and impractical to use as it looks.

Wooden Rudder Assembly

Though fairly complex, this type of rudder is not terribly difficult to build. The pintles will be the most expensive part, but it doesn't take much wood. Mahogany would be the logical choice, but ash or other hardwood could also be used. I'm not fond of plywood for the blade, but good-quality marine plywood could be used for the housing. Plywood's exposed end-grain will need careful sealing. A plywood rudder won't look as good as solid lumber, and it will also probably cost more.

The **filler piece** is slightly thicker than the blade.

Plan the radius and clearance on both the top of the blade and the corresponding area on the filler piece carefully, so the blade will rotate on the pivot-bolt properly as you retract it.

The "bump" on the trailing edge to anchor the pull-up line could be omitted and replaced by a simple eye-strap attached with screws.

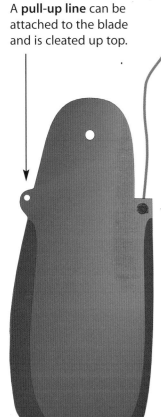

A **pull-up line** can be attached to the blade and is cleated up top.

A **pull-down line** comes up through the housing and the yoke, and is cleated on top.

A hole down from the top joins a hole drilled halfway through the blade from the side. A stopper-knot at the end of the line fits flush in the hole in the side.

Near side panel removed to show filler piece.

Vertical hole, ¼ " or so, bored down through filler piece to take the pull-down line, which is cleated at the top.

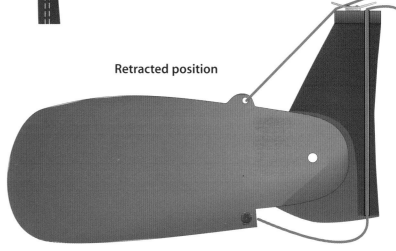

Retracted position

Starboard side of housing has been removed for clarity.

As with a leeboard, the blade is rounded on the leading edge and tapered on the trailing edge. The upper section, where the blade bears against the inside of the housing, should be left flat, with just a slight round on the corners. It is a good idea to use large low-friction (plastic) washers between the blade and the housing at the pivot point.

The blade should be about 8 to 9 inches wide and ¾ inch thick, and should extend 15 to 18 inches below the waterline. A metal blade can be substituted for wood, in which case the filler piece should be correspondingly thinner. The housing should end a couple of inches above the waterline and can be shaped to the end profile of the canoe if desired.

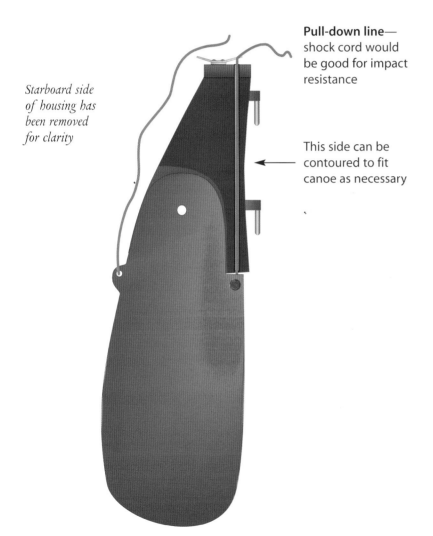

Starboard side of housing has been removed for clarity

Pull-down line— shock cord would be good for impact resistance

This side can be contoured to fit canoe as necessary

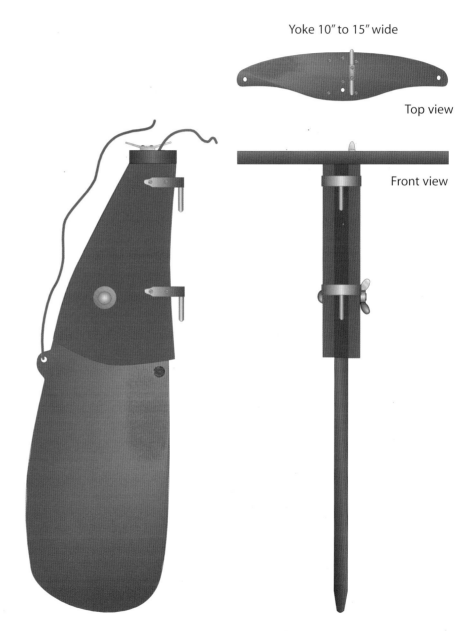

Yoke 10" to 15" wide

Top view

Front view

The Hand-Carved Rudder

Some of the more interesting rudders are combinations of carving, strip-building, and veneer lamination, similar to the construction of laminated canoe paddles. Though not as heavy-duty as the slab-built variety, they are good for smaller canoes that aren't sailed in extreme conditions. They may, or may not, kick up, or be retractable. This "blade on a stick" approach can also be used with metal, combining a plate with tubing, rod, square stock, or castings.

The horizontal-blade rudder is good in shallow water, but does not have the performance of a tall, vertical blade when the wind is up and the boat is really moving. It is more of a "light-wind, beautiful-evening" type of rudder, for those conditions when a canoe will outsail a lot of very expensive sailboats.

If woodworking is one of your hobbies, sculpting a beautiful rudder blade is a good winter project. The optional "fence" on the bottom of a shallow rudder can boost performance by (in the simplest terms) keeping the water from sneaking around the bottom of the shallow blade and robbing the blade of its turning power. As the boat heels, putting the rudder at an angle, the fence effectively adds length as well.

Going "horizontal" when designing the shallow-draft blade is necessary in order to keep enough rudder in the water to turn the canoe. As a rule, though, designing a rudder blade that trails behind the boat, rather than a vertical fin, may cause steering problems and put more strain on the gudgeons than is good for them.

If you're after a general-purpose rudder assembly for a sailing canoe, your best design option will be a vertical fin that has the ability to kick up and is equipped with both pull-down and pull-up lines. Should you encounter shallow water, the blade can be raised partially into a more horizontal position and cleated there. Once you return to deeper water, it can be returned to vertical. You will then notice a definite improvement in handling.

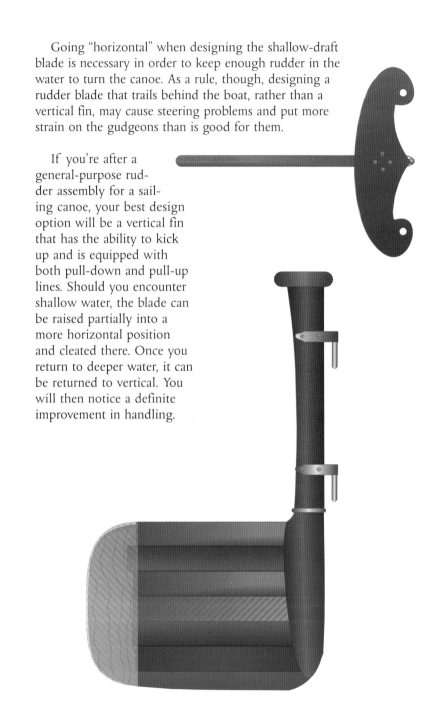

Top view

Aft view

Side view

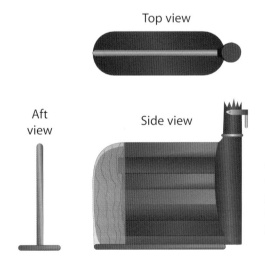

This blade has a fence, a shelf-like horizontal piece fixed to the bottom to improve performance.

Rudder Size

As with sail and leeboard area, it is difficult to establish a blanket formula for determining how much area a rudder blade needs to steer the canoe. As long as the rudder is deep enough and has enough area to turn the boat, we can adjust the lateral balance of the rig by experimenting with leeboard bracket location, a luxury of using leeboards in the first place.

If the rudder is too small for the job, the obvious symptom is that properly controlling the boat will be difficult. If it is larger than necessary, it will cause unnecessary drag, though the drag won't be extreme unless the blade is huge. Considering these two factors, it would seem to be best to err on the large side.

Wind and water conditions may also play a role in determining what is an adequately sized blade. In light air, a small blade may be sufficient and the extra drag of a large one will be magnified by the slower speeds and light wind. In higher winds, when the boat is heeling more and the water is choppy, the larger, and especially the longer, blade will be much better.

Any rudder mounted on the stern of a boat as responsive as a canoe will have quite a bit of turning power. The balance between the center of effort of the sails and the lateral plane of the boat will be easily as important in making the steering work properly as the size of the rudder blade. Since the final design phase always involves actual on-water testing, it will be important to remember that incorrect balance can cause symptoms that would appear to indicate inadequate rudder area.

Balance problems will manifest themselves as an excessive amount of either weather helm, where the canoe tries to turn upwind, or lee helm, where it wants to turn downwind. Remember, we would prefer to sail with just a bit of weather helm, as with such a condition the canoe will point up and come to a stop if the sailor falls overboard. If the balance creates too much helm—weather or lee—the rudder blade will be going through the water somewhat sideways, causing a tremendous amount of drag.

Having to use so much rudder might, at first, seem to indicate a blade that is too small to do the job. The boat will be unresponsive to any turning action, except to weather, or lee, depending upon the balance equation and which way it is forcing the boat. Switching to a larger rudder blade might give you enough area to muscle the boat in the desired direction, but only with a corresponding increase in drag.

It is quite possible that moving the leeboard brackets a few inches forward or aft will change the balance enough to tame the beast nicely. For excessive weather helm, the leeboards should be moved aft, moving the canoe's center of lateral plane farther aft of the sail's center of effort and forcing the bow away from the wind. Lee helm should be corrected by moving the leeboards and the canoe's C.L.P. forward.

Only after careful experimentation with balance as above can a rudder be judged too small for the job.

As a starting point, a typical cruising canoe in the 16-to-18-foot range of length should start with a rudder having around one square foot of submerged area. This would be a blade 8 inches wide and 18 inches submerged depth, or 9 inches wide and 16 inches submerged depth. Think of either one as being about the size of a good-sized paddle blade.

On a high-speed twin, a 6-by-24-inch high-aspect-ratio blade would be even more efficient, but at a certain point the depth of the blade will start limiting your shallow-water sailing ability. This can make launching and landing, when you're most likely to run into something or damage your canoe, difficult.

If anything, the above examples are generous-sized blades. Your canoe may be able to sail quite well with less blade area, but this is a good place to start. Obviously, if your canoe is only 12 feet long and has a 25-square-foot sail plan, you will want to scale down the size of both the rudder the and leeboards to minimize drag.

Stem Construction and Reinforcement

Once our rudder and its potential relationship to the canoe's stem profile have been planned, it is time to take a careful look at the construction of the stern of the canoe prior to drilling any holes to mount the gudgeons. Since the end of the boat was probably not designed with rudder mounting in mind, some internal reinforcement may be needed to prevent the gudgeons from pulling out or damaging the boat.

The first thing to determine is whether or not you can even get to the inside of the stem area. If the boat has built-in flotation, access may be a problem. Traditional wooden canoes and many of the modern thermoplastic boats have open interiors at both ends, getting their flotation from the hull and sometimes the seats. Though the hull may need a bit of reinforcement to back up the gudgeons, at least the area will be readily accessible.

Wood-strippers, aluminum canoes, and most fiberglass models will probably have flotation tanks that block your access to the stem area. Most of these tanks contain molded-in-place foam blocks. Opening up the tank, digging out the foam, and rebuilding the tank after gudgeon installation is major surgery not to be taken lightly. A better option may be to rely on adhesives combined with fasteners to mount the gudgeons, leaving the tank intact.

In any case, the strongest part of any canoe's stern is the area within an inch or two of the stem. This is the part of the boat where the sides are closest together, the shape has the most extreme curves, and the builder has reinforced the structure to withstand that occasional unplanned meeting with a dock or other unyielding object.

As you move forward from the stern stem, the structure above the waterline only needs to be sturdy enough to keep water out. It is to our advantage to use the strongest part of the canoe's end for mounting the gudgeons, though different constructions may need different solutions.

On a wood-and-canvas canoe, the hardwood stem pieces (inside, outside, or both), though fairly small in cross-section, are the sturdiest part of the stern structure and the best area for taking screws. Moving forward as little as an inch will probably mean that you will be trying to attach the gudgeon to one layer of canvas and a $3/16$-inch-thick piece of soft cedar planking. The first rib will still be several inches forward of this point; without internal blocking, the planking won't be strong enough for for fastening the gudgeons.

So, for a wood-and-canvas canoe, a gudgeon like the Willits Brothers model (page 169), or the single-tube/long-flange type that allows the screws to be driven into the stem piece rather than the planking, is preferred. If the design of your gudgeon does require screws or bolts through planking alone, hardwood blocking, epoxied to the plank and spreading the strain of the gudgeon over several square inches of the plank, is recommended. Otherwise, the screws may tear out of the soft planking.

A metal plate or large fender washer might also work as an interior backup for the gudgeons, but neither will be as effective in preventing planking splits as will a reinforcement that has been bonded to the plank. If you are equipped with the right tools and patience, you can cut and carve wooden blocks that can be epoxied to both sides of the planking and the stem piece all at once, forming a very strong anchor for the gudgeon.

Bedding compound or a marine sealant should be used under the gudgeon and any back-up plates or washers. Avoid silicone sealer on anything that you may ever need to paint. If you will be drilling through the canvas, be careful. A drill bit will often grab a strand and pull out several inches of it, winding it around the drill bit. The best technique to avoid having to repair a large area of mangled canvas next to the gudgeon is first to cut a small hole in the canvas with a knife and then drill into the wood.

Rudder Installation on Non-Wooden Canoes

Mounting gudgeons on plastic, wood-strip, and fiberglass canoes that don't have flotation tanks built into their ends is fairly simple. You won't generally have a stem piece inside the stern to drive screws into, but you should be able to back up screws or bolts with internal wooden blocks or metal plates bonded to the hull, or with large washers.

There are types of epoxy resin that will stick to almost any plastic. If your boat is Royalex or polyethylene, you will need to contact the manufacturer to find out which formulation will work and what, if any, special preparation will be needed prior to bonding. Before resin will stick to it, some polyethylene must be polarized by quickly running a propane torch over the surface.

If you are planning to glue wooden blocking into the boat, it would be wise to seal all sides of the block with two or three coats of epoxy beforehand. Otherwise, the blocking may eventually rot. Small chunks of marine plywood can be used as blocking as long as they are carefully sealed.

On 'glass boats, multiple layers of 'glass cloth or mat will strengthen the area, but screw-holding power will never be very good. A piece of wood or plywood epoxied in place to take the screw makes a better anchor.

If your boat has flotation tanks preventing access to the ends, your options for gudgeon mounting and back-up are limited. On an aluminum boat, the best I can think of would be to rivet the gudgeon to the boat with sealant under it. The heavy aluminum strip along the stem is quite sturdy. If you can find gudgeons with fastener holes in the right places, riveting the gudgeon through those heavy stem strips with stainless-steel pop rivets would create a strong joint.

If your fastener holes are too far forward to allow riveting into the stem strip, you will have to rivet or screw the gudgeon to the hull skin. I would use aluminum pop rivets for this, as stainless rivets require so much force to set that they might pull through a single layer of aluminum. Another option here would be sheet-metal screws.

A high-powered polyurethane marine adhesive/sealant, such as 3M 5200, might add strength to a mechanical fastening. As mentioned previously, aluminum is difficult to glue anything to because it oxidizes so fast. Seconds after you clean, sand, and prepare aluminum, it has already started to oxidize, preventing a good bond. Adhesive/sealant will help, but the rivets will do most of the work. Luckily the tear strength of aluminum is quite high compared to other canoe-building materials.

On a fiberglass or wood-strip boat, with end tanks, you can get a very good bond with a combination of polyurethane adhesive and screws. Use a gudgeon that has as much surface contact area as possible.

It is also possible to drill from both sides and through-bolt the gudgeon, though you may need to bend the bolt for it to fit. To bend the bolt, screw on the nut, bridge the bolt on two solid surfaces, and hit it with a hammer (carefully). The bolt should have enough bend to pass cleanly through the stem and the gudgeon and allow the nut to sit flat.

Keep in mind that in a fiberglass or wood-strip canoe there is more material close to the stem, so try to find a gudgeon that has favorable holes. Away from the stem, the hull will be very thin.

I would recommend trying the adhesive-and-hardware mix before considering opening the flotation tank and digging out the foam. There is a very good chance that your gudgeons will hold, especially if you won't be pushing the limits when you sail your canoe. Here again, the tender nature of the boat will act as a stress reliever, heeling to take strain off the rig, which will take at least some of the strain off the gudgeons as well.

Rudder Alignment

Throughout much of this book, I have given rather vague guidelines regarding certain aspects of converting your canoe for sailing. In most cases, since I haven't seen your boat and don't know anything about its design, size, or construction, it is difficult to be more specific. My descriptions of the theory involved and my rough guidelines should have given you the information that you need to make educated decisions and put together a functional rig for your canoe.

The topic of rudder alignment is different. READ AND UNDERSTAND THIS PAGE! The final planning stage before drilling holes in your boat for gudgeons is critical. On this page "exact" means EXACT and "must" means MUST. The concept involved is fairly simple, but we don't want to miss it. So, pay attention:

For a rudder to work properly—for it to turn smoothly without putting undue strain on the gudgeons and their attachment—there must be ONLY ONE pivot line. This pivot line must pass through the center of the pin holes in the gudgeons and the corresponding center of the pins of the pintles or pivot pin(s), depending on the system used.

If the stem profile of the canoe doesn't interfere, you should be able to drop a long rod through both gudgeons, and their pin holes will line up exactly. If they don't, your rudder will be trying to pivot on two different axes at once, which is impossible. A major misalignment will jam the rudder; a minor one will eventually tear the fastener holes for the gudgeons as the gudgeons try to align themselves.

Because of the stem profile, you may or may not have a clear line of sight through the gudgeon holes. To understand this, see the illustrations to the right.

The rudder does not have to pivot on a perfectly vertical line (try not to get this line too far off vertical, however), but there must be only one line. The only margin for error in the equation is the slight difference between the inside diameter of the pin holes in the gudgeons and the outside diameter of the pin, or pins.

After alignment has been checked and rechecked, it is finally safe to get out the drill and mount the gudgeons.

No matter the end profile of the canoe, the gudgeons must line up. Though the rudder can be shaped to follow the canoe's end profile or can be mounted to pivot on a non-vertical line, the pintles on the blade and the gudgeons on the boat must be aligned. This prevents the blade from trying to pivot in two directions at once.

Gudgeon pivot line

Gudgeon pivot line

Upper gudgeon pivot line

Lower gudgeon pivot line

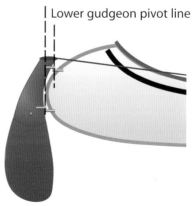

Alignment is critical!

The installation of the yellow boat's rudder looks fine—until you try to turn the rudder. Since the placement of the rudder hardware has created two separate pivot points, the rudder cannot turn.

Rudder Control Systems

Considering how complex the installation of a rudder assembly can be, the actual rudder control mechanism is usually quite simple and straightforward. Essentially, all we need is something that will pull on the ends of the rudder yoke to turn the blade. This is most often line, strung in a continuous loop from one side of the yoke, forward to the center thwart or leeboard bracket, through a couple of blocks, and back to the other side of the yoke (page 182).

The loop is then snugged up to reduce slop. Steering, by pushing and pulling, can be accomplished from anywhere the sailor can reach the line. It would even be possible to run the steering line all the way to the bow deck before sending it back to the yoke. With a couple of extra blocks to route the line near the gunwales, steering would be possible from anywhere in the canoe, even by a person in the bow.

Some of the small canoes in which the canoeists sit on the bottom and use a double-bladed paddle are fitted with individual steering ropes connected to foot pedals (page 183). As long as the sailor won't be hiking out and can stay in a seated position, foot steering is great. It frees the hands for trimming sails or eating lunch; steering the canoe becomes second nature. The amount of steering-line travel needed to turn the yoke is not great and can be adjusted by working with the yoke's width, so foot pedals don't have to move much to steer the canoe through turns and tacks.

The most common non-steering-line system uses a one-armed yoke atop the rudder and a Norwegian-style steer-stick, which is literally a stick about ¾ inch in diameter, long enough to reach the middle of the canoe and connected to the yoke's horn by a simple universal joint (page 184). Steering is accomplished by pushing and pulling on the stick. One action turns the canoe to starboard, the other to port. Moving the steer-stick across the boat, as you would with a tiller, won't do anything.

Unlike using a normal sailboat tiller, steering with a steer-stick is the same (port/starboard) while traveling in any direction. If the yoke is on the rudder's port side, pulling the stick turns the boat to port and pushing it turns it to starboard. With a starboard-side yoke, pulling the stick will turn the canoe to starboard and pushing, to port.

If you're used to sailing tiller-equipped sailboats, where pulling-in the tiller turns the boat downwind, regardless of port and starboard, and pushing it turns the boat upwind, getting used to a steer-stick will take a little practice, but it's not a big deal.

Remember the drawing on page 173 showing the uncomfortable steering position? The sailor had to reach up and back to get hold of the tiller and then move it crossways to steer. The steer-stick works much better. As long as the stick reaches the sailor's position, steering is just a push-pull, fingertip exercise.

The universal joint connecting the stick to the yoke arm can be a pair of interlocking eye-bolts, a very short piece of line, or a mechanical fitting. It is not a complex construction project. The stick itself can be as fancy as you choose to make it—round, eight-sided, straight or curved, bare or with a grip wrapped with leather or twine and French whipping.

How about this option? If you make yourself a helmet with a single yoke arm on top, mounted on the side opposite the rudder yoke arm, and connect the loose end of the steer-stick to it, you could have "what you see is where you go" steering! Now, that's more advanced than even a modern jet fighter. Plus, your head will be protected in the event you are "boomed."

Canoe sailors already get plenty of strange looks. WYSIWYG steering might really make you a curiosity.

Rope Steering

The knot between the turning blocks provides an easy, no-look, rudder-straight reference point. It also provides a better grip on the steering line. Additional knots can be tied as needed along the sides. For light winds, when the sailor sits on the bottom of the canoe, the line along the gunwales is easiest to reach.

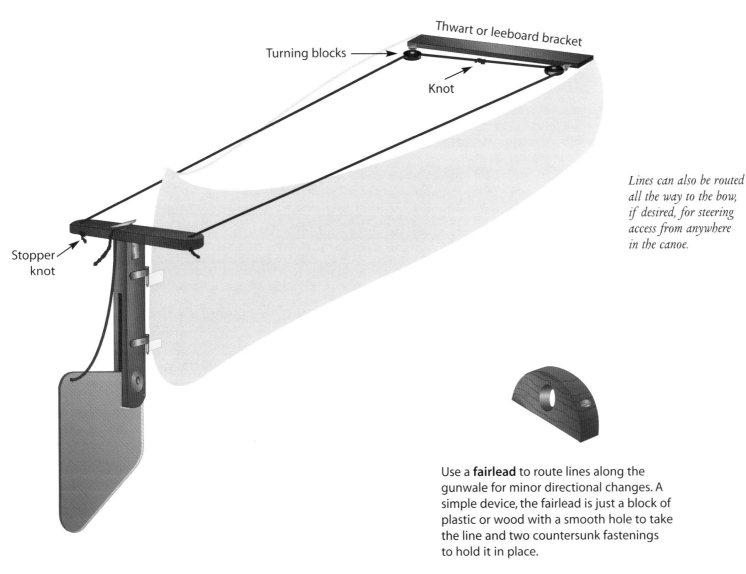

Thwart or leeboard bracket

Turning blocks

Knot

Stopper knot

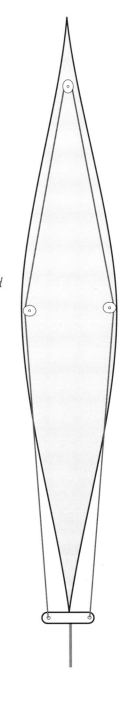

Lines can also be routed all the way to the bow, if desired, for steering access from anywhere in the canoe.

Use a **fairlead** to route lines along the gunwale for minor directional changes. A simple device, the fairlead is just a block of plastic or wood with a smooth hole to take the line and two countersunk fastenings to hold it in place.

Foot-Controlled Steering

Pedals and foot-bars are popular canoe-steering devices. Pedals can be hinged to the bottom of the boat, the sides, the deck, or some other structure. The steering lines can be routed with fairleads or blocks to get them out of the way under the gunwales or the deck. On decked boats the decking is often pierced by a piece of metal or plastic tubing for routing the lines from the yoke, through the deck, and forward to the pedals.

Foot-bar steering can be set up for push-right/turn-right, or push-right/turn-left control, depending on what feels natural to you. If you own more than one foot-steered boat, set them up the same; otherwise, it can be very difficult to learn to react instinctively while steering.

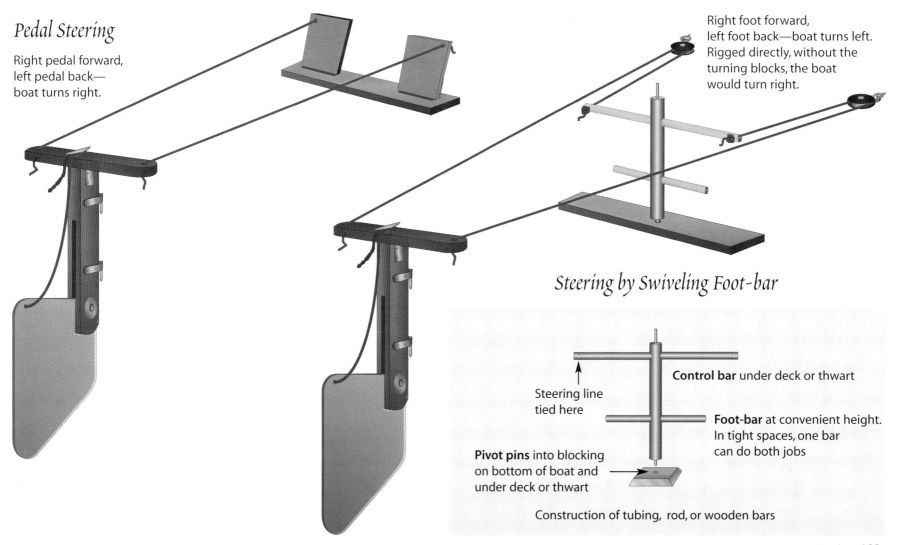

Pedal Steering

Right pedal forward, left pedal back—boat turns right.

Right foot forward, left foot back—boat turns left. Rigged directly, without the turning blocks, the boat would turn right.

Steering by Swiveling Foot-bar

Steering line tied here

Control bar under deck or thwart

Foot-bar at convenient height. In tight spaces, one bar can do both jobs

Pivot pins into blocking on bottom of boat and under deck or thwart

Construction of tubing, rod, or wooden bars

The Steer-Stick

Though this rudder has a one-armed yoke, a steer-stick could be mounted on either side of almost any yoke if you wish to switch back and forth between rope and stick steering. You could mount the stick on whichever side you wanted.

Set up as illustrated, pulling the steer-stick turns the boat to starboard and pushing it turns you to port. If the yoke arm and stick were mounted on the opposite side of the rudderhead, the directions would be reversed (pull-port and push-starboard).

There are many possible ways to connect the steer-stick to the yoke arm. Here are three relatively simple ones.

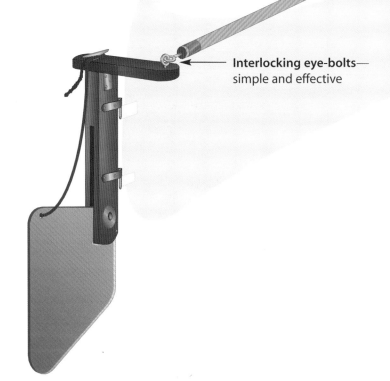

Interlocking eye-bolts—simple and effective

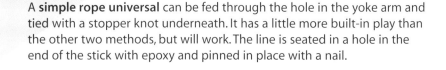

A **simple rope universal** can be fed through the hole in the yoke arm and **tied** with a stopper knot underneath. It has a little more built-in play than the other two methods, but will work. The line is seated in a hole in the end of the stick with epoxy and pinned in place with a nail.

A brass ring around the end of the stick helps to keep the stick from splitting; it is a good idea on any steer-stick, regardless of which connection is used.

Mechanical universal joint—very little play

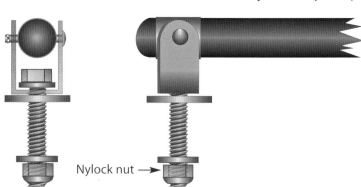

Don't overtighten the bolt. The fitting should spin freely.

Nylock nut →

The Slave Tiller

Though somebody must have tried this concept in the past, I haven't seen it yet. The idea struck me one day when I was underneath my iceboat, adjusting the steering cables. Many iceboats use a yoke-like arrangement mounted to the front runner to steer the boat. The yoke is often connected by rods or cables to another yoke, the latter attached to the tiller.

It got me wondering about using a similar arrangement on a sailing canoe. An iceboat has two yokes, because the front, steering runner is too far from the sailor to be used with a directly connected tiller. On some boats a direct tiller would have to be 15 feet long.

For a high-performance sailing canoe, where the sailor is crosswise in the center of the boat and hiking out, a tiller would be great, especially if the sailor were used to other sailboats that are tiller-equipped. The problems are tiller length and clearing the high stern stem.

If a second yoke were mounted on the stern quarter thwart, connected to the rudder yoke by ropes, and had a small tiller and extension, the steering would be very similar to that of most high-performance dinghies. The second yoke would be fixed on a single pivot bolt through a hole in the thwart.

For most canoe sailors who spend much of their sailing time sitting, facing forward, on the bottom of the canoe, this "slave-tiller" system will not be much more comfortable than the tiller illustrated on page 173. It is the speed sailor who sails sitting on the gunwale, back to the wind and balancing a large rig, that this system might benefit.

It would also be possible to intercept normal steering lines at the stern quarter thwart, tie in the slave tiller, and continue forward to the turning blocks, thereby having both systems for both sailing positions. This is a complex arrangement, but possible.

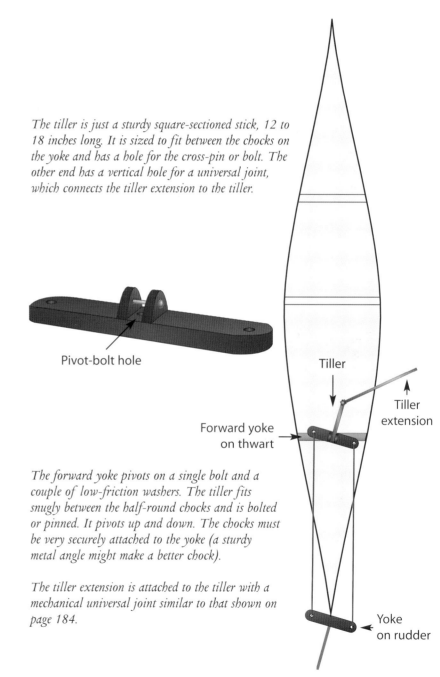

The tiller is just a sturdy square-sectioned stick, 12 to 18 inches long. It is sized to fit between the chocks on the yoke and has a hole for the cross-pin or bolt. The other end has a vertical hole for a universal joint, which connects the tiller extension to the tiller.

Pivot-bolt hole

Tiller

Tiller extension

Forward yoke on thwart

Yoke on rudder

The forward yoke pivots on a single bolt and a couple of low-friction washers. The tiller fits snugly between the half-round chocks and is bolted or pinned. It pivots up and down. The chocks must be very securely attached to the yoke (a sturdy metal angle might make a better chock).

The tiller extension is attached to the tiller with a mechanical universal joint similar to that shown on page 184.

Kayak-Style Rudders

Most modern sea kayaks are now equipped with a rudder that hangs from a single pivot at the top of the stern stem. This type would be a workable idea for downwind sailing, as it is for paddling. In both cases, the power being applied to the boat is pushing it forward.

For sailing close-hauled and reaching, the power is being applied from the side of the boat and the underwater foils must resist that force, channeling it into forward motion. A top-mounted, single-pivot rudder will probably deflect, losing effectiveness, or break something under these circumstances. Even if you can only put 6 inches between the two gudgeons on the stern of your canoe, that distance will really help stabilize and support the rudder while sailing.

The kayak-style rudder is very effective when used for its designed application. As a sailing rudder on anything except a very small boat it will probably be less than adequate, unless the leeboards can be positioned to do nearly all of the lateral resisting, leaving the rudder for steering only. This could make balancing the sail plan and the hull quite a challenge.

Top view of yoke

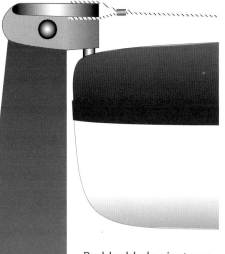

Cable-controlled yoke pivots on vertical stainless-steel shaft set into stern

Rudder blade pivots on single pin set crosswise through yoke

Steering Adjustments

Since any paddling-canoe-to-sailing-canoe modification is somewhat experimental, and because there are so many possible variations in boats and sails, it will take some sailing time to really determine how well the various parts of a rig work together. A boat with a plumb stem and straight keel, built for distance cruising, will be less responsive to its rudder than a more maneuverable hull. In turn, it should sail faster, just as it paddles faster.

To a great extent, the hull's paddling characteristics will carry over into its sail handling. That your long, lean cruiser doesn't spin on a dime when you tack probably has nothing to do with the size of its rudder and a lot to do with the shape of its hull. Every boat will be a compromise between speed and maneuverability under sail, just as it is when under paddle.

The element that we will be looking for during our first sailing trials will be balance. Can the boat be set up with just a bit of weather helm? What happens when the position of the leeboards is changed or when they are tilted a bit? What is the best way to approach a tack?

At times, I have owned up to five sailboats at once. Each one required slightly different timing in order to make a smooth tack. A boat that's fast in a straight line should be turned slowly, keeping up as much speed as possible until the bow has passed through the eye of the wind. An abrupt, hard turn to windward is likely to stall the boat; it will end up "in irons," or stopped dead with the boat pointed straight into the wind and the sail flapping.

Shorter, wider hulls are a bit more forgiving, because they generally maneuver faster. A good sailor can link tacks and jibes, making figure-eights, and keep up enough speed to continue doing that indefinitely if he chooses to. If the sailor in a long, fast hull tried that, the boat would lose speed at every turn and eventually stop. The long hull needs more time to regain speed between maneuvers.

With its long, narrow hull, your sailing canoe will be more like the longer, faster sailboat. Carrying as much speed as possible into a maneuver and making less abrupt turns will probably work best. The configuration of the rig will, no doubt, be another factor that will affect the canoe's turning characteristics, as will the wind and water conditions of the day.

That canoes are light and often carry large amounts of sail for a small hull will make them quick to accelerate, so any speed lost during a maneuver should be quickly regained. Practice and experimentation will be the keys to learning to sail and handle various conditions.

Getting a real feel for your steering system will probably take some time. After you've played with leeboard positions, boat balance, and turning methods, if you still think you need more steering power, try building another rudder blade. It won't cost much for the experiment, and you might even end up with both light- and heavy-air blades. Rather than making a new blade that's just bigger, try instead making one that's longer. It should still fit in the same housing, and the extra length should give more steering control while adding the least amount of drag to the system.

WHY NOT USE YOUR FEET?

Chapter Eleven

Sails

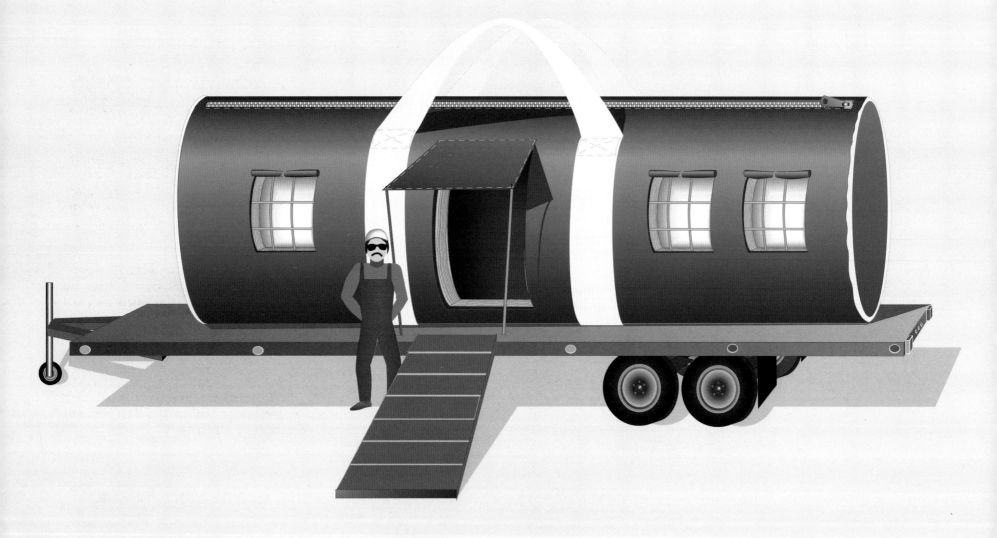

In the Beginning...

In some ways, this entire book is a fluke. It was never my intention to become a canoe-sail specialist. Being the only sailmaker in a town built around several large lakes, most of my business is repair work for local sailors, making sail and boat covers, and building one-of-a-kind sails for unusual or old boats. Someone will call me needing a replacement sail for a thirty year-old dinghy that they keep at their cabin. Since boat manufacturers come and go fairly quickly (mostly go), many of these people can't just call up the builder and order a new sail, so they call me instead.

Then there are the weird calls, such as the one from the guy who owned a 50-foot-long hollow log as big as a mobile home. He moved it around on a flatbed trailer and sold log tours. He wanted a cover for it—with a built-in awning. I generally can't afford to turn down work, but I really had no desire to have a 50-foot log parked in my driveway for a week. In a case like that one, you bid high—really high. If you do get the job, at least you'll make a lot of money.

I never did have to make a canvas cover for that log, nor did my friends and relatives have to see the newspaper headline, "Log rolls off trailer, squashes local sailmaker." The log must have gone elsewhere…or perhaps it rotted or became infested with termites. I would like to have at least seen it, though. Might even have taken the tour.

Considering the long history of sailing and iceboating in my area, I've always been disappointed by the lack of interest in old boats. There are a few nice refurbished mahogany powerboats, but it's tough to find traditional small boats or anyone interested in them.

One of my unusual phone calls, however, came a few years ago from a man with an old Peterborough sailing canoe. The original cotton sails were shot, and he wanted replacements built. The job sounded interesting. I had him bring the sails and spars over, so I could get a look at them.

To make a long story short, I built a pair of new sails, using Dacron fabric, in a color made to mimic old cotton sailcloth. I tried to stay historically accurate with any changes that I made and to retain the look of the original sails. I really enjoyed the project.

The owner was pleased with the results. As it turned out, he was formerly President of the Wooden Canoe Heritage Association and a frequent contributor to the association's magazine, *Wooden Canoe*, and through him the word spread.

As word got out that there was someone interested in building authentic-looking traditional canoe sails and willing to take the time to do it right, more orders and requests for information started coming in. I eventually put together a small catalog of drawings and explanations, just to have something to send to prospective customers. A few of those drawings were the basis for this book.

Building canoe sails offered me an opportunity to use the traditional sewing skills of a sailmaker, many of which have completely disappeared from most of the modern production sail lofts. These days, you can buy a very good sail, built by people with absolutely no knowledge of how sails were made even thirty years ago, and no need or desire to know anything more.

If you can convince them to build you a canoe sail, and if they can figure out how to do it at "normal, factory speed," meaning in about two hours—total production time for such a small sail—they can build you a perfectly fine, reasonably inexpensive sail.

On the other hand, if you are looking for a sail that looks as if it belongs on your antique or traditional canoe, you are limited to about three choices. You can have it built by one of perhaps twenty sailmakers who specialize in traditional sails, you can learn the techniques and build it yourself, or you can rent some technology and have a sail kit built for you with emphasis on traditional style, and assemble it yourself.

Cotton, Polyester, or Other

Your first and possibly most important decision relating to your canoe's sails is what they will be built from. It will have a bearing upon their cost, their look, their durability, their construction, and even their builder.

Nearly all of the original sails for now-antique canoes were cotton, the premium grade of which was Egyptian cotton. As it was told to me back in about 1970 by a sleeping-bag hustler, Egyptian cotton has longer fibers than normal cotton, allowing it to be spun into finer yarns and woven into a tighter, less porous weave. I never checked up on his story, but it made sense to me. The down has never come through the Egyptian cotton cover of my sleeping bag, so, at least in principle, he seems to have been right.

Today, you occasionally see advertisements for sheets made from Egyptian cotton, but whether it really is, or not, I couldn't tell you. I will tell you that you can't run down to the nearest fabric store and buy a chunk of it. The stuff is very rare, and most of the sailmakers now using it for classic boats just happened to come across a bolt of it and put it away for future use. If you hunt around, it is possible to find fairly similar cotton fabric suitable for canoe sails, though maybe not quite as fine and tight as true Egyptian.

As I see it, there are only three possible reasons to consider cotton sailcloth. First, if your canoe is a true, collectible antique and will spend much of its life on display as such, cotton sails look more antique and correct. Second, should you choose to build sails from locally gathered ingredients, you probably will have more luck finding suitable cotton than you will finding real polyester sailcloth. That cotton won't necessarily save you any money, but it will probably be available. Third, cotton is soft.

Most of the Dacron (DuPont's trade name for their polyester fiber) sailcloth, as well as the similar polyesters from overseas, are hard, slick, stiff, and noisy. Though the polyester fiber itself is fairly soft, the finishing techniques and resin applications that turn the base fabric into sailcloth make it very firm. Some of the firmest grades are actually so stiff that they will fracture if you bend them in a tight radius. These fabrics make excellent airfoils for serious racers but are quite impractical for average sailors.

Luckily, the polyester sailcloth made for classic boats is much more forgiving. It still has a very different feel from cotton, but it is a drastic improvement over cotton in performance, durability, and resistance to stretch, shrinkage, mold, rot, and sunlight. These are the characteristics that make polyester the logical choice for the vast majority of canoe sails.

Since very few sailmakers still work with cotton cloth or even have a source for it, you can pretty well assume that your sails will be polyester. In the long run, it is the best all-round choice for anything that's going to spend more time on the water than in a museum.

It is very possible to buy or build a sail for your classic canoe that works beautifully but looks as if it had been made in a factory, from modern materials, in about two hours. This is what every stock offering from all canoe companies and most sail lofts has looked like for as long as I can remember. It was the challenge of changing that standard that originally interested me in canoe sails and eventually led to this book.

I can't teach you how to build sails in one chapter, but I can point you in the right direction. I can show you how to make a sail that looks as if it fits a classic canoe. By mixing some old technology and styling with new materials, it's possible to eliminate the modern, factory-made look, and most of the modifications that turn a stock sail into a classic one just take more time and careful work, none of which is particularly difficult.

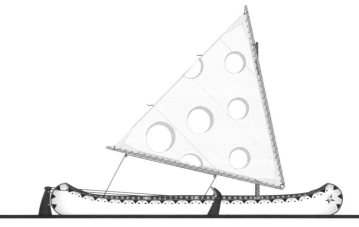

Wisconsin Regional Variation

What About Other?

Other fabric choices are pretty limited. I have always wondered about some of the cotton/polyester blends used for high-tech outerwear for hikers and climbers. When I was in the backpacking and canoeing business, blends like "65/35 Cloth," using a cotton-covered polyester yarn, were more stable and durable than plain cotton, and they were wind-tight enough for shell garments and limited-use raingear. Here again, the problem is finding the really good stuff. Though a blend is an interesting concept, it will never sail as well as unadulterated polyester sailcloth.

Nylon sailcloth, in weights suitable for mainsails and jibs, disappeared years ago. It was strong, but it had too much stretch and poor resistance to sunlight. Avoid the temptation to head down to the local fabric store to pick up some nylon for building a sail. It will be a waste of money.

The two modern spinnakers featured in Chapter Three are the only sails in this book that should be made from nylon fabric. Spinnakers must be very light to fly properly. These sails should be built from either .5-ounce or .75-ounce spinnaker nylon. The .5-ounce will fly better; the .75-ounce comes in more colors.

You will be surprised at how "crunchy" these nylon fabrics are. The base fabric is very similar to that of a sleeping bag or a down parka, but it is coated to stabilize it and reduce porosity, making it feel like heavy tissue paper. Coating also makes working with it much easier. Modern construction methods for spinnakers involve sticking the pieces together with double-stick sailmaker's tape and sewing to reinforce the tape bond. Soft fabric store "ripstop" nylon could be used, but real sail fabric will result in a better sail that is easier to build.

Small spinnakers are quite easy to build from kits, or by doing the math and laying out the pieces on your own. They are also fun to use, requiring only a pole for a mast. Anyone who is reasonably handy could crank out a spinnaker in a weekend.

Oceanus, a Possibility with Promise

By far the most interesting fabric for our purposes is somewhat new. North Cloth, the fabric manufacturing division of sailmaking giant North Sails, produces a fabric that combines filament Dacron (continuous fibers) like those in normal sailcloth with spun Dacron (fuzzy, shorter fibers). Called Oceanus, this new cloth looks and feels like the cotton sail canvas used on the old square-riggers. It was designed just for such ships that still remain, and it is absolutely beautiful stuff. It makes a sail that has most of the durability characteristics of polyester, yet the soft look and feel of cotton. You could keep your antique sailboat on display in a museum during the week and race it on weekends.

For classic canoe sails, Oceanus would be perfect. The only problem is that at the time of writing North doesn't make it in a light enough weight to be suitable for canoe or dinghy sails. The lightest weight offered is 7-ounce fabric. By comparison, in regular polyester, we use 3.8- to 4-ounce and would often go lighter if it were available. If Oceanus were offered in as heavy a weight as 5-ounce, it would be usable, but 7-ounce is too heavy for a canoe sail.

Unfortunately, the average canoe or dinghy sail only uses a few yards of fabric. North would probably have to refit every dinghy in the U.S.A. to get a return on the investment required to develop dinghy-weight Oceanus. Still, there is a chance that it will eventually happen, so if you are having a sail made, check with your sailmaker for current availability.

Sailcloth is never cheap, and Oceanus might cost twice what Dacron would, but when you only use five or six yards for the whole sail, the difference isn't that bad. If you are really going for the classic look, the best will be worth it. I've even thought about recanvasing my Old Town canoe with one of the heavier grades of Oceanus, though I think I'd do some canvas-filler adhesion tests before trying it.

Back to Dacron

Since cotton works best in museums, and Oceanus may never be available in a light enough weight, standard polyester sailcloth is still our best bet for canoe sails. The cloth offered in the 4-ounce range is available from several sailcloth manufacturers and in a rainbow of colors, as well as "natural," which means white.

Most sailboat sails are white, but back in the days of cotton, sails were what most people today think of as "natural"—a light, creamy-tan color, like unbleached muslin or untreated canvas. The fabric manufacturers, in an effort to cater to the traditional boat market, have brought out cream-colored polyester, approximating the color of cotton, and "tanbark," a reddish-brown sailcloth that imitates the cotton sails that were treated with tannic-acid-based preservatives.

The cream-colored fabric is called "Egyptian Dacron," "Egyptian Cream," or "Classic Cream," depending on which brand you buy. They are, slightly different shades of cream, but they all look pretty good once you get them up and the light shines through them. Oceanus, in North's "Canvas" color, is just about perfect, but unfortunately that doesn't make it weigh less.

Tanbark is a bit weird. Up close, it has a rather sleazy look. I'm not sure why, but the brown color seems to magnify the fact that the cloth is essentially plastic. From a distance, especially outdoors, tanbark is a rich, beautiful color and really looks good on a traditional boat. It is quite acceptable for canoe sails, though I doubt many canoe sailors ever felt they needed treated sails. If there were any "barked" originals, they would have been rare.

The traditionalists seem to hide the fact that in the old days there were also treated cotton sails that were red, blue, yellow, orange, green, and black, some of them quite bright, depending on the exact chemicals used to treat them. If you show up at a classic boat rendezvous with bright green sails, most folks will think you have a screw loose. You may have quite a battle trying to justify your choice of sailcloth.

Of course, you can also use white (natural) Dacron. Some people just think sails should be white. If, on the other hand, you really want your sails to look right on a classic boat, white is too bright! On the water, cream-colored Dacron is toned down just enough to make a classy understatement. It also works much better with the faux-antique construction tricks and traditional techniques that we will use to make sails that look as if they fit traditional boats.

If the construction and design are right, the corner reinforcements made properly, and the grommets, rings, and hardware all traditionally rendered, it is possible to build a sail that, from 20 feet away, looks as if it had been made in 1900. Up close, the fabric will be obviously modern, but if the work is good enough, you won't get any complaints.

In addition, it will be a good sail. It may weigh a few ounces more than a two-hour, factory-built quickie, but most of that extra weight will be reinforcement that the factory would have put there if they could have budgeted three hours for it and still made a profit.

To get a better idea of what is special about building functional, believable, traditional sails for canoes, there are four main aspects to consider. First is design: getting the sail to work with the canoe and its spars. Second is panel layout: how the body of the sail is constructed. Third is placement and shape of fabric reinforcement at the corners and stress points. And fourth is trim-out: the selection and installation of grommets, rings, and other hardware used to connect the sail to the spars and control lines.

Once you've been through the process, you will have a better idea of how to get your sailmaker to build the sail that you want for your boat, or whether you might want to try building it yourself.

Designing a Canoe Sail

There are two factors that make designing a canoe sail a bit different from designing a sail for most small sailboats. The first is the canoe's tender nature. With its narrow beam and light weight, a canoe can easily be overpowered by its sail. Sail area has much to do with this, as does the height of the sail above the water and its corresponding heeling leverage. Draft, the depth of the sail's belly, also is a factor.

When designing a sail, the draft is built in using mathematical formulas and calculations. The most common way to add draft to what would otherwise be a flat assembly is by shaping the luff along the mast, and the foot along the boom. Instead of cutting straight edges to match the edges of the corresponding spars, extra fabric is added to create curved sail edges. These added areas are known as "luff-round" along the sail's luff and "foot-round" along the foot of the sail. When these curved edges are attached to the straight spars, the extra fabric creates the draft. There are some special seaming or cutting techniques that are used to help move the belly into the center of the sail so it won't pile up along the spars, but for now all we need to know is that a curved luff or foot forms draft. The amount of draft, or camber, is determined by just how much extra material is added.

Normally, the sail's general dimensions are measured from the sail plan, which is usually drawn as if the sail were perfectly flat, with straight edges. Other than providing a good profile drawing, sail plans are used more for rig design than as sailmaking instructions. To build the sail, a more detailed and complex version of the sail plan must be generated.

Once the basic profile is laid down, horizontal lines are drawn across the plan at 25 percent, 50 percent, and 75 percent of the sail's height. These are the "chords." They are the spots where the calculations for draft will be made and specific amounts of extra fabric added. Between these specific points, the curve of the edge will be faired in with a batten. At both ends, the curve will taper out, back to our original, planned corner.

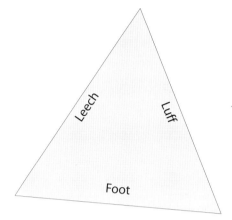

The designed "reference shape" is taken from the original sail plan and used primarily for sail-size calculations and rig design.

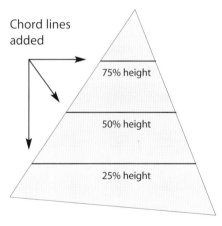

After the chord lines have been drawn, a percentage of each chord will be added to the line, projecting forward from the luff.

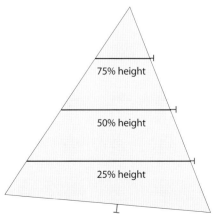

On many sails, the foot will also be shaped by adding a percentage of its length outside the reference shape. This will determine the maximum amount of foot-round and its position along the edge.

Figuring Luff Round

Designing-in Draft

Heavy, beamy boats need powerful sails to push them through water and waves. Power is generated by sails with fairly deep draft. Light, fast boats, such as catamarans and canoes, develop more speed with sails having fairly shallow draft. Since their skinny hulls accelerate quickly and offer less resistance, deep-draft sails would tend to overpower them, causing excessive amounts of heel.

The percentage added to each chord for the luff curve on a canoe sail is usually only 1 to 1½ percent of the chord length. This would mean that a 75-inch chord would be lengthened by less than 1 inch, so you can see that these are subtle curves. Some canoe sails are even cut straight-sided and flat, with nothing added for draft. They get their shape from the pressure of the wind, which will push some curvature and, hence, draft into the sail.

Cotton has so much stretch that a small lightweight sail will have a certain unavoidable amount of draft without any luff curvature being added. Learning to estimate and control stretch comes only from the experience of building a lot of similar sails from the same weight and weave of fabric. The scarcity of suitable fabric makes this very difficult and is a contributing factor to the experimental nature of trying to build good cotton canoe sails.

Dacron, being much more stretch resistant, generally benefits from designed-in draft, even if the added percentages are slight. To move the draft formed by curves in the luff and foot away from the spars and into the middle of the sail, "tapers" are either cut or sewn into the seams joining the fabric panels together.

Traditionally, the fabric panel width was kept constant and the seam overlaps were slowly increased as the seam neared the curved edges. This was also done according to formulas, dictating where the tapers would start and the final seam width at the edges. Usually, tapered and non-tapered seams would be mixed to achieve the finished shape.

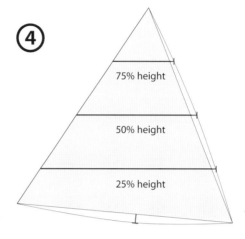

④ A batten is used to connect the reference points and fair the curves into the sail's corners, which remain unchanged from the original plan.

The percentage of the chord widths added to the original, straight-sided plan and the added foot-round will determine the final luff and foot curves. These, in turn, will determine the amount of draft in the finished sail.

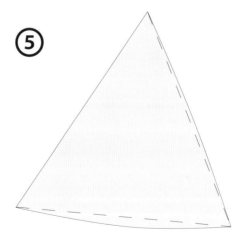

⑤ Luff and foot curves after adding draft calculations.

Today, many sail lofts and the companies building sew-it-yourself sail kits use computer plotters to cut out the pieces of their sails. Rather than changing the seam widths (called "broadseaming"), to adjust draft, computers generally maintain the seam width and cut the panel-to-panel overlaps with mating, curved edges. The method is still referred to as broadseaming, but it really is more like "panel shaping." Though a trained eye can readily tell the difference, either technique will work fine in Dacron. Cotton panels are always traditionally broadseamed. The woven, selvedge edge keeps the edge from raveling, something that is not a problem with hot-cut Dacron.

So, in comparison to regular boat sails, the first design difference for canoe sails is that they are cut with less draft. A lateen, for example, on a 17-foot canoe may have only half of the built-in draft that a similar sail used on a dinghy might have. Since lack of sufficient power to push the boat is rarely a canoe sailor's problem, the flatter sail will work better.

Spar-Bend Allowance

The other major difference between designing a canoe sail and a sailboat sail is our old nemesis, spar bend. There are no sailing craft with lighter, more flexible spars than sailing canoes. The curvature that we just added for draft is there under the temporary assumption that the spars will be straight. Once you handle your canoe spars, you will realize that, like it or not, they are going to flex in use.

If we added an inch of extra chord length for draft to the sail and our spar flexed just an inch, the spar would be curved to match the luff of the sail and our draft would be gone. In reality, some spars may flex 3 or 4 inches. Not only will flexing eat up our draft, it will distort the entire sail. On lateens, lugs, and other sails with long, bendy spars, we need to measure the spar's potential bend and allow for it in the design of our sail.

To help give us the best possible sail shape in most conditions, it is advisable to measure the spars for bend and add a factor for that into the design of the sail, just as we did with the draft calculations.

Spar Bend

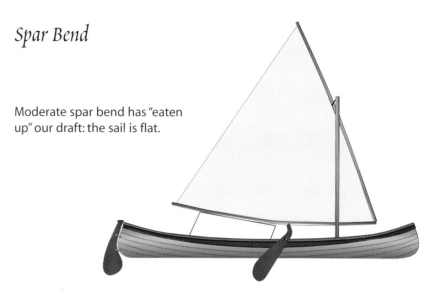

Moderate spar bend has "eaten up" our draft: the sail is flat.

Having the sail flatten when it is sheeted in tightly isn't necessarily a bad thing. The sailing situations that tend to induce the most spar bend are the times when the mainsheet is pulling hard to trim the sail. This happens when sailing close-hauled, working upwind, or when high winds are putting a lot of pressure on the sail and you must pull the sheet hard to control sail position.

In both upwind and high-wind sailing, a flatter sail will work better and help keep you from being overpowered. The spars' ability to bend actually can help us in these situations.

Extreme bend pulls the sail too tightly across the middle and may not pull it tightly enough elsewhere, resulting in very poor sail shape.

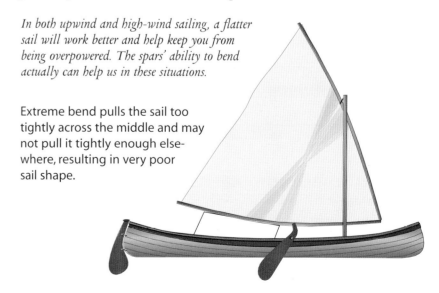

Measuring Spars for Bend

We know that our seemingly straight spars won't actually be straight in use, so we strike a compromise and allow for a certain amount of bend by adding even more curve to the edges of the sail—in addition to the curve that was added for draft.

Compromise is the key word here. We can't possibly calculate wind loads, spar bend, and sail trim for all possible conditions. Furthermore, any canoe spar can probably be over-bent enough to exceed a reasonable amount of spar-bend allowance built into the sail. What we can do is measure the spars and use a bend allowance that reflects the type of conditions that canoes usually sail in. This relationship between sail shape and spar bend is also different from larger sailing craft in that the cloth may actually be determining, to a large extent, the final shape of the wood.

Bend is measured as an addition to each chord and faired in, just as the draft percentage was. If we look at one of the long mid-sail chords on a lateen sail, for example, we may end up adding an inch to the chord for draft and adding 3 inches more for spar bend. Our final reference point, the one used to draw the cutting line on the sailcloth, would be 4 inches past the original straight line that represented the luff on the original plan.

Once the sail fills with wind and is sheeted in, the spars will bend and thus use up the bend allowance; we are back to a sail with the desired shallow draft. The major compromise comes in light winds. In conditions requiring very light sheet tension, the spars won't bend as much as planned and the sail will have deeper than ideal draft. To get good, all-around performance, we must live with this as it is simply the nature of such a flexible rig. Canoe sailing is all about compromise.

If your sail has short spars, such as a bat-wing, you may not need to build in any spar-bend allowance. The spars might bend a bit, but nothing like a 10-foot-long yard on a lateen or lugsail. I would start thinking about measuring for bend any spar that is over 6 to 7 feet long. Of course, if you want to, you can measure any spar just to see how much it bends. The decision of when bend deserves its own allowance is a tough one. Anything over an inch of bend is probably a good place to start.

It is possible that you could end up with a long yard and boom with as much as 10 to 12 inches of bend when measured. Though not ideal, the sail could be cut accordingly. Most sailmakers would probably hedge a bit, adding 60 to 75 percent spar-bend allowance to the sail and hoping that the cloth will help control the bend.

If you study some of the old sailing-canoe regatta photographs from the Rushton era (late nineteenth century), you will notice that some of the yards on the decked sailing canoes had a tremendous amount of bend. Even though the sails were stretchy cotton, the sailmakers would have had to build substantial allowances into those sails to handle all that bend.

One last compromise involves lateen sails. Since the yard and boom are often nearly identical, most canoe sailmakers measure the bend of the yard, figure the bend and draft allowances, develop the desired luff curve, and simply use the same curve for the foot of the sail. A separate foot-round can be calculated, as we saw on the previous pages, but for a canoe sail just matching the luff curve seems to work fine—and it's less work. If the yard and boom are of different lengths, which is sometimes the case on older lateens, the curve on the shorter foot edge is reduced proportionally.

The following two pages describe the process used to measure a spar's bend with little more than a string, a ruler, and a sack of potatoes or other suitable weight.

This simple test will help keep spar bend from ruining sail shape on canoes with long, bendy spars. I "borrowed" it from Jim Grant at Sailrite. It can be performed on booms, too, but the upper spars (yards) of lateens and lug sails are the most important. A boom will also bend, but careful placement of the mainsheet blocks (so they are not pulling down on the center of the boom) will eliminate much of the boom bend.

A yard is a different story. It must be lifted by a halyard tied to a specific spot on the spar; the whole rig pulls down on the yard, inducing the bend at that spot.

The spars are suspended from their ends with THE SIDE THAT WILL BE AGAINST THE SAIL ON TOP—the top of a boom, the BOTTOM of a yard. A reference string is hung above the spar, and measurements are taken from the string to the spar at one-quarter-length intervals along the unweighted spar. It is important to note which end of the spar is the tack end and which is the peak or clew end, because many spars are skinnier on their tail ends.

A weight equal to one-third of the sail's square footage in pounds (60 square feet: 20-pound weight) is then suspended from the spar. The distances at the quarters from the reference string are remeasured and the differences are noted. These amounts will be built into the sail's edge curve to accommodate the bend of the spar.

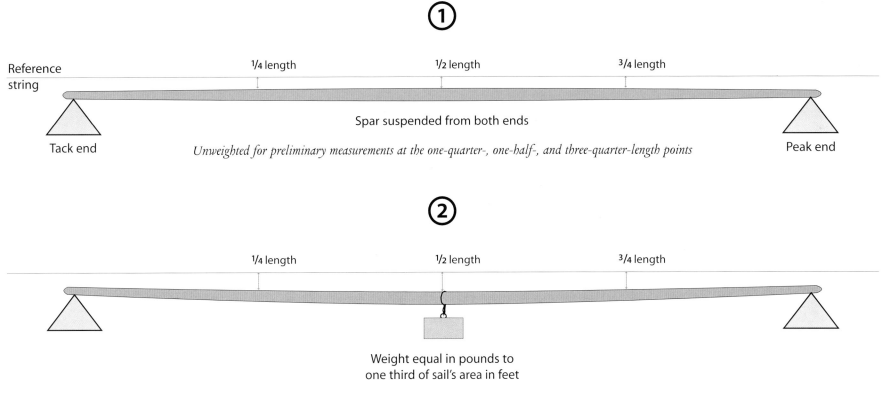

①

Reference string | ¼ length | ½ length | ¾ length

Spar suspended from both ends

Tack end

Unweighted for preliminary measurements at the one-quarter-, one-half-, and three-quarter-length points

Peak end

②

¼ length | ½ length | ¾ length

Weight equal in pounds to one third of sail's area in feet

Weighted for bend measurements at the one-quarter-, one-half-, and three-quarter-length points

Charting Spar Bend

If you plan to do your sailing in light winds, as many canoe sailors do, you could probably reduce the measuring weight a bit. Twenty-five percent, in pounds, of sail area will give you a flatter sail in light air that might perform better. To keep track of your findings, you may want to make a spar-bend chart similar to the one below. Though not absolutely necessary, a chart sometimes helps prevent mix-ups and math errors as you start figuring the chord-length additions.

As you can see, allowing for spar bend is merely an estimate on a boat with such skinny, bendy spars. The result can only be a compromise. Every canoe will sail better in certain conditions than others because of the spar-bend/sail-shape equation that was chosen at the start. Allowing for spar bend is, by far, the most difficult and unpredictable part of designing a canoe sail, compounded by the fact that every spar is different and there are so many different-sized rigs being used.

Spar Bend Measurement Chart

		Tack end of yard	1/4 length	1/2 length	3/4 length	Peak end
The	Weighted measurements—string to spar	3.75"	5.25"	6.5"	5.75"	3.75"
Less the	Unweighted measurements—string to spar	3.75"	3.25"	3"	3.5"	3.75"
Gives us the	Measured bend of that spar	0"	2"	3.5"	2.25"	0"

Weighted measurements – unweighted measurements = **Measured bend of the spar**

Panel Layout Basics

Modern sailcloth is produced in widths from 36 to 54 inches. Nearly all of the fabric in the 4-ounce range comes 36 inches wide. This means that most canoe sails can be built from three or four 36-inch-wide panels, making them fast to produce. Unfortunately, wide panels immediately prove to knowledgeable observers that they are modern sails. They're a tipoff, like a supposedly 2,000-year-old mummy that was dug up holding a Pepsi can.

Back in the days of cotton, fabric was woven in narrower widths, often as narrow as 18 inches. In light weights, even these narrow panels were often further reinforced against stretch by a technique called "false-seaming." A false seam looks just like a panel-joining seam, but it is made down the center of a panel by folding the cloth back on itself, twice, and sewing the fold in place. In cross-section, the fold is in the shape of a "Z."

A well-made cotton sail in the old days would appear to have had panels that were as narrow as 9 to 12 inches, though only some of the seams actually joined different pieces of fabric. The false seams between the panel-joining seams helped reduce bias stretch, which was and still is the number one obstacle to making a good airfoil from a piece of cloth.

Dacron, with its resin coatings, is much more stable than cotton, allowing the elimination of false-seaming. For a big production sail loft, faced with the task of building hundreds of similar sails, the use of wide fabric saves time and money. For our purposes, however, wider panels tend to work against the visual image that we are trying to create. Any panel layout using full-width panels will instantly stamp "modern" on our sail.

Dacron can be false-seamed, but it is quite tedious and creates rather bulky seams. As an alternative, we can build a sail from narrow strips of Dacron, with real seams. These narrow panels aren't really needed for stretch control, but they help generate a sail that looks as if it's from an earlier era.

Most cotton sails were sewn with a straight stitch. The zigzag stitch began being used somewhere between 1930 and 1940. On Dacron, zigzagging makes a stronger seam, as it spreads out the stitching holes rather than running them in a perforated line. Even though a zigzagged seam may not be authentic, then, it is a better bet on Dacron replicas of old sails.

Seaming Styles

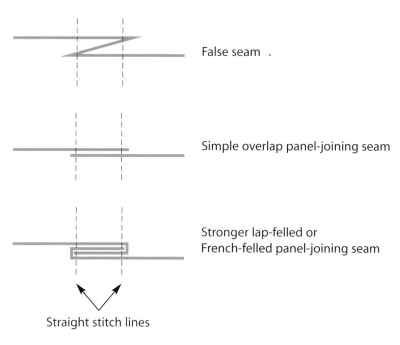

Cross-sections of false seams and panel-joining **seams for cotton**

False seam

Simple overlap panel-joining seam

Stronger lap-felled or French-felled panel-joining seam

Straight stitch lines

Seaming Dacron with panel-joining seams only

Zig zag stitch lines

Finished seams

I've been working for several years on a design for a two-person schooner about the size of a big kayak. The concept intrigues me, because the boat looks as if it should be 75 feet long. In the process of prototyping some parts, I started building one of the jibs. If it were to look like a miniaturized version of a big schooner's jib, it would need panels that were only about 6 inches wide. I cut some 4-ounce tanbark strips and started sewing panels together.

After I had several panels sewn together, I noticed that the seams were not as smooth as normal. I checked my sewing machine for thread tension, needle size, foot pressure, and anything else that I could think of and finally decided that it was a function of putting so many seams so close together in light fabric. I was just about to throw the partially completed sail in the scrap box when the notion struck me.... The sail looked old.

Yes, it was still 4-ounce tanbark, but it had lost some of the hard, shiny, slick look that all Dacron seems to have. The normal slight puckering along the seams was helping to camouflage the modern synthetic look of the cloth. I didn't think much more about this—until the order came in for my first replacement sail for an antique canoe.

The boat's original cotton sails had been made by a seamstress, not a sailmaker. The orientation of the frabric weave and some of the trim details were either peculiar or wrong in any era. This left me a bit of maneuvering room. There was no reason to duplicate bad work.

I decided to build Egyptian Dacron replacements and try the narrow-panel technique with 8-inch-wide panels. The result was a pair of modern Dacron sails that from a few feet away looked like fancy cotton sails. Up close, it was apparent that they weren't actually cotton, but the corner construction, the hand-sewn rings, and especially the panel layout made them look believable. They fit the look of the boat and its wooden spars.

Building a little sail using twenty panels when it could be made from three is, obviously, extra work. It adds about one more afternoon to the construction process, but it does wonders for the way the sail looks. I don't care whether it's going on a 1928 Old Town, or a 1998 Mad River, a narrow-paneled canoe sail just looks richer.

Nearly all of the sails in this book are shown with 8- to 12-inch-wide panels, even though they could be built with full-width Dacron. You may have to twist your sailmaker's arm to get him to build a canoe sail with narrow panels, but the effort is worth it, especially on an older boat. If you're planning on building your own sail, from scratch or from a sail kit, don't be scared off by the extra work. Sewing panel seams is the easiest part of sailmaking.

Determining the exact width of your panels depends on the fabric chosen and its manufactured width. You will probably also need some thin strips of fabric (2 to 3 inches wide, called Dacron tape) for binding the edges. A 10-yard chunk of 36-inch Dacron, for example, will yield four 8-inch strips (120 linear feet) and two 2-inch by 30-foot tapes. It could also be cut into three 10-inch strips (90 linear feet) and three 2-inch or two 3-inch strips of tape. Sometimes one panel width may be more cost-effective than another.

Sailcloth manufacturers sell a variety of precut widths and weights of Dacron tape, but it is rarely available in the colors that we need. Most of it is white, which doesn't necessarily look bad, but it doesn't look correct, either. You should plan on cutting your tapes from the same roll of fabric as your panels. This makes determining mileage for both panel material and tape a bit more challenging, but it isn't a big problem.

Fabric Panel Orientation

Fabric is much more resistant to stretch when the stress is applied square to the weave. The unsupported leech of the sail is its most vulnerable area, and panels are always laid out with that in mind. The panel seams and the weave of the fabric should be either parallel or perpendicular to the leech, or in the case of sails with hollow edges or a slight roach, to a straight line between the head and the clew.

Most Dacron is actually woven to resist stretch best when used in a cross-cut configuration. For canoe sails and other small sails, Dacron will work almost as well for vertically cut sails, especially if they are narrow paneled.

Miter-cut sails are somewhat unpredictable in Dacron. Most of the sail-design computer programs and many modern sailmakers don't do miters. I have done a few, and can't say that I'm really comfortable with them. Miters involve a lot of guesswork; by the time you get to see if you guessed right, the sail is finished.

If the shaping of the miter seam is not right, fixing it involves taking virtually the whole sail apart. Luckily, almost any sail that is shown on a sail plan as a miter can also be cross or vertically cut, thus increasing the chances it will be shaped properly.

Bat-wings and other sails with big roaches are best if the weave and panel layout follow the leech, around the roach. This means building sections from narrow panels and then joining the sections together. If the sail were simply cross-cut, or vertically cut, there would be areas where the strains on the leech would be pulling diagonally on the weave, which is bound to stretch out prematurely.

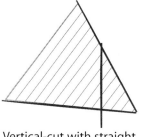

Vertical-cut with straight leech

The **vertical-cut sail** *is the oldest method of panel layout. Panel seams run parallel to the leech. Vertical-cut sails were eventually replaced by cross-cut sails for racing; the theory was that cross-cut seams provided a smoother shape and less wind resistance.*

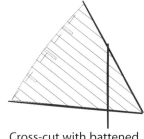

Cross-cut with battened roach

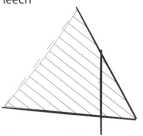

Cross-cut with hollowed leech

In **cross-cut sails**, *seams run perpendicular to the leech, which may be cut straight but is usually hollowed a bit to prevent fluttering. Also common are cross-cut sails with an outwardly curved "roach" (which requires small, wooden battens to support the extra area and keep it from flapping), as can be seen at left.*

Miter-cut

The sprit-boom sails in this book are **miter-cut sails**. *They have panel seams that are perpendicular to both the leech and the foot, meeting at the diagonal "miter seam" in the middle.*

Bat-wing

Bat-wing sails *have full battens, running all the way across the sail and supporting a very large roach. They are usually cut with panel seams parallel to the leech, like a vertical cut, but divided, section by section. The seams make a pattern resembling a spider web.*

Corner Patches

Corners need to be built up with multiple layers of fabric to take the stresses of grommets and corner rings. These layers are called "corner patches." The modern industry standard is a stack of simple triangular patches. Though these aren't necessarily historically inaccurate, most well-built old sails used "tongue patches" instead. Tongue patches are longer and often wrap around the edge of the sail.

Here again, tongue patches take more time but help create the classic look. Cotton sails often had very small corner patches. It is not unusual to see a cotton canoe sail with 3-inch-long patches. On a Dacron sail, patches need to be built longer. The fabric's low stretch requires a smoother transition from several layers at the corner to one layer in the body of the sail.

The largest patch should be 8 to 10 percent of the length of that particular edge of the sail (luff, leech, etc.), and the other layers, which are placed under the largest patch, are each reduced by an inch or two as they near the corner. Four to six layers of fabric is enough to anchor a corner ring or grommet securely. To prevent wrinkles, the weave of the patches should be aligned to match the weave of the base sail panel.

Sometimes patches of different shapes can be combined on the same sail. A gaff sail, for example, might have tongue patches at the head, clew, and tack, but a circular patch at the throat. If the sail has a line of reef points, the tack and clew tongue patches along the luff and leech are sometimes cut long enough to reinforce both the regular tack and clew and the reef tack and clew.

There are no hard-and-fast rules concerning patch style and selection. The choice is pretty well up to the individual sailmaker. In fact, it's sometimes possible to tell a sail's builder by the shape and layout of its corner patching.

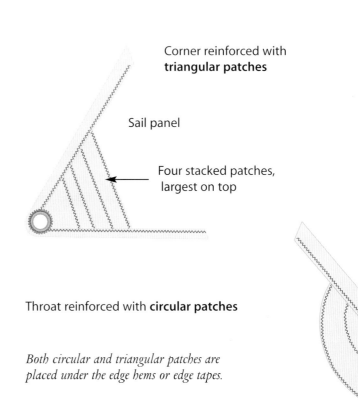

Corner reinforced with **triangular patches**

Sail panel

Four stacked patches, largest on top

Throat reinforced with **circular patches**

Both circular and triangular patches are placed under the edge hems or edge tapes.

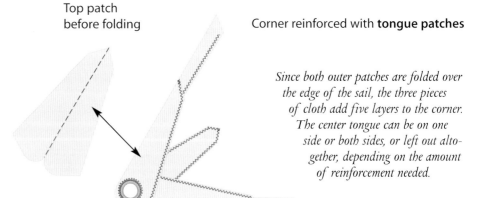

Top patch before folding

Corner reinforced with **tongue patches**

Since both outer patches are folded over the edge of the sail, the three pieces of cloth add five layers to the corner. The center tongue can be on one side or both sides, or left out altogether, depending on the amount of reinforcement needed.

Radial Corners, Strong But Wrong

If you're ordering or building a traditional sail, the one corner construction that you will definitely want to avoid is called a radial or fan corner. They are actually superb structures on the right panel layout, but have no place at all on a traditional sail or a classic boat. I don't remember ever seeing one before the 1987 *America's Cup*.

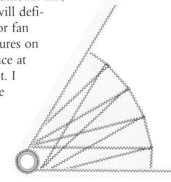

These days, they are used on all kinds of sails, in some cases because they work best, in others because they look sexy. Some sailmakers use them for almost everything, betting that the customer doesn't know that they really only work well on some sails. They are

Though not unattractive, a modern radial corner has no place on a traditional sail.

definitely the fanciest-looking corner, adding perceived value to the sail, yet they are among the easiest and fastest corners to assemble, which saves labor and therefore money.

Radial corners were developed for radially cut sails, a modern technique where a sail's panels are fanned out from the corners, aligning the weave of the fabric with the stresses on the sail. Many of the new high-tech sail fabrics are built specifically for radial cuts. Since the panels themselves fan out, the corner patches should fan in order that their weave is aligned with that of the sail.

For a radial corner, a stack of strips are cut from the same fabric as the sail. The strips might be 6 to 12 inches wide on a sail for a 20- to 30-foot boat. The strips are fanned, like opening a poker hand. They all overlap at the corner ring, but as they move inward they eventually spread until just a single thickness exists, on top of the sail itself.

Technically, on anything but a radial sail, radial corners are structurally incorrect. The sailmakers who are using them on modern cross-cuts either don't know any better or don't care. My pet peeve is seeing a classic boat with new narrow-paneled Egyptian Dacron sails with radial corners. If your sailmaker wants to put them on your antique canoe sail—find another sailmaker!

This is a sail plan that I drew for the radial mainsail on the trimaran that my wife and I own. It is built from a Mylar laminate with polyester (white) and Technora Aramid (black) fibers. The sail's panels fan out from the corners.

In reality, the weave follows this fan shape as well. The panels are cut with the warp yarns of the fabric running lengthwise down the center of each panel. The corner patches are also radial, as they should be on this type of sail—which is about as traditional as it looks.

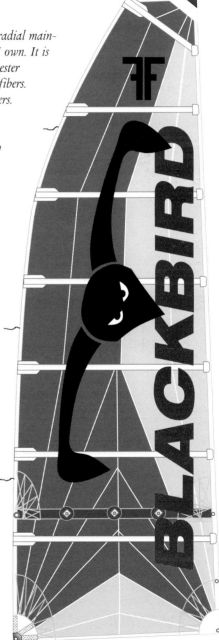

Sail Hardware

I really enjoy installing the grommets, rings, and other hardware on a traditional sail. The sail is nearly finished, and adding bits of brass and hand-sewn detailing is like adding jewelry. Unlike modern sails, where stainless and plastic corner rings are squashed in place under thirty tons of pressure in a hydraulic press, traditional sails use the sailmaker's skill and twine to hold these fittings to the sail. Surprisingly, the hand-sewn ring is nearly as strong and durable as its modern descendant, and probably less apt to fail.

For a canoe-sized sail, various sizes of "spur grommets" can handle all of the lacing and corner loads. A spur grommet is similar to a hardware-store washer grommet, but it has metal teeth that pierce the fabric around its edge and lock the grommet's washer and barrel together. This makes the spur grommet very strong.

Spurs come in sizes. The smallest, #000, is about twice the size of a shoe's lacing eyelet. The largest commonly used on sails is a #5. It is designed for a ⅝-inch hole and has a maximum diameter of 1¼ inches. For canoe sails, #2 spurs in ⅜-inch holes are strong enough for corner rings; lacing grommets can be #1, #0, #00, or #000 grommets.

Spur grommet setters, the tool for fixing them in place, are expensive. I have several hundred dollars invested in them and don't even have a full set.

I generally use #2s, #0s, #00s, and #000s for canoe sails. One of the instant-aging tricks that I discovered while looking at old canoe sails and building replicas was that a lot of small lacing grommets, spaced fairly close together, looks more antique than fewer, bigger grommets with more space between them.

On a typical lateen, most sailmakers will use #1 or #2 spurs, 8 to 12 inches apart. I use #000s spaced 4 inches apart, or #00s spaced 6 inches apart. Functionally, it doesn't matter, but visually, just as with narrow fabric panels, many small closely spaced grommets help make the sails look as if they really are part of an antique boat's sail rig, not a modern replacement.

Hand-sewn rings consist of a brass ring sewn to the sail and a brass liner, pressed inside, to protect the stitching from chafe. Rarely is there a need for them, structurally, on a canoe sail, but they are beautiful and scream, "This sail wasn't stamped out in a factory!" From what I have seen, there aren't very many people in the modern sailmaking business who still remember (or ever learned) how to neatly sew one.

The liners and setting tools are scarce and expensive, and the sail hardware manufacturers are letting their supplies run out—for good. Unless somebody makes an investment in tradition, simply for preservation, the hand-sewn ring won't be around much longer.

"Cringles," brass thimbles woven into a loop of rope and anchored to a series of connected rings, are another tradition falling by the wayside. Again, they are stronger than required for the corners of a canoe sail, but they add to the beauty of the sail. Like sewn rings, only sailmakers who specialize in traditional sails use them.

If you plan to build your own sails, hand-sewing your corner rings and "sticking" cringles is the least expensive way to build super-strong corners. It sure beats laying out a couple thousand dollars for a hydraulic press.

It takes years (literally) of practice to really get good at the hand-sewing skills of a sailmaker. Every stitch is visible, and any misalignment is obvious. On the other hand, a careful beginner can sew in a ring that, though maybe not beautiful, is strong enough to pick up the whole boat with and swing it around.

The drawing on the following page shows the relative sizes and appearance of the hardware I use for canoe sails. All of these fittings have been around as long as there have been sailing canoes, and various combinations of them can be used to get both the desired strength and the traditional appearance.

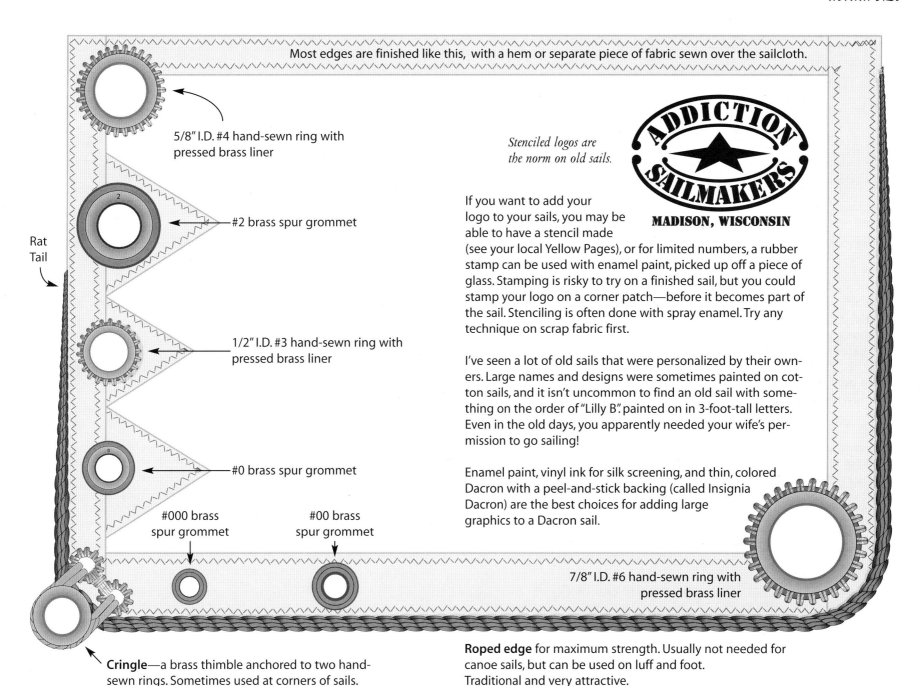

Most edges are finished like this, with a hem or separate piece of fabric sewn over the sailcloth.

5/8" I.D. #4 hand-sewn ring with pressed brass liner

#2 brass spur grommet

Rat Tail

1/2" I.D. #3 hand-sewn ring with pressed brass liner

#0 brass spur grommet

#000 brass spur grommet

#00 brass spur grommet

7/8" I.D. #6 hand-sewn ring with pressed brass liner

Cringle—a brass thimble anchored to two hand-sewn rings. Sometimes used at corners of sails.

Stenciled logos are the norm on old sails.

ADDICTION SAILMAKERS

MADISON, WISCONSIN

If you want to add your logo to your sails, you may be able to have a stencil made (see your local Yellow Pages), or for limited numbers, a rubber stamp can be used with enamel paint, picked up off a piece of glass. Stamping is risky to try on a finished sail, but you could stamp your logo on a corner patch—before it becomes part of the sail. Stenciling is often done with spray enamel. Try any technique on scrap fabric first.

I've seen a lot of old sails that were personalized by their owners. Large names and designs were sometimes painted on cotton sails, and it isn't uncommon to find an old sail with something on the order of "Lilly B". painted on in 3-foot-tall letters. Even in the old days, you apparently needed your wife's permission to go sailing!

Enamel paint, vinyl ink for silk screening, and thin, colored Dacron with a peel-and-stick backing (called Insignia Dacron) are the best choices for adding large graphics to a Dacron sail.

Roped edge for maximum strength. Usually not needed for canoe sails, but can be used on luff and foot. Traditional and very attractive.

Roping

Roped edges, as shown on page 207, are pure luxury on a sail as small as a canoe sail. You will find this out if you ask your sailmaker how much it will add to the price of your sail. Traditionally, the luff, foot, and head (on a four-sided sail) were roped for strength. A few sails, such as those on Chinese junks, were roped on all sides, but most had unroped leeches. A three-stranded rope rounded the clew or head and rapidly tapered out on the ends of the leech, leaving most of the leech bare. The tapered ends, also shown on page 207, are called "rat-tails."

The rope was sewn, by hand, to the sail and actually was on one side of the sail's edge. Strand by strand, the roping was stitched to the edge. It is a tricky and very labor-intensive task, which most sailmakers no longer perform and most customers couldn't afford even if they did.

At one point I decided I wanted to be able to rope small sails. To keep the scale right, it would have to be small rope. I chose ¾₆-inch polyester three-strand. The variety that I decided to use is from New England Ropes and is a fairly hard, low-stretch (for three-strand) filament polyester. They also make a softer, fuzzier version, but I didn't want soft rope (or fuzzy rope, for that matter).

Once the proper rope had been located, there were only three remaining problems. First, it was the wrong color, being snow white, which would never look right on an antique reproduction. Second, I wasn't sure it would rat-tail well, and though some workboat sails had roping that abruptly stopped, without rat-tailing, at the leech, it was somewhat crude in appearance. Third, it would require 10 carefully placed hand stitches per inch. That could mean as many as 2,500 stitches on a canoe-sized lateen sail! Who could afford that? Not to mention that I'm too impatient to sit all day, stitching a few feet of rope.

Since I now owned 1,200 feet of this rope, however, and because roping is so elegant, these problems had to be overcome, one way or another.

Coloring Rope

Rope used on traditional sails and rigging should look traditional; though clean white rope is very nice-looking, it is not the least bit traditional. Polyester does not readily take dye, so dyeing was out. Traditional tar-based treatments would work, but they eventually get all over the sail, the sailors, the boat, and anything else they came in contact with, so they were out. Then, the answer came to me.

If you get oil-based enamel or stain on a shirt, you can wash it with thinner, soap, etc., but unless you get to it quickly, you will always have a stain. It can be washed until it isn't sticky or stiff, and until it won't come off on other clothing, but some of the color will still be there for the life of the shirt.

A little experimentation yielded colored rope. The way I do it is to open the can of wood stain (something close to "cherry" seems to work best), stir it well, and slowly coil the chunk of rope into the can. After a couple of minutes, I grab one end of the rope and slowly pull it out, wiping it down with a rag as it comes out.

Next, to keep it from being sticky and stiffening the rope, I dunk it in thinner for a couple more minutes. (I use naphtha—highly flammable and definitely not something you want to breathe. Use caution.) The rope loses some color, but when it is removed, wiped, and allowed to dry, it feels about like it did before the stain, and the color doesn't come off on you or the sail. Problem #1 solved.

Rat-tailing

For quite a while, I wasn't sure whether my rat-tailing failures were because of me or the rope. I could rat-tail manila, but not polyester very well because it was limp. The process is to tape or whip the rope 8 to 10 inches above the end and separate the three strands. Each strand is then unwound and its fibers scraped with a knife until they form a long taper, which is waxed and twisted back together. When all three strands are individually tapered, they are retwisted together to make a long, tapered rat-tail.

Pre-roped Edging

Through practice and persistence, not to mention the motivation of owning 1,200 feet of rope, I learned to rat-tail the stuff, but not without developing a plan of attack. First, I developed a guide. On a board, I drew eight parallel lines about an inch apart. The stopped-off rope is clamped to the board with the whipping at the first line and the other lines under the three strands.

Each strand is then unwrapped until all of its fibers can be clamped down at their loose ends, flat on the board, side by side. I use a sharp blade from a utility knife, without the handle. Holding the blade straight up and down, I start at the first line, by the whipping, and scrape all the way down, as evenly as possible with a firm, but not too aggressive stroke. The next stroke starts at the next line, an inch closer to the end, and goes all the way to the end.

Each new stroke starts at the next line down, the final strokes being very short. Then it's back to the top, and the process repeats. As progress is made, fuzz-blobs build up at the bottom. The strands are rubbed down with wax (sailmaker's wax is a yellow beeswax blend) as the tapering progresses. Once the taper looks even, the fuzzy end is cut off and the fibers are twisted and waxed into a tapered strand.

After all three strands are tapered and rebuilt, they can be twisted and waxed back into a rope. I stain the rope before rat-tailing and normally have to touch up the stain on the tail once it's done.

Making a rat-tail is a fairly tedious job, but it can be done with polyester rope. It just takes practice and consistent scraping for a proper job.

Problem #2 solved. Now I had brown rat-tailed rope. The next task was to find a reasonably efficient way to attach it to the sail.

A quick test proved that hand-sewing the rope to the sail at a rate of ten stitches per inch was time-consuming and tedious, so a new plan had to be developed. For years sails have been built with preconstructed roping. The rope is sewn to a strip of Dacron tape, which is then folded over the raw edge of the sail and sewn, leaving the rope centered on the edge and standing proud.

Standard preconstructed roping, or roped tape, is pretty good-looking but has its drawbacks: Both the rope and the tape are white; the size of the rope is a bit large for small sails; and the ends can't be rat-tailed, so sailmakers have to hide them under corner patches or just allow them to stop abruptly. I decided to try making my own roped tape, using Egyptian-colored tape and stained rope with rat-tailed ends. I tried it several ways—even considered building some sort of feeder to keep the rope lined up properly—but finally developed a technique that works.

First, 2-inch-wide tape is folded in half lengthwise and creased along the fold. I run a pencil along the outside of the crease to make a small guideline. The rope is positioned under the straight-stitch foot of the sewing machine and the creased Dacron is placed on top of the rope, like a pup tent. The top tension on a sewing machine is much easier to adjust than the bobbin tension, so having the rope underneath allows you to set the top tension tight enough to nearly bury the stitches into the rope.

The only problem is that you can no longer see the rope, as it is under the Dacron tape. With fingers close to the presser foot on both sides, you pull the tape in and down on the rope, and guide the rope under the needle. Sewing and feeding slowly, you straight-stitch along the pencil line and down the center of the tape and the rope.

With a little practice, you can even guide the stitching right down the middle of the rat-tail and onto bare Dacron once past the rat-tail. With nothing but a pencil line and your fingers, you can make pre-sewn roped luff tape.

Sewing the Rope

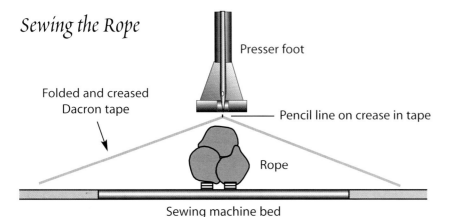

Presser foot

Folded and creased Dacron tape

Pencil line on crease in tape

Rope

Sewing machine bed

Fingertips on both sides pull fabric tight and guide rope....
Try to keep yours (fingertips, that is) attached to your hands.

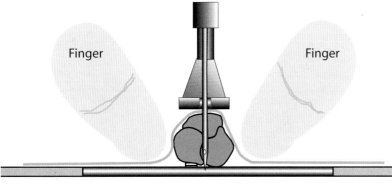

Finger

Finger

Edge of sail will be sandwiched between these flaps of fabric and sewn

Stitch line

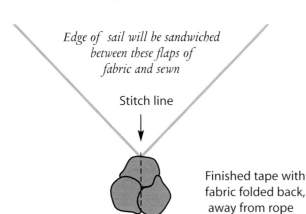

Finished tape with fabric folded back, away from rope

Using the Pre-roped Tape

I found out the hard way that cutting the pieces to size and rat-tailing both ends of the rope before sewing it to the tape is a mistake. The roped tape doesn't end up as long as the original pieces were. Now I rat-tail one end and start with about 15 percent more rope and tape than the sail's edge measurement.

Once the rope and the tape are sewn together, the tape is folded back the opposite way along the crease, leaving the rope standing proud along the crease and two flaps of fabric to be sewn down, sandwiching the edge of the sail. The roping usually runs continuously from the top of the clew patch, on the leech, down around the clew, across the foot to the tack, around the tack corner to the luff, up the luff, and around the head; it ends at the bottom of the upper leech patch. (See the leg-o'-mutton sail on the following page.)

Where the roped tape goes around a corner, the tape is slit as needed to make the bend and then sewn down. The slit will always be under a corner ring, so you won't be aware of it once the sail is finished. I start at the clew end and work my way down the leech, across the foot, up the luff, and around the head. It is usually easier to baste the tape in place with double-stick sailmaker's tape than to try to position the tape as you sew it down.

Once I'm about a foot away from the end, I stop sewing. The rope and tape are cut to terminate at the same spot as the upper leech corner patch and separated from each other for the last foot. The rope is rat-tailed and sewn back onto the tape, and then the tape is sewn the rest of the way. Rat-tailing is a bit difficult when you're dragging the whole sail around as you work, but it's the only way to get the rope to end where it's supposed to.

Leg-o'-Mutton Sail

This is a simple sail. It has a straight leech, no battens, and no exotic shape, yet it makes a good showpiece for the techniques and detailing described in this chapter. The narrow panels, hand-sewn head and tack rings, clew cringle, small lacing grommets, tongue patches, and roped edges all combine to make the sail very elegant. It would be just as functional made from four white panels and a handful of grommets, but it wouldn't have anywhere near the visual impact it does now, especially on a wooden canoe.

Even with machine sewing, roping a sail like this adds the better part of two days' work to the construction time. It also adds substantially to the cost, but the sail really looks great when it's done. A roped edge has a richness that isn't obtainable with any other material. It even feels good to the touch.

One concession that has to be made when using roped tape is that it must be the top layer. If you have used wrapped tongue patches around the corners of the sails, the rope and its tape will be applied over the patches, as shown here, but it still looks good.

Triangles and circular patches aren't affected by roped tape, since they are always placed under some type of hem or edging. If you know the sail will be roped using this technique, tongue-shaped patches could be applied in a similar manner, saving some time.

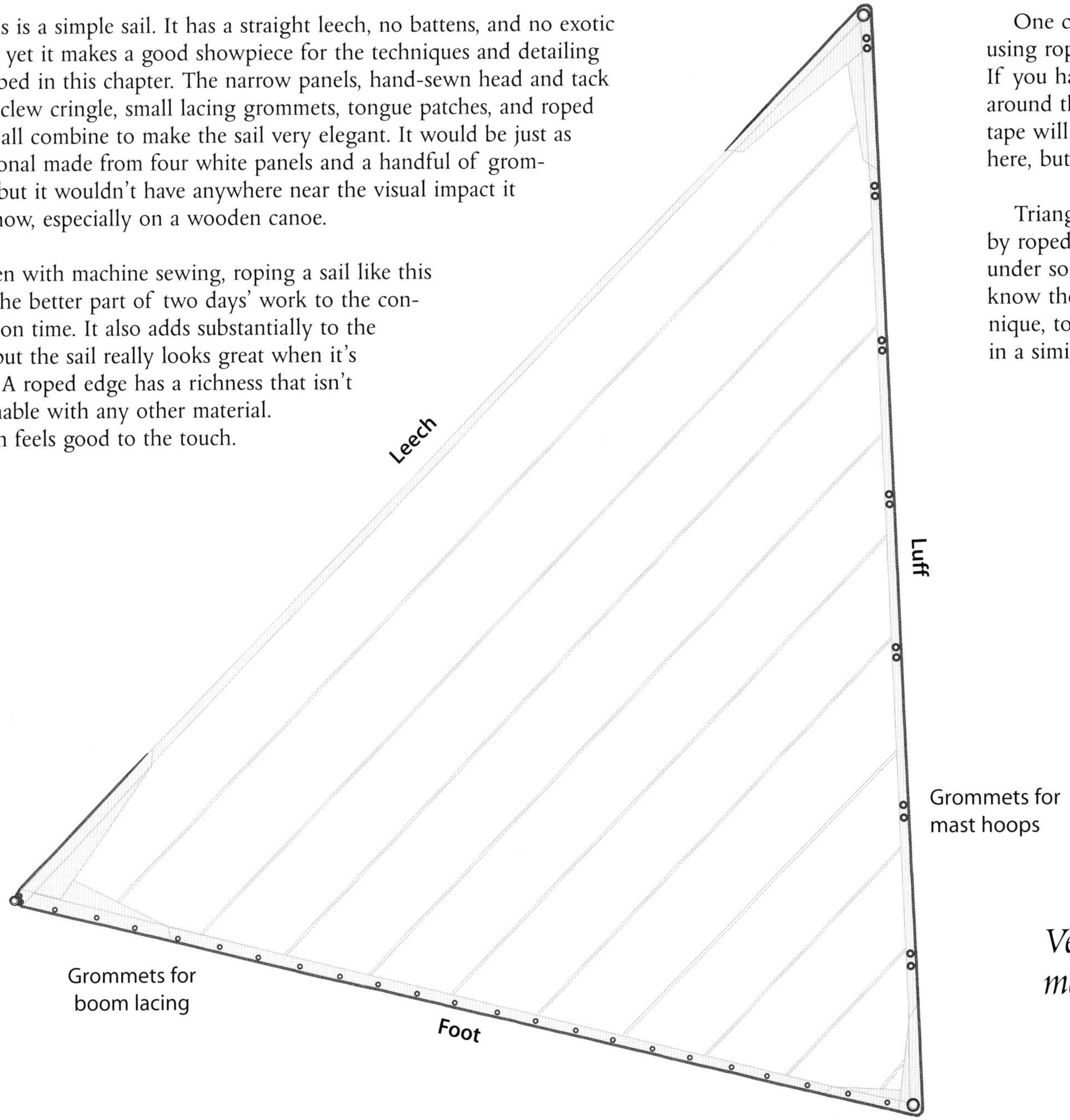

Leech

Luff

Grommets for
mast hoops

Grommets for
boom lacing

Foot

*Vertical cut with
machine-sewn roped edges*

Leech Battens

Battens for canoe sails fall into two categories: leech battens, the short battens that are used to support a small roach; and full-length battens that run from the luff to the leech, such as those on a bat-wing sail or a Chinese-style lugsail. In either case, wood is the logical material for making them.

Leech battens fit into cloth pockets sewn to the sail perpendicular to the leech. There are several different styles of pockets with differing methods of retaining the batten. Some pockets are open ended, requiring a couple of hand stitches to lock the batten in place; others use flaps, openings along the side of the batten, or internal elastic to keep the batten in the pocket. Your sailmaker may have one particular style that he prefers, but any of them will work fine.

The leech batten should be around three times as long as the amount of roach that it must support (3-inch roach: 9-inch batten). A typical canoe sail might have as few as two or as may as four battens. Three, spaced evenly at 25, 50, and 75 percent of the height of the leech above the boom, would be normal.

Batten width and thickness vary, but a wooden batten 1 to 1½ inches wide and ⅛ to 3⁄16 inch thick will work for most applications. The thickness can be uniform or taper toward the inboard end for better sail shape. Thinning the inner end will allow the batten to flex more, conforming better to the curve of the sail. I don't recommend going much below ⅛ inch thick anywhere on a wooden batten, because it raises the potential for warping and splitting.

Leech battens can be made from ash, spruce, pine, cedar, basswood, or almost anything you have available. Smooth all edges carefully to prevent them from wearing holes in the pockets or the sail, and varnish them well. Raw wood, if it gets wet, will become moldy, as will the inside of the batten pocket. Varnishing the battens and carefully drying wet sails will prevent unsightly mold spots.

Internal, Full-Length Battens

Full-length battens can be contained in long batten pockets that cross the entire sail, or they can be mounted externally and laced or tied to the sail. For pocket-mounted full battens, you may want to go as thick as ¼ or 5⁄16 inch on the leech end. A 1¼-by-¼-inch ash batten that tapers on the luff end to 1¼ inches by ⅛ inch will generally have enough stiffness to support a big roach, yet enough softness to allow the sail to form a curved airfoil.

Most full-length batten pockets are open at the leech end and have grommets on the pocket and on the leech of the sail that correspond to a hole bored through the end of the batten. A small tie keeps the batten in place and allows the adjustment of compression tension on the batten, giving it a bit of bend. The inner, luff end of the pocket should be reinforced with fabric patches or leather to keep the batten from poking through.

You won't need very much tension on the battens if they are a good match for the sail. If they are too thick and stiff, and your sail is as flat as a board, thin out the battens rather than force a lot of bend into them with the batten ties. Your sail will last longer that way.

Strips of straight-grained ash are the best choice for full-length battens. They should protrude about an inch from the leech end of the pockets, and all edges should be carefully smoothed. Cutting or sanding a consistent taper on a 5-foot-long batten can be tricky, but mostly it just takes time and a good eye. I use a stationary belt sander (moving the batten, not the sander, of course) and then push the luff end of the batten against a wall (pushing from the leech end) to flex the batten and check for stiffness and airfoil shape.

Here again, sealing the batten well with varnish will protect both the batten and the sail. Ash tends to become stained deeply in the grain with a nasty black mold or fungus if it isn't well protected. You don't want that stuff on either your battens or your sail.

External, Full-Length Battens

I really like external full battens on canoe sails. Though any of the sails that use them could also be built with pockets, varnished wooden battens, laced to both sides of a bat-wing or battened-lug, have a very unusual and distinctive look.

The battens are placed either where sections of the sail are joined or over protective strips of fabric sewn to the sail. This prevents sail abrasion and provides enough fabric thickness to support the lacing grommets. The inboard end of the battens can fit into short leather or fabric pockets near the luff, or can be secured with lacing holes drilled through their ends and laced through additional grommets. On bat-wings, I like the idea of lacing the forward end of the battens through the same luff grommets that are used for attaching mast hoops or for luff lacing.

External battens are used in pairs, with one on each side of the sail. Traditionally, one batten of a pair is thicker than the other, the thinner one being there more for completing the sandwich than for shaping the sail. Since two are being used where normally there would be one, the thickness of both could possibly be reduced somewhat to keep the assembly from being too stiff.

The thin "keeper batten" could probably be ⅛ inch thick for its full length. For the heavier batten, I suggest starting about ³/₁₆ or ¼ inch thick at the leech and tapering to ⅛ inch at the luff. Stiffness is required to support a big bat-wing roach, but we don't want to add unnecessary weight. I might even sail the canoe a couple of times to check performance before varnishing the battens; pare them down if you determine it is necessary, then varnish.

External battens can be laced on with spiral or continuous lacing, or tied with individual ties, which may be more convenient. The panel-seam/batten intersections are the logical place to put lacing grommets, one just above the batten, one just below it. The arrangement looks better than random spacing, and the seam gives us another layer of cloth for strength.

If you want something other than straight-sided slabs for external battens, shape the battens by tapering the width at the ends. Remember, the leech end should be stiff. If you want to taper it for appearance, you may have make it thick for stiffness.

Batten Types and Installations

Typical wooden leech batten

Luff end

Straight stitching on cotton, zigzag on Dacron

Opening on top side for batten

① One type of simple, traditional leech batten pocket

② Full-length batten in pocket — Leather chafe patch on luff end

Leech hem

Luff tape

Hoop grommets

③ External full-length batten with mate on back side

A short leather or fabric pocket will also work at the luff

Cross-section of external double-batten installation

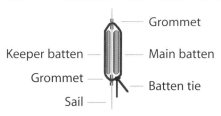

Grommet

Keeper batten — Main batten

Grommet — Batten tie

Sail

Sources for Sails

Some sailmakers might resist making a sail like those shown in this book. They might not be interested in spending so much time on something so small, or they might not be set up (or trained) to do some of the hand sewing required. Most will think my roping technique is an incredible waste of their time. You might try approaching them in the winter, when most of us will do almost anything (even write books) to make some money.

The few professional sailmakers who specialize in traditional sails will understand my point of view, and though they may have different ways of doing some things, they should be able to build you a fine sail. They realize that part of what makes traditional sails special is their appearance and detailing. They are used to building sails the way you will want yours built. For the names and addresses of traditional sailmakers, look in magazines specializing in traditional boats, such as *WoodenBoat*, *Wooden Canoe*, and *Classic Boat*.

Really choice canoe sails with a lot of elegant trim are as expensive per square foot as the ultra-modern, top-secret, racing sails used by the *America's Cup* contenders. Luckily, our sails are much smaller than theirs, so the total price is, too. One of the things that I enjoy most about canoe-sail building is that the detailing and trim can be rather extravagant without the price getting crazy. Yes, these little sails can be very expensive, but a fancy canoe sail usually costs less than a very plain jib for the typical 25-foot recreational sailboat.

I also enjoy the variety. When canoe makers approach me about making quantities of sails for their canoes, I say no. Making a stack of sails, each one the same, is boring. Making a custom sail is not. That a sail is different from the next is what drives me to build it in the first place—I want to see what it will look like and how it will work. Most traditional sailmakers share that enthusiasm and have little tolerance for the production of two-hour quickies.

Textbooks on Sailmaking

As I mentioned earlier, I can't teach you how to build sails in one chapter. We have looked primarily at the things that can be done differently to produce sails for traditional canoes. If you want a better understanding of sailmaking and traditional techniques, there are two books that are well worth your time and money.

The first is *The Mainsail Manual*, by Jim Grant, founder of Sailrite, the leading supplier of sailmaking supplies, sewing machines modified for sailmaking, precut sail kits, and correspondence courses that turn regular folks into sailmakers. *The Mainsail Manual* is part of a series devoted to the design and construction of various types of sails. It is a fairly small book, and in many ways it reduces sail design to tape-measure and calculator work.

Though *The Mainsail Manual* also deals with the other aspects of sailmaking, I think its greatest strength is the simple way that it lays out the design process. If you're not sure how much foot-round to add, it will give you a formula and explain both how it works and why.

If you want to build a spinnaker, Jim Grant has another small manual for that, *The Spinnaker Manual*. Years ago I built a spinnaker over a weekend on my kitchen floor, using the book as a guide. It has the same well-written understandability of *The Mainsail Manual*.

If you plan to build sails without turning pro and setting up a bunch of wholesale accounts, you are bound to end up dealing with Sailrite and the Grant family. They've been selling sailmaking information and supplies to amateurs for a long time and show no signs of slowing down.

Sailrite, 305 W. VanBuren St., P.O. 987, Columbia City, IN 46725; telephone (219) 244-6715 and (800) 348-2769.

Sails Built from Kits

The Sailmaker's Apprentice, written by Emiliano Marino and illustrated by Christine Erikson, is your other principal textbook. Published in 1994 by International Marine, it is available in bookstores.

The Sailmaker's Apprentice has done more to preserve the art of traditional sailmaking than all other books combined. It takes you through all the intricate sewing and construction techniques—hand-roping, ring sewing, cringle making, thread weights, needles, sewing machines, and much more. It's like a museum in a book—with instructions.

Marino believes that sails should be built to last, a refreshing approach when compared to some of the products that are being shipped from many modern sail factories. Christine Erikson's drawings are wonderfully clear, showing you, stitch by stitch, how things are supposed to be done. Those of us who draw by clicking a mouse and bending lines envy people who can draw with their hands.

The Sailmaker's Apprentice is not cheap, but it's nearly 500 pages long and never gets tedious or boring. If you are truly interested in building authentic, traditional sails and learning the hand work that has always been a part of them, you will find it to be one of your most important tools.

There are other good sailmaking books on the market, many of them containing more scientific data on wind flow, drag coefficients, and other technical material, but starting with Grant's *The Mainsail Manual* and Marino's *The Sailmaker's Apprentice*, you should be able to handle any of the technical problems encountered while building sails for your canoe. Just don't expect to stop building after one sail. Sailmaking is addictive (I should know: Addiction Sailmakers); there is always something you want to try…on the next sail.

It is possible to have custom sails supplied to you in kit form and designed to be as traditional as the sails in this book. You sew the seams, but the design work and fabric cutting are done by a computer plotter. Working from dimensions and parameters that you supply by providing some preliminary measurements, the manufacturer can assemble the kit with Egyptian or tanbark Dacron, and narrow, cross-cut, or vertical panels.

The corner patches and other reinforcement will be made from scrap fabric; hardware, like grommets, is included. The grommet and ring setters can be rented to complete the job, or they can be purchased if you have the feeling that you may want to build more sails later.

The kit will arrive as a roll of numbered, precut panels with seaming lines marked on them. Seam-basting tape, instructions, and even the thread are included. A good home sewing machine should be able to do all the sewing on a canoe-sized sail.

By sewing your own sail, you will probably save 30 to 50 percent of what it would cost to have a sailmaker build it. Sailrite is the major supplier of kit sails in the U.S.A. Other kit suppliers come and go from time to time and usually advertise their products in the sailing magazines; check the classified and small display ads.

How good are kit sails? Sailrite's plotter system and the computer that runs it cost over $100,000. For that kind of money, you get accuracy. When I build intricate, radially cut sailboat sails from modern, and very expensive laminated fabrics, I rent time on Sailrite's plotter. The computer saves me a lot of calculator work, and the plotter cuts a much cleaner line than I can with a pair of scissors.

The workmanship on a kit sail is up to you. If you take your time, your sail will be something to be proud of. So will your second…and third…and….

Chapter Twelve

Running Rigging

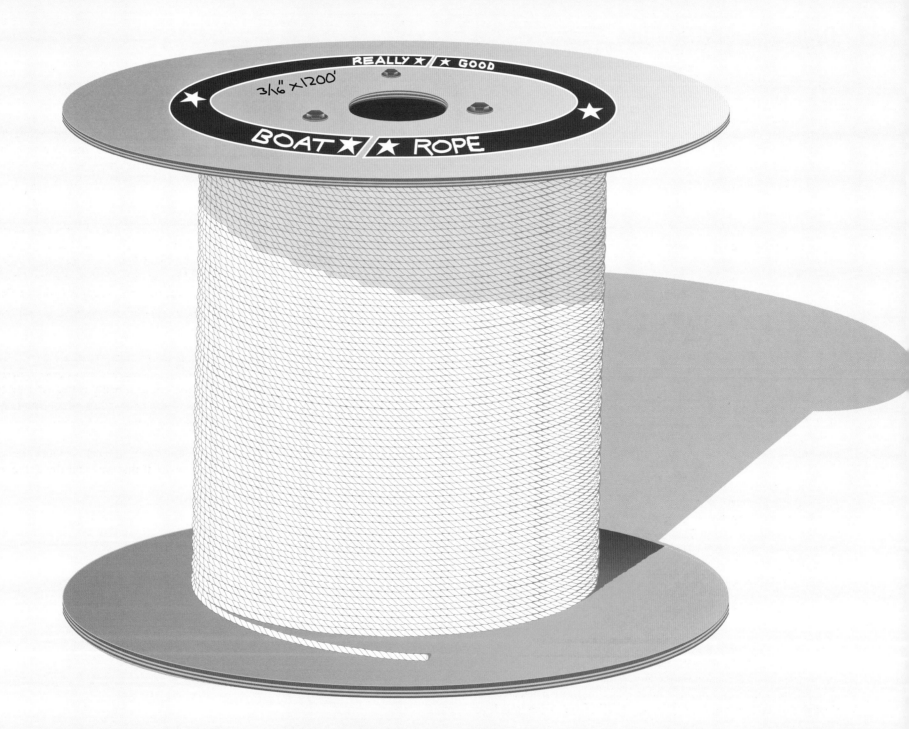

Rope and Lacing Line

Running rigging is a term used to describe the lines, wires, and supporting hardware that are frequently adjusted while a boat is sailing. The halyards that raise and lower the sails, the sheets that control and trim the sails, and the blocks and cleats that the halyards and sheets run to and through, all fit in this category. For our purposes, we will also add sail-to-spar lacing lines to this chapter, even though they are usually set once and left alone.

The best choice for rope used in running rigging is polyester. Three-strand construction is the most authentic but not always the most practical, as it has a tendency to "hockle," or kink, when pulled through blocks at high speed. For a halyard, this usually isn't a serious problem, but for a mainsheet it can be. Having the sheet knot-up at the mainsheet block when you need to ease the sail to stay upright has obvious drawbacks.

Three-strand is also less kind to your hands than other types of rope. I would use it for halyards but would be inclined to use something else for a mainsheet.

A good choice for the mainsheet is twelve-strand yacht braid, which is quite soft to the touch, bordering on limp, and resistant to jamming in the blocks. If you plan on splicing any eyes in your lines, a splice in braided line is more complex than three-strand, but it can be done. Alternately, an eye can be seized with sail twine instead of being spliced.

Most modern yacht braid is built using "kernmantel" construction in which a woven sheath surrounds a separate core. On normal rope, the core is braided. Ropes having reduced stretch are made with cores that have little or no braiding. The more up-and-down weaving or braiding you build into the core, the more slack you incorporate and the more it can stretch. Some of the new high-tech no-stretch ropes use Kevlar, Spectra, Technora, or Vectran fibers in the core and are sheathed on the outside with polyester. They make great halyards but are a bit high-tech for an old sailing canoe; in addition, they are very expensive.

Ropes of any construction that are intended for hand-held control lines have soft, fuzzy surfaces. This makes them easy to grip and easier on the hands, which is important on tender boats such as canoes, because at least one hand is holding the mainsheet. (It isn't particularly wise to cleat the sheet and forget about it, as a puff of wind can knock you over before you have time to uncleat the sheet and ease the sail.)

Most of these ropes are only available in—you guessed it—bright white. Many have little colored specks woven in as well. If an authentically traditional color scheme is of concern to you, they can be stained, just as we stained the sail-roping in the last chapter. Any shade of tan or brown will be more historically accurate than white. Rinse the rope very well to keep it from getting stiff.

Nothing looks more unseamanlike on a boat than lines that are too big in diameter for their jobs. Try to keep halyards and small control lines in the 3/16-to-1/4-inch range, and hand-held lines, such as sheets, no more than 3/8 inch in diameter. Sail lacing should be 1/8 inch and can be of twine (twisted) or kernmantle construction, which is easier to find. Polyester "leech line," used inside the leech hems on large sails, works pretty well and takes stain.

I like to stain lacing line dark brown with walnut stain. I just like the look of it. There is currently a dark polyester twine available called "tarred marline." It has a good color, but as it really is treated with tar, it is a little sticky. I would worry about the tar coming off on the sail, and if it did, it would be very difficult to remove.

Lacing is the first step in rigging the sails in a canoe. Once the sails are laced to the spars, they are usually left that way and the entire works is transported as a unit.

Bending Sail

Dacron sails don't require the long breaking-in period that cotton sails do, but it is a good idea to start them out in light to moderate winds. Sails with lots of panel seams and grommets will take a while for all the parts to really start working as one unit. As they do, the seams and edges will generally smooth out to the sail's final shape. Light winds are also better for getting used to controlling your canoe under sail power and working out any bugs in the leeboard and steering systems.

To attach the sail to the spars, first attach the corners to their respective fittings and stretch the edges just enough to pull out the wrinkles. Now you are ready to lace the edges to the spars.

WARNING: Pulling a piece of lacing line through the grommets and up against the fabric at high speed can actually MELT Dacron. Lace slowly and carefully.

Spiral lacing is the simplest way to attach the sail (it's also the easiest to draw, which is why I use it in most of the drawings of rigs in this book), but there are other possibilities as well.

Robands are simply short, independent pieces of line that pass through a single grommet and around the spar, and are tied with a square knot. Each grommet has its own roband. Being separate from each other, robands are infinitely adjustable and immune to any kind of group failure should the line break.

Marling hitching is a continuous-line lacing similar to spiral lacing; the extra friction where the line crosses itself may help to keep the sail-to-spar distance more uniform and less prone to migration.

In any case we want the edge of the sail close to, but not smashed up against the spar. The lacing should be fairly loose at first, as you will often be lacing a curved sail edge to a straight spar. It is easy to loosely lace an entire side and then go back later to even out the spar-to-sail distance.

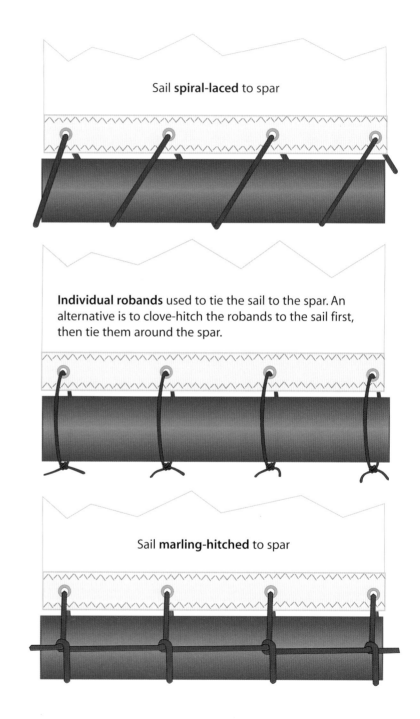

Sail **spiral-laced** to spar

Individual robands used to tie the sail to the spar. An alternative is to clove-hitch the robands to the sail first, then tie them around the spar.

Sail **marling-hitched** to spar

Halyards

Halyard systems are quite simple on canoes. For the halyard itself, I prefer the traditional look of stained three-strand polyester, with a diameter of ³⁄₁₆ or ¼ inch. Three-strand will stretch more than the newer braided constructions, but halyards are very visible, so the older style looks better. On most rigs, a little extra halyard stretch isn't a major problem. It is, however, a concern for peak halyards on gaff sails. The ability to firmly peak up the gaff makes the boat point better. If three-strand doesn't seem to perform well, the halyard can be replaced with a modern low-stretch yacht braid.

The halyards on most canoe rigs are cleated to small horned cleats screwed to the sides of the mast, just above the mast thwart. The cleats can be carved from wood, cast from metal, or made with a sheet-metal horned plate on a wooden or metal spacer. If it's possible, I prefer to cleat the halyards to the thwart. Then, if the boat goes over, the halyard tension will help keep the mast in place, whereas if the halyard is cleated to the mast, the whole rig could fall out. This is one reason why I like the idea of using belaying pins, set through holes in the seat frame or mast thwart (see page 130).

An alternative is to position a fairlead (see page 182) on top of the thwart next to the mast hole. The halyard could then be routed through the fairlead and off to a cleat on the thwart, or even tied to the gunwale. The halyard would still be exerting downward pressure on the mast to keep it in the boat in the event of a capsize.

At the masthead, the only fitting usually required for the halyard is a dumb sheave (page 106) or a small block. If you wish, a shackle can be spliced to the halyard for attaching it to the sail, but it really isn't needed. A bowline tied to the head grommet will work fine. Most canoe rigs are so short that you could splice the halyard directly to the sail and reach up and thread it through the masthead while rigging the boat. For longer masts, the boat could be rolled slightly until you can reach the top of the mast and reeve the halyard.

On lateens, lugs, and other sails where the halyard is tied to a yard, rather than the sail, it is actually better to leave the halyard attached to the yard and thread it through the mast when rigging the canoe.

The knot that joins the halyard to the yard is an important one. You don't want it to slip, so take the time to tie it correctly before you get underway. A clove hitch, rolling hitch, or topsail halyard bend will all work. We've had the same rolling hitch on the yard of our Sunfish for about twenty years, and it hasn't moved yet. I find the clove hitch more prone to slipping; the other two knots use more turns around the spar and seem to grip better.

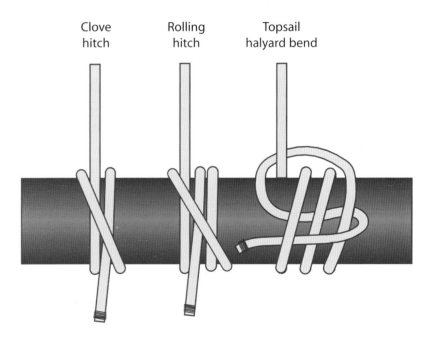

Knots for attaching halyards to spars

Blocks

Blocks are the pulleys used to route lines and/or create mechanical advantage for raising sails and trimming the mainsheet. There are single blocks, double blocks, triples, fiddles, and a host of other configurations available. Since we are dealing with small sails, there is generally little need for high-powered, multi-purchase tackle systems on a canoe. In fact, for the average sailing canoe, you could tie the yard or sail directly to the masthead, attach a piece of line to the boom for a mainsheet, and sail away without a problem.

A few blocks added to the system do have a tendency to make life easier, though, but finding suitable traditional-looking blocks in a small size can be a somewhat annoying challenge. The vast majority of what is available is too modern and looks it.

The sailboat block market is dominated by ball-bearing-equipped blocks made by or based on those developed by the Harken brothers of Pewaukee, Wisconsin. The modern block is a marvelous thing, but just doesn't look good on a traditional sailboat or canoe.

Some hardware stores sell small cast-metal blocks—better call them pulleys—with brass sheaves. They are reasonably traditional looking, inexpensive, and strong enough for the job. If I didn't recognize them as pulleys, not blocks, and know their source, I would probably find them acceptable. If you polish them up and mount them elegantly, I won't tell anybody where you got them.

There are some absolutely beautiful bronze blocks being built for classic boats, and some of them are small enough to work on a sailing canoe. Be glad that you're looking for the little ones, because these little gems are priced as if they were. Some manufacturers are making them with modern ball-bearing sheaves inside a traditional bronze shell for the best of both worlds. Check the boating magazines for sources. Once you get over the sticker shock, you will find that the blocks are great and will outlast your canoe.

The most interesting option is to build your own wood-shelled blocks. I've seen plans for them in several books on traditional rigging and boat-building. They can be made from small chunks of any fairly dense hardwood—ash, lignum vitae, teak, walnut, rosewood, or whatever you can find. The sheaves can be wooden, bronze, or even the brass sheaves surgically removed from those inexpensive hardware-store pulleys.

Wood-shelled blocks can be stropped with metal or a rope becket set in grooves carved in the cheeks. Essentially, the becket is just a rope grommet that has been tightly seized to the block. A metal axle for the sheave and sometimes a couple of small plates to cover ends of the axle are the only other major components required.

At one time I came up with a scheme to make "penny blocks," small wooden blocks with polished pennies tacked over the ends of the axles for cover plates. I haven't gotten around to it yet, which is probably why I'm not in prison for defacing American currency. On the other hand, how much time can you get for drilling holes in pennies? I guess to avoid legal problems, Americans should use Canadian coins and Canadians should use American.

Penny cover plates or not, I urge you to try making your own wooden blocks. Doing so is rather enjoyable and only moderately difficult. Of all the block options, a carefully built wooden block, finished with oil, is the least expensive and the most attractive.

Assorted Blocks

Modern Harken blocks with ball-bearing sheaves—they work great but look as if they were made last week.

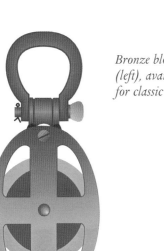

Bronze block (below) and bronze cage block (left), available from suppliers of hardware for classic boats—beautiful but pricey.

Penny Blocks

Pins

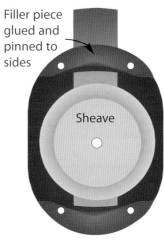

Filler piece glued and pinned to sides

Sheave

Axle cover plate

Axle

Guess who?

Top view

Groove on inside for strap

Inside

Bronze strap

Pin holes

Outside

More Blocks

This bronze block is attached to a gaff bridle saddle and connects the peak halyard to a simple bridle fixed to the gaff. The saddle is free to move along the bridle and distributes halyard tension on the bridle for an even pull.

Here is a bullet block seized inside a rope grommet. The loop can go over a boom or masthead and can be held in position with a thumb cleat.

Sheet Horses, Travelers, and Vangs...oh my

Those who aren't yet sailors are probably wondering what in tarnation I'm talking about. Sheet horse, traveler, vang—all three basically perform the same function but in somewhat different ways. They are sail-shaping devices, and though not critical for a sailing canoe, they can be helpful when sailing downwind.

As you change headings and begin a broad reach or a run, sailing off the wind, the first thing to do is to ease out the sail, sometimes quite far. Your boom may even be perpendicular to the keel line on a run. As the sail is let out, the mainsheet controls its angle to the wind and the keel line, but the sheet starts to lose its ability to keep the boom level.

The wind hitting the sail tends to lift the outboard end of the boom, creating a big bag in the middle of the sail, twisting the top of the sail to leeward, and spilling wind—and power. What is needed is a way to let the sail swing out to the proper angle in relation to the direction of the wind, but still maintain its shape by keeping the boom down and the top section from twisting. With those two problems corrected, the middle of the sail will take care of itself, and we will have good sail shape from top to bottom.

The same sail-shape problem can arise when reaching or sailing close-hauled, though it is not as severe or as obvious. Any time the sail is eased, whether it's done due to a change of heading or just to de-power the rig a bit, the top will twist off to leeward; the only way to bring it back in line is to trim in the mainsheet.

If it's windy and you are getting overpowered, letting the top of the sail fall off will help you control the boat. The twist reduces pressure on the sail, which reduces the heeling force that the sail is exerting on the canoe and you—the ballast. There are times, though, when you are sailing, comfortably in control, and you want the entire sail to be working for maximum speed whenever possible. A traveler or a sheet horse can help, but only to a limited extent.

Rope Travelers

At the after end of the canoe, the mainsheet is usually tied off to a painter ring mounted on the stern deck, or run through a hole in the deck and ending with a stopper knot. From there, the sheet goes up to and along the boom.

The only time a mainsheet can exert direct, downward pressure on the after end of the boom, and thus the sail, is when it is trimmed in so tightly that the boom is parallel to the keel, or centerline. On a canoe, such a situation is rare. Trimming in the sail that much will usually stall the airflow, creating considerable heeling force and little lift for pulling the boat forward.

Travelers and sheet horses are systems that allow the after termination point of the mainsheet to move athwartships, or side-to-side, as the boat maneuvers. Moving the termination point to leeward allows us to exert a bit more downward pressure on the boom and therefore reduce sail-top twist when the boom is not centered.

The most common traveler on a small, simple rig is a slightly slack piece of line. On a canoe, the ends of the line are tied to each gunwale, crossing the boat in the vicinity of the stern seat. The after end of the mainsheet has a small block or ring spliced into it that can move side-to-side along the rope traveler. Since a canoe is quite narrow, this arrangement might only allow the mainsheet to move 8 to 10 inches out from the centerline, but there are times when even such a small amount can improve sail shape.

A rope traveler is also a convenient way to anchor the mainsheet to the stern of a boat that has no stern painter ring when the owner doesn't want to drill a hole in the after deck. The traveler rope can be tied to the seat frame, the ends of a thwart, or through slotted gunwales without having to drill any holes in the boat. This convenience alone can sometimes make a rope traveler worth incorporating into your rig.

Sheet Horses

A sheet horse does the same job as a rope traveler, but uses a metal rod across the boat instead of a rope. It is usually bent into an upside-down-U shape and anchored by flanges attached to the gunwale on either side or to the decking on a decked boat. The end of the mainsheet is fixed to a block or saddle that slides or rolls along the rod.

A sheet horse could be used on an open boat, but it would be rare. Other than adding another bit of polished bronze to the rig, it won't have any real advantage over a rope traveler, which costs only pennies.

For a decked sailing canoe with a fancy fan centerboard and other luxury gizmos, a bronze horse built from polished ¼-inch rod with decorative flanges, might be a nice touch. Remember that during its golden years, canoe sailing was often a formal social experience. When was the last time you saw a man in a coat and tie and a woman in a long dress launching their canoe at your favorite put-in?

In the old days, I'm sure there was a little healthy rivalry to see whose boat was the best appointed as well as the fastest. A bronze sheet horse would do the job and in a very classy manner, even though it certainly wouldn't be required for performance.

Despite their complex descriptions and functions, travelers and sheet horses are simple devices that may sometimes improve the shape of your sails. A rope traveler in particular may be the easiest way possible for terminating the after end of the mainsheet. It requires no fittings or holes in the gunwales or the stern deck, as it is simply tied to the canoe.

By allowing the anchored end of the mainsheet to move from side to side, the sheet will have more downward pull on the boom, reducing sail twist.

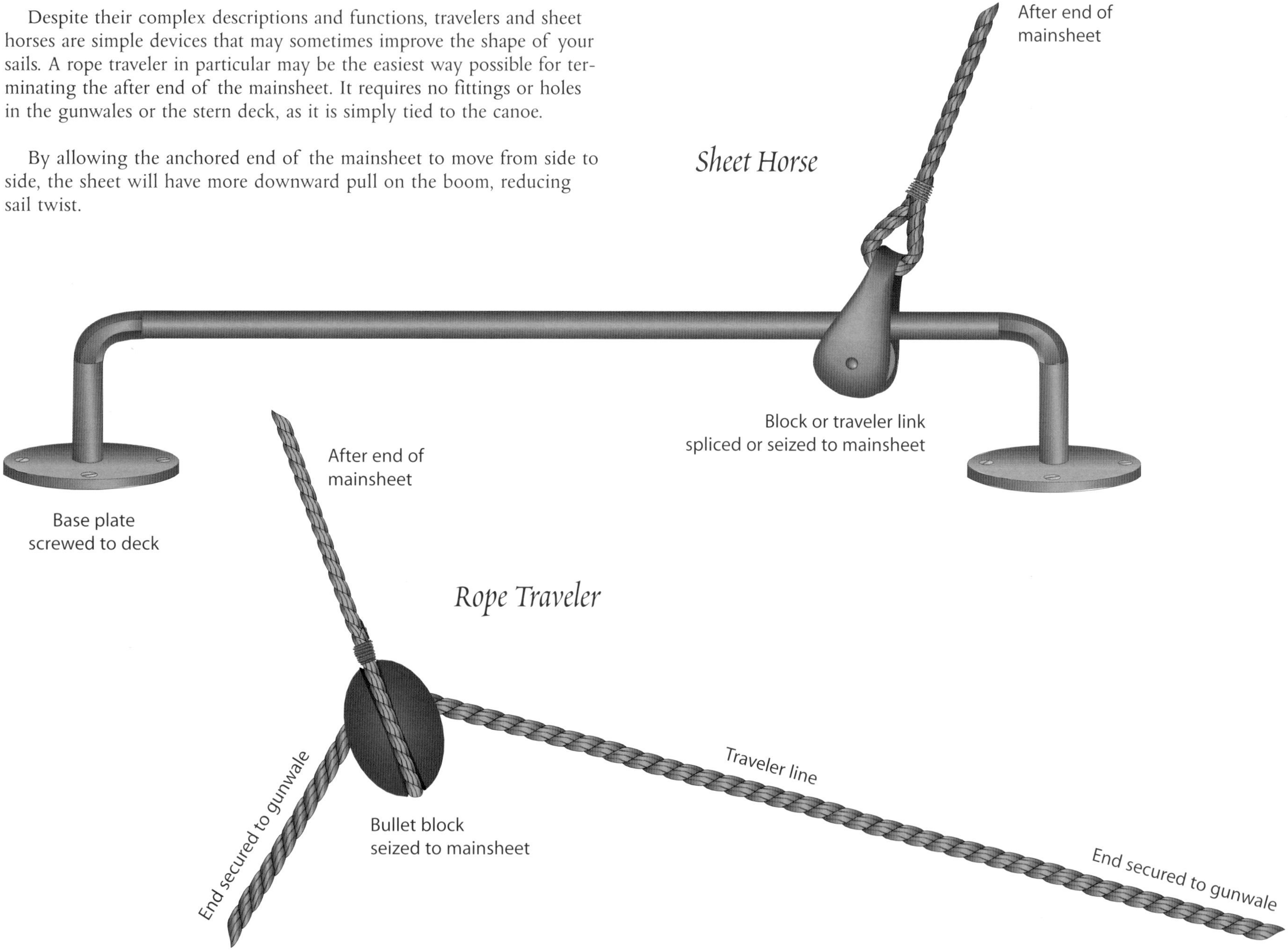

After end of
mainsheet

Sheet Horse

Block or traveler link
spliced or seized to mainsheet

Base plate
screwed to deck

After end of
mainsheet

Rope Traveler

Bullet block
seized to mainsheet

End secured to gunwale

Traveler line

End secured to gunwale

The Boom Vang

Despite its unusual name, a vang can be a very handy device. In short, it is a small block-and-tackle system, the lower end of which is attached to the mast near the deck; on an open boat, it is attached just above the intersection of the mast and the mast thwart or seat. The upper end of the system is attached to the boom, about a foot aft of its junction with the mast. Near one of the end of the vang (usually the lower) there is a cleat for setting the vang tension.

As the boom vang is tightened, it pulls down on the boom. Though the vang is attached near the forward end of the boom, the tension it exerts is used to control the after end of it. When the sail is eased out to the side on a reach or a run, and the mainsheet can only control the angle of the sail to the wind, the vang is very effective in keeping the after end of the boom from lifting. Even though the boom may be hanging way out to the side, the vang will keep it down; this, in turn, will prevent the top of the sail from twisting to leeward and spilling wind.

By playing with the vang while sailing, you can actually watch the top of the sail move as you adjust vang tension. The old rule of thumb for sailors is to apply enough vang to keep the top mainsail batten parallel to the boom. Since many canoe sails don't have any battens, you may have to use your imagination.

As you turn and head upwind, the sail is trimmed in and the mainsheet will start to take over the duties of the vang. On a close reach or when sailing close-hauled, the vang won't be needed, and all downward pressure on the boom and sail can be applied by the mainsheet and, if you have one, the traveler.

Thousands of canoes have sailed for years without a vang, traveler, or sheet horse. You don't need any of them for successful sailing, but they can be helpful at times, especially if you are trying to squeeze every last ounce of forward drive out of your sails.

A Simple Boom Vang

with a three-to-one mechanical purchase

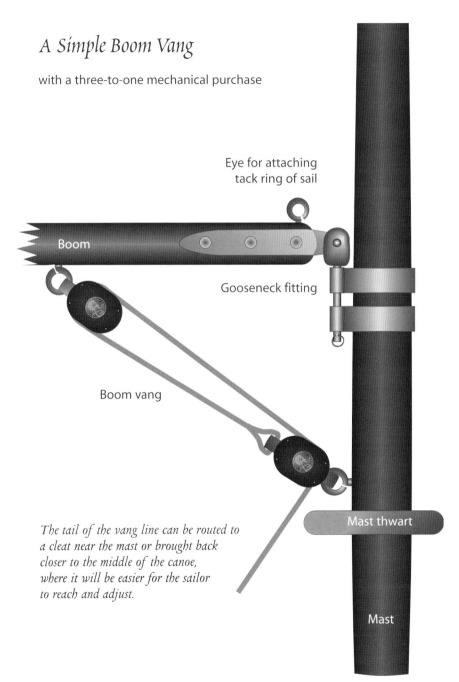

Eye for attaching tack ring of sail

Boom

Gooseneck fitting

Boom vang

Mast thwart

The tail of the vang line can be routed to a cleat near the mast or brought back closer to the middle of the canoe, where it will be easier for the sailor to reach and adjust.

Mast

Mainsheet Systems

As I mentioned earlier, the mainsheet for a sailing canoe can be as simple as a 10-foot piece of line tied to the boom and held by hand. In some ways, it's the ultimate in quick-release sail-handling systems. All you have to do is let go, and the boat will pop back to upright and stop.

In spite of its ability to quickly depower the rig, this form of sail control does have a few drawbacks that make it less than ideal. Though easy to release completely, a piece of line is not so easy to release partially without producing rope burns. I also find the fact that the sail trim will change every time you move your arm to be a bit tedious. Furthermore, for the mainsheet to be easily reached and convenient for the sailor, who is positioned in the center of the canoe, the mainsheet must be tied at or near the middle of the boom. Applying mainsheet loads at that point encourages the boom to bend. As we can't get away from spar bend, it isn't wise to do anything that might contribute to it unnecessarily.

A better option, one that provides mechanical advantage, is to fix blocks to the boom and run the mainsheet through them and along the boom. This is the most common type of system. It's easier on your hands, and when properly placed near the ends of the boom, the blocks minimize bend. Here's how it is arranged, starting at the stern:

The after end of the mainsheet is fixed to a thwart, the after deck, or a traveler or sheet-horse assembly. It runs, first, up to a block hanging just under the boom, near its after end. From this block, the sheet heads forward along the underside of the boom to a second hanging block at the forward end of the boom. At this point, there are two options for leading the sheet.

Some sailors end the mechanical system at that point. The loose end of the mainsheet dangles from the forward boom block; the sail is trimmed by pulling in on the sheet and eased by letting out on it. Since the blocks are mounted near the forward and after ends of the boom, the sheet tension is less likely to cause the boom to bend. It is a definite improvement over the line tied directly to the boom.

My biggest complaint with this improved system is my aversion to mainsheet systems that are trying to lift me out of the boat, which is what is happening when the wind is blowing hard and there is a lot of upward and outward pull on the sheet.

If we add another block, this one anchored low on the after side of the mast or, better yet, on the mast thwart or even the mast step, we can run the sheet along the boom as before but then drop it down to deck level or below. The block on the thwart will route the mainsheet straight back to the sailor, who now pulls back to trim, not down. High loads may be trying to pull you forward in the boat, but not out of it.

This arrangement also allows us to mount a cleat or friction-creating device to take some of the strain off our hands. But a narrow sailing canoe is not what would normally be considered a "cleat it and forget it" sailboat. The ability to instantly release the mainsheet can be what keeps you from capsizing on windy days, so it's often wiser to hold the tail of the sheet in your hand, rather than cleat it. Having the final block in the system level with or below the gunwales will make the job easier.

The system works well on sails having as much as 75 square feet of area. For more mechanical advantage, the after end of the sheet could be tied off to the after end of the boom and brought down to a block on the stern deck or the traveler, sent back up to the boom, and then routed forward and down as before. The drawbacks to this are that more line will have to be trimmed, and eased, for the boom to move the same amount, and since more blocks are involved, there are more opportunities for kinks to develop in the sheet that could jam in the blocks.

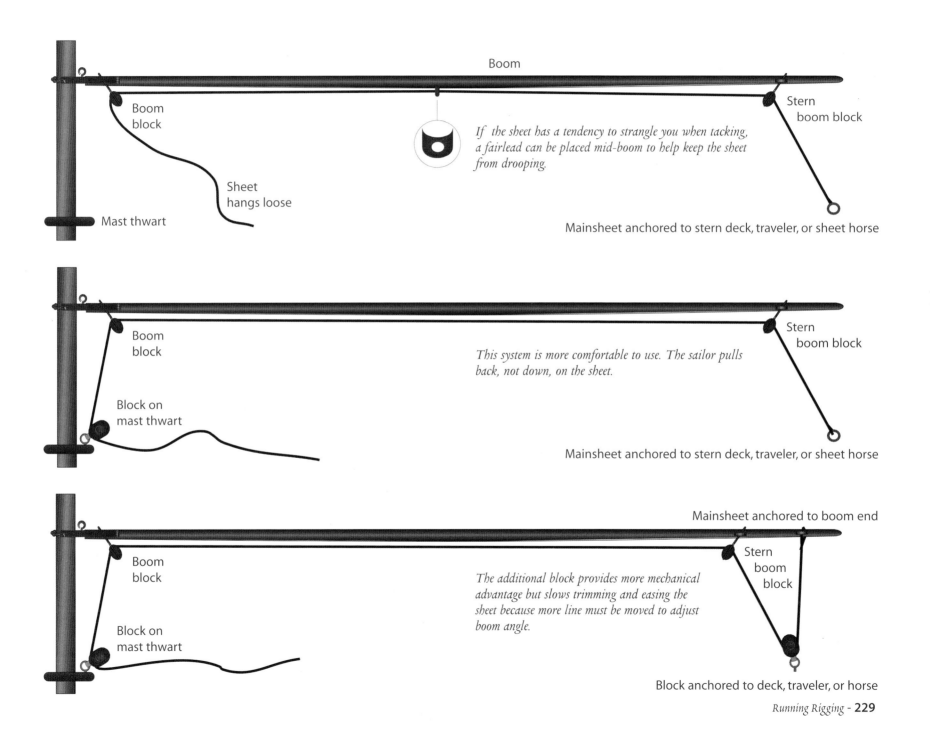

Boom

Boom
block

*If the sheet has a tendency to strangle you when tacking,
a fairlead can be placed mid-boom to help keep the sheet
from drooping.*

Stern
boom block

Sheet
hangs loose

Mast thwart

Mainsheet anchored to stern deck, traveler, or sheet horse

Boom
block

Stern
boom block

*This system is more comfortable to use. The sailor pulls
back, not down, on the sheet.*

Block on
mast thwart

Mainsheet anchored to stern deck, traveler, or sheet horse

Mainsheet anchored to boom end

Boom
block

Stern
boom
block

*The additional block provides more mechanical
advantage but slows trimming and easing the
sheet because more line must be moved to adjust
boom angle.*

Block on
mast thwart

Block anchored to deck, traveler, or horse

Luff Tension Adjustment

For best performance, the luff of the sail should be tightened for upwind sailing, pulling the draft forward by gathering in close to the mast the excess fabric that forms the luff curve. Tightening the luff is also a good way to de-power the sail on windy days.

For reaching and running in normal winds, more draft will power-up the rig for more speed. This can be accomplished by using just enough tension on the luff to pull the wrinkles out of it, and no more.

If your rig has a fixed gooseneck (see page 114) fitting joining the boom to the mast, halyard tension is the only adjustment available for changing luff tension. It is not practical to try to adjust the halyard every time you change headings, so you set it once when you raise the sail, making your best guess about the sailing conditions, and live with it.

A gooseneck that slides up and down on the mast, or a boom/mast connection using jaws on the boom, is easier to adjust for luff tension. Adding a downhaul—a short piece of line, connected to an eye on the bottom of the gooseneck or the boom jaws—is one way to do it. A small cleat is attached to the mast, below the boom; pulling or easing the downhaul and then cleating it allows luff tension to be adjusted without having to mess with the halyard.

An easier method, which often works better, is the self-tending system, mentioned in the chapter on spars. With the forward boom block mounted very close to the mast, as seen on page 229, the mainsheet tension will pull down on the forward end of the boom as the sheet tension increases and tighten the luff of the sail for upwind work. Easing the sheet for reaching and running will automatically ease luff tension.

In high winds, pressure on the sails and the increased mainsheet tension required to control them will keep the luff tight and de-power the rig for more control. This type of "no-system" downhaul is also common on dinghies and iceboats, and works very well.

Twin-Sail Sheeting

As you might imagine, sailing a twin-sailed rig can be a complex experience. A solo sailor will have two sheets to trim while steering and tending the leeboards—all while balancing the boat. This adds up to the best reason for first learning to sail a twin rig well in light air before venturing out on a windy day.

The sheeting systems for a second sail, such as a mizzen, are the same as those for a single-sail rig. The final block should lead the sheet forward to the sailor's position amidships. Since mizzens are often quite small and their shorter spars less likely to bend drastically, the mizzen sheet can often be tied to the boom, and run through a block on the stern deck and forward to the sailor, without the need for further mechanical advantage.

Trying to hand-hold and trim two sheets and steer the canoe at the same time is difficult, so the best option is usually to trim the mizzen and cleat it. This allows the sailor to steer with one hand and work the mainsheet with the other. Should the boat become overpowered, easing the mainsail without touching the mizzen will usually be enough to bring the boat back under control. Even if you let go of the mainsheet, the cleated mizzen will swing the stern around, the boat will come up into the wind, and the canoe will coast to a stop.

The mizzen can be left to tack and jibe itself. The only time it will need major adjustment will be during a drastic course change, such as going from a close-hauled course to a reach or run. At that time it would be reset and cleated for the new heading.

Mizzen trim will also affect helm balance and the feel of the steering system. You may find from experimentation that undertrimming or overtrimming the mizzen on certain headings makes the canoe handle better. You will also find that you can steer the boat largely by trimming the sails rather than using a heavy hand on the rudder.

Cleats

Several types of cleats can be used on a sailing canoe. Their functions can be divided into those for halyards and those for control lines.

The biggest obstacle you are likely to run into when selecting cleats is finding small ones. Another is that those you find will be plastic. Structurally and functionally, plastic cleats are fine, but if you're outfitting an old canoe, something made from metal or wood will be more appropriate.

The traditional horn cleat (page 232) is at its best for securing infrequently adjusted lines, such as halyards. A line figure-eighted around the horns isn't likely to slip. On the other hand, for frequently adjusted control lines, such as the main or mizzen sheets, a horned cleat would be dangerously slow to release in situations where avoiding capsize depended upon quickly easing the sail.

Some of the old canoe rigs I have worked on used horn cleats made from a piece of sheet brass screwed to the mast over a small brass or wooden spacer, which allows the line to pass under the horns. They are inexpensive and simple to build, and work fine for halyards. If desired, such cleats can also be carved from hardwood blocks.

The two types of cleats that work best for the mainsheet, mizzen sheet, and similar control lines are the cam cleat and the Clamcleat (page 233). They hold securely but release the line almost instantly for easing the sail quickly. Most sailors mount them on top of the leeboard bracket. If you think you may occasionally need to hike out to balance the canoe, it would be a good idea to mount the cleats on both sides of the bracket, near the gunwale. You should be able to reach them from a hiked-out position, which might not be easy if a single center-mounted cleat were used instead.

It's a good idea to keep the tail of the mainsheet in your hand at all times when sailing a canoe, even if the line is cleated. Not having to find it in an emergency may some day keep you from getting wet. On windy days, you may not feel comfortable cleating the sheet at all. Smooth boat handling means learning to uncleat the sheet and take over by hand before you get to the point where you have to ease the sail. Waiting until both sheet and cleat are under a lot of tension and then popping the sheet free usually results in rather jerky sailing.

Cam cleats have a flat baseplate and two spring-loaded, toothed cams that pinch the rope between them. They have been around for a long time. Though most are currently made from plastic or aluminum, the companies specializing in classic hardware build bronze reproductions of the older versions.

Cam cleats often have a built-in fairlead just ahead of the cams. For a sailing canoe, which may require cleats for the mainsheet on both the port and starboard sides, a cleat without a fairlead will probably work better.

Clamcleats are fairly recent. I don't recall seeing them on any boats built before about 1970. From a function standpoint, they are probably the most efficient way to cleat the sheets on a canoe. A Clamcleat has no moving parts. It is a small block of plastic or aluminum with a notched V-shaped groove molded into the top of it. The line is simply dragged into the groove, and the notches hold it there. The more the load on the sheet, the deeper the line is forced into the groove.

To release the line from the Clamcleat, the sailor simply tugs back on the sheet and lifts it out of the cleat. A cleat about 2 inches long and ¾ inch wide is strong enough to hold any canoe sheet and costs only a few dollars. One on each side of the leeboard bracket, aimed at the mainsheet block on the mast thwart, would be the lightest, simplest, and probably most effective solution to your cleating needs.

If you don't care for the modern appearance of the Clamcleat, some of the custom bronze casters can invest and burn out a plastic version, leaving a hollow mold, and cast one for you in bronze.

Easily Constructed Halyard Cleats

Here is a simple two-piece horn cleat for halyards. If mounted on the side of the mast, the bottom of the wooden base can be contoured to fit the curvature of the mast.

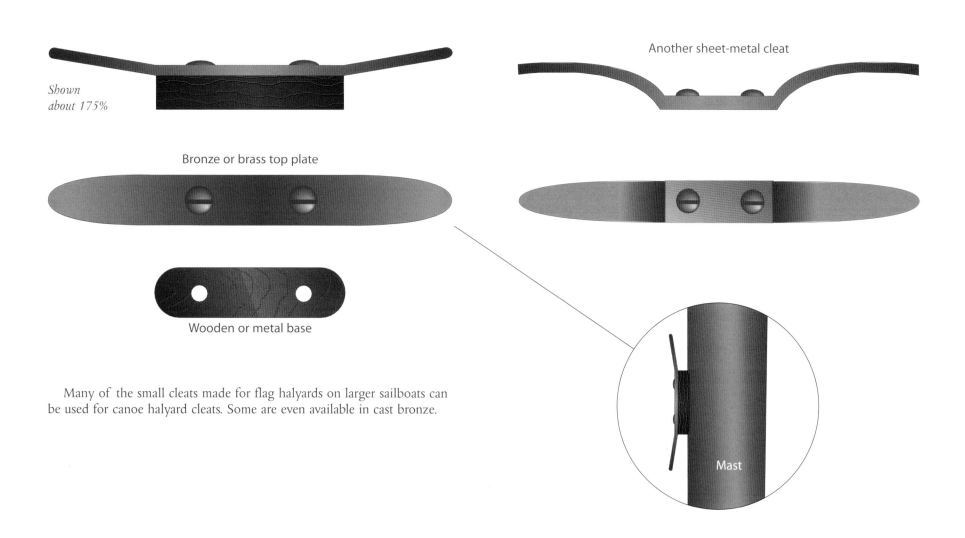

Shown about 175%

Another sheet-metal cleat

Bronze or brass top plate

Wooden or metal base

Mast

Many of the small cleats made for flag halyards on larger sailboats can be used for canoe halyard cleats. Some are even available in cast bronze.

Quick-Release Control-Line Cleats

This small tubular jam cleat can be made from bronze or brass sheet metal. The line is pulled into the V to cleat it. A jam cleat isn't great for a mainsheet, as the line remains captive inside the tube, but it works well for frequently adjusted auxiliary lines, such as boom vangs and downhauls.

These are traditional bronze cam cleats. You are looking at the back side, which would be facing the sailor. The bottom cleat has a fairlead built into the base. As the line is pulled into the cleat, the spring-loaded cams open to receive it. The teeth and the shape of the cams grip the line. To release, the line is pulled up and slips out from between the cams. Cam cleats work well, but they are fairly expensive in bronze.

Cam cleats with a fairlead are also often available on a swiveling base. A single swiveling cleat could be mounted centrally on the leeboard bracket to replace port and starboard cleats.

Clamcleats come in several varieties and in both plastic and aluminum. Their angled ridges hold the line securely, yet make releasing it fast and easy. Though there is nothing traditional about a Clamcleat, it is so small that it doesn't attract too much attention. In use, this is the easiest and least expensive method of cleating sheets and control lines.

Chapter Thirteen

Loose Ends

Preflight and Sail Care

Once all of the parts of your rig are accounted for, it's a good idea to pick a day with little or no wind and "dry-sail" your canoe across the front yard. This will give you a chance to check the halyard and control systems without getting wet or distracted.

Most canoe sails are stored on their spars. When you're ready to drop the sail, try to bring together any full-length battens, the yard, and the boom, and then wrap, roll, or bundle the cloth close to them. Some of the more complex sail types can be difficult to pack into a tight bundle, but you should at least be able to get them down into a manageable pile.

If the sail will be stored for quite a while, it's a good idea to ease the outhaul tension along the boom or yard to keep from stretching the edges. Be absolutely sure the sail is dry, and store it out of the sun and weather, preferably in a bag made to hold the spars with the sail attached.

You would not believe how much money I make every year repairing sails that have been chewed by mice. Mice don't eat Dacron, but they do crawl into bags and chew their way through sails when they want out. Store your sails with this in mind. The best thing to do in the off season is to remove the sails from the spars, fold or roll them, and stow them in a closet or other suitable inside storage area.

Sailcloth manufacturers have a fabric test called a "flutter test." The easiest way to conduct your own is to tie a piece of cloth to your car's radio antenna and drive away. The flutter test determines how many minutes (and yes, it only takes minutes) the flapping piece of fabric will last before being destroyed. The moral of the story is not to car-top a sail unless it is protected inside a suitable bag or tube.

The main enemies of your sails are unnecessary flapping, deterioration from sunlight, and mold from wet storage. Sun damage is cumulative and nearly always due to poor storage, not sailing. Mold will not ruin Dacron, but it will discolor it and is very difficult to remove. Whenever you dry your sails, be sure to allow time for the hidden areas, such as the inside of the batten pockets, to dry as well. If you sail in salt water, the brass rings and grommets will turn green and corrode. To prevent this from happening, rinse the sails with clean, fresh water and dry them before storage.

Both Tanbark and Egyptian Dacron will crease when folded. Though the creases won't affect performance, they are visible and should be kept to a minimum. If possible, roll the sail. For a long sail that is difficult to handle as a roll, accordion-fold it into a long pile 12 to 18 inches wide and then roll or fold the pile into a manageable size.

Accordion-Folding a Sail

To accordion-fold a sail, start by pulling the foot straight and flat on a flat surface. The sail is then carefully flaked, back and forth, all the way to the head, being careful to prevent wrinkles in the fabric. Once it has been flaked into a long stack, it is customary to start at the luff end of the pile and roll or fold (like a flat roll) from the luff to the leech. The sail is then placed in a bag (even a plastic bag can be used as long as the sail is completely dry) and stored out of the sun, away from mice, and in a dry place.

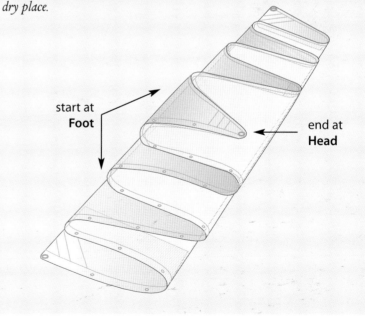

start at **Foot**

end at **Head**

Furling a Lateen Sail

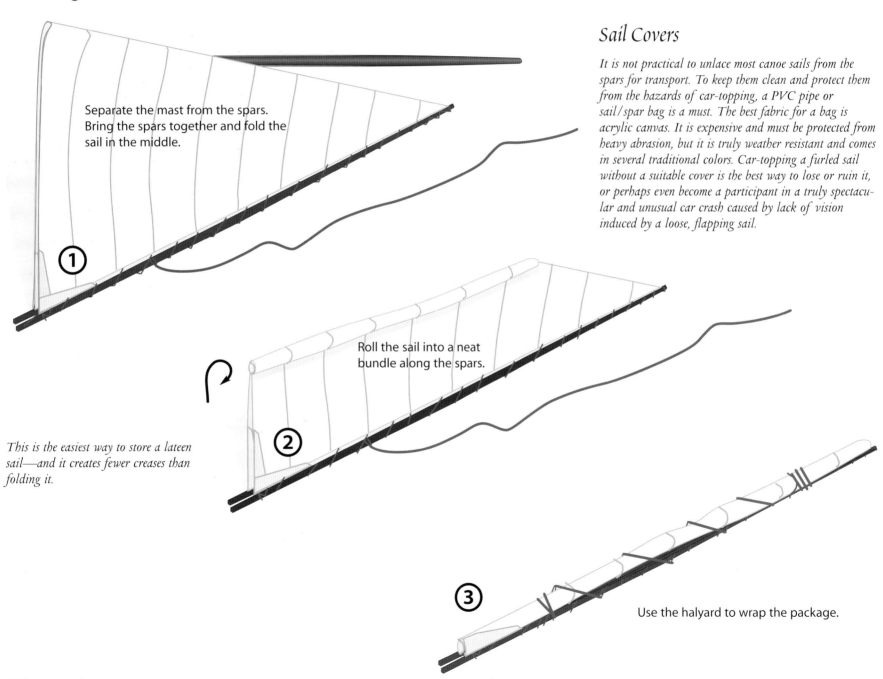

① Separate the mast from the spars. Bring the spars together and fold the sail in the middle.

This is the easiest way to store a lateen sail—and it creates fewer creases than folding it.

② Roll the sail into a neat bundle along the spars.

③ Use the halyard to wrap the package.

Sail Covers

It is not practical to unlace most canoe sails from the spars for transport. To keep them clean and protect them from the hazards of car-topping, a PVC pipe or sail/spar bag is a must. The best fabric for a bag is acrylic canvas. It is expensive and must be protected from heavy abrasion, but it is truly weather resistant and comes in several traditional colors. Car-topping a furled sail without a suitable cover is the best way to lose or ruin it, or perhaps even become a participant in a truly spectacular and unusual car crash caused by lack of vision induced by a loose, flapping sail.

The Sailing Canoe and the Law

In many parts of the United States, canoes don't have to be registered, but in nearly all states, sailboats do. When you turn your canoe into a sailboat, you may be required to register it and even put registration numbers and a state sticker on it. Without opening a debate on the need for a number to identify a 17-foot yellow Old Town Molitor with a black stripe along the gunwales and a 60-square-foot Egyptian Dacron twin bat-wing sailing rig, let me just suggest that you check with local regulations before launching.

Some states also require a throwable flotation device in addition to passenger PFDs on sailboats over 16 feet long. Canoes and kayaks are sometimes exempt from this regulation, but again, check locally. Sailing canoes may be treated differently from paddling canoes.

Understand that a sailing canoe is a curiosity and it attracts attention, both from normal folks and from rangers, wardens, and other officials. The latter are likely to motor over to check out your boat just because it's something interesting, but they are not likely to leave before making sure that you are in accordance with safety and registration laws. It's their job; yours is to comply. Start by wearing your life jacket. It is both safe and a demonstration that you aren't some weirdo in a contraption that the rescue squad is going to have to drag the lake for sooner or later.

You may also be required to carry some sort of auxiliary propulsion device in case the wind dies. Tie a paddle in the canoe so it doesn't fall overboard, and enjoy the fact that you are in the easiest of all boats to paddle home should conditions deteriorate from either too little or too much wind. It's also a good idea to carry a flashlight on late-afternoon sails just in case the wind drops and it takes you a while to get back to the car. A bass boat, moving 40 miles per hour, won't have much time to avoid you in the dark.

Sailing Tips

Most of the damage that happens to small-boat and dinghy rigs is caused by objects connected to the land, not by anything in the water. In a canoe, you may be most vulnerable while getting the sails raised and maneuvering away from the shore or dock. A couple of strong paddle strokes may be all that is needed to get you clear safely, out where you can get the boat moving under sail power alone.

If there is a lot of boat traffic, you may want to paddle out to open water or down the shore to a less congested area before raising your sail. As a paddle craft you have right-of-way over other traffic, but once you raise your sails, you will have to yield to rowing, paddling, and some sailing boats (port-starboard situations: refer to Chapter Two).

You should also remember that many motorboaters don't understand how sailing craft move. Normal tacking and jibing situations for sailors can bewilder powerboaters, who are doing their best to stay clear but may not realize that you may need to change directions. Don't assume that your right-of-way status will protect you if you don't allow the other boat room, or time, to stay clear.

When crossing paths with other sail-powered craft, you may hear the skipper of an approaching boat yell "STARBOARD!" This translates as, "I have the right-of-way here, and I intend to use it." (Again, refer to Chapter Two.) You should avoid such situations by tacking away, preferably before anybody has to yell anything.

I won't kid you. Sailors, as a group, aren't as relaxed as paddlers. Many of them sail just to compete, and any time they are on the water they're competing with somebody for something. To someone like you or me, who came out of the paddling community, they can seem obnoxiously aggressive. The best thing we can do is to learn the rules, the limitations of our sailing canoes, and how to sail our boats beautifully. Nobody can argue with that. Good sailing!

Measured Plans
for Sails and
Leeboards

About These Plans

The following are measured plans for most of the sails in this book. They are reference plans, not construction plans, and are included to give you and/or your sailmaker the basic dimensions and proportions of the sails. Spar and batten lengths can also be calculated from the measurements provided here.

No allowances have been made for spar bend, luff curve, broadseaming, or other draft and shape modifications. These should be added by your sailmaker, by the company plotting your sail kit for you, or by you if you choose to build sails from scratch. If you like a particular sail's proportions but want to change its size, follow the instructions in Chapter Six to reduce or enlarge its area.

At the end of this section, I have added profiles of some of the leeboard shapes from Chapter Nine with a grid superimposed over them. By counting squares and plotting where the edge of the profile crosses them, it is possible to generate a pattern for cutting a leeboard blank.

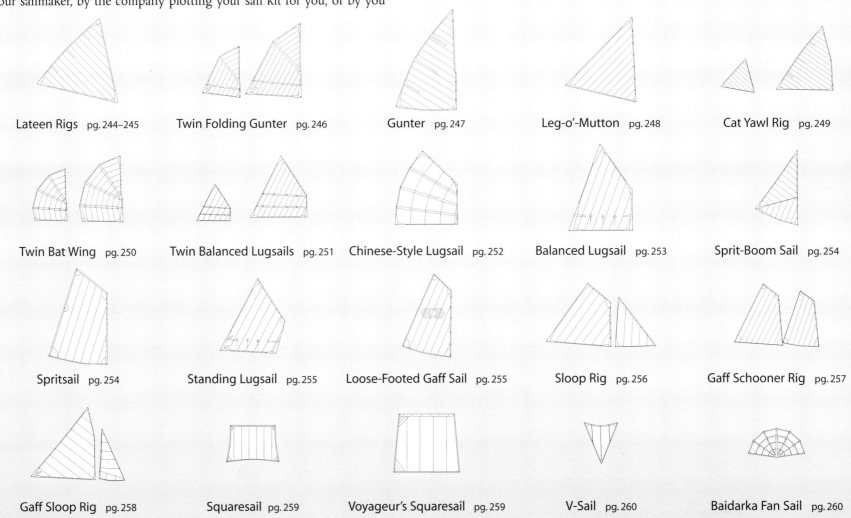

Lateen Rigs pg. 244–245

Twin Folding Gunter pg. 246

Gunter pg. 247

Leg-o'-Mutton pg. 248

Cat Yawl Rig pg. 249

Twin Bat Wing pg. 250

Twin Balanced Lugsails pg. 251

Chinese-Style Lugsail pg. 252

Balanced Lugsail pg. 253

Sprit-Boom Sail pg. 254

Spritsail pg. 254

Standing Lugsail pg. 255

Loose-Footed Gaff Sail pg. 255

Sloop Rig pg. 256

Gaff Schooner Rig pg. 257

Gaff Sloop Rig pg. 258

Squaresail pg. 259

Voyageur's Squaresail pg. 259

V-Sail pg. 260

Baidarka Fan Sail pg. 260

Lateen Sail, 55 Sq. Ft.

Shown cross-cut with a battened leech roach, this sail can also be built with a straight or slightly hollow leech and no battens. Hollowing the leech about 1 inch for every 10 feet of leech length will help keep a non-battened leech from fluttering as the sail ages. Spar bend and draft allowances are yet to be added to the plan.

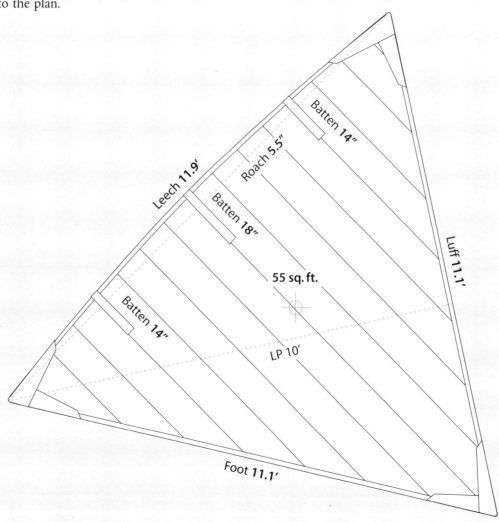

Twin Lateen Sails, Mainsail and Mizzen

75 Sq. Ft.

The mainsail and the mizzen for the Twin Lateen Rig are the same exact shape, but the mizzen is smaller. Here again, a slight hollow is recommended for the leeches of both sails, and spar bend and draft allowances will need to be added.

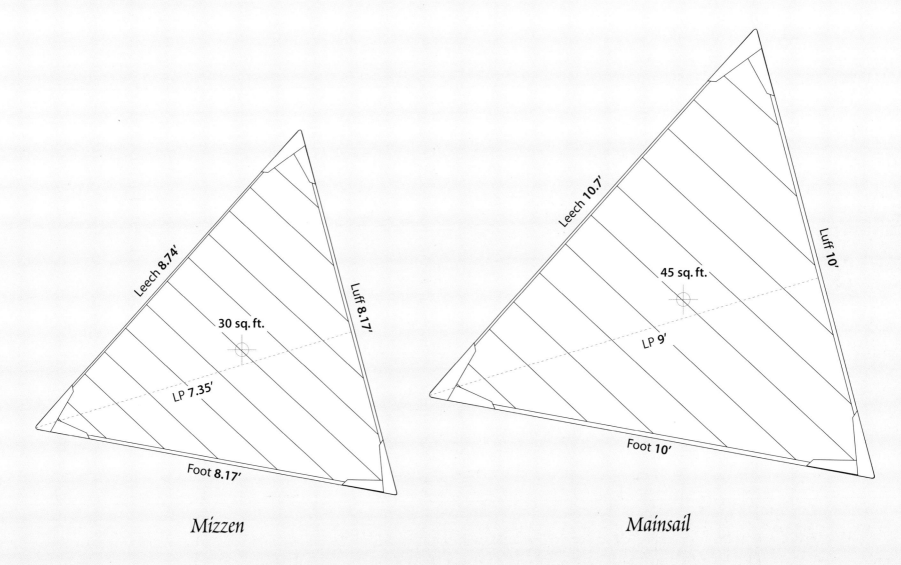

Mizzen

Mainsail

Twin Folding Gunter Sails, Mainsail and Mizzen

These sails are cut flat, with no luff curve. The spars are short enough that spar bend is not really a problem, so no modification to the sails is required to account for it. The single battens must be fairly substantial to support the roach; they were spruce on the boat these sails were originally designed for. The original sails had no reef points; I added them because the canoe was small and narrow, and would often be overpowered.

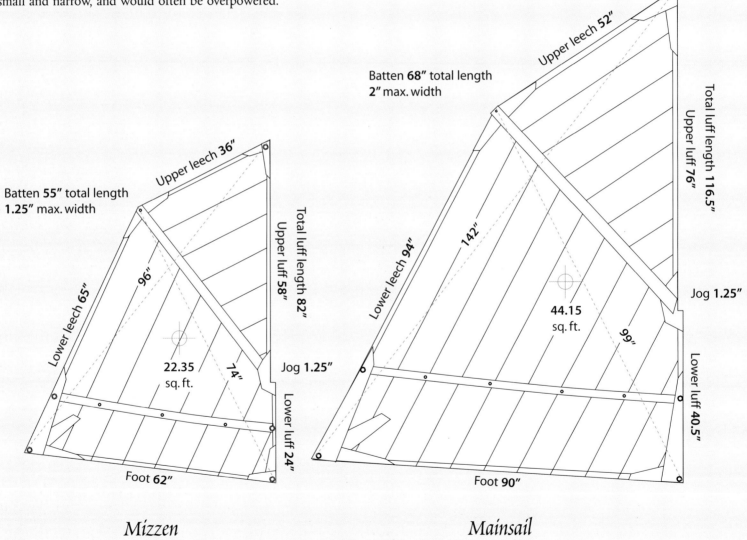

Mizzen

Mainsail

Gunter Sail, 52 Sq. Ft.

If desired, less roach can be cut into this sail. The topmast is not quite vertical, so the luff is not a straight line from tack to head. Draft has yet to be added to the plan.

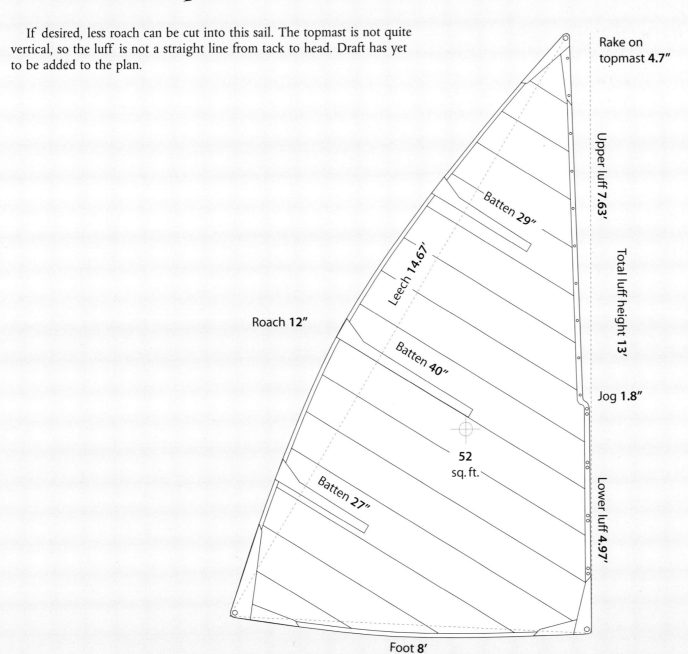

Rake on topmast **4.7"**

Upper luff **7.63'**

Total luff height **13'**

Jog **1.8"**

Lower luff **4.97'**

Batten **29"**

Leech **14.67'**

Roach **12"**

Batten **40"**

52 sq. ft.

Batten **27"**

Foot **8'**

Leg-o'-Mutton Sail, 50 Sq. Ft.

This sail is vertically paneled with a straight leech. Draft should be added to the luff and foot, and, depending on mast stiffness, some bend allowance may be needed on the luff. On any vertically cut sail, a slight leech hollow (1 inch per 10 feet of leech length) may be added to the plan and cut into the leech panel. Should the leech eventually stretch, this will help prevent flapping.

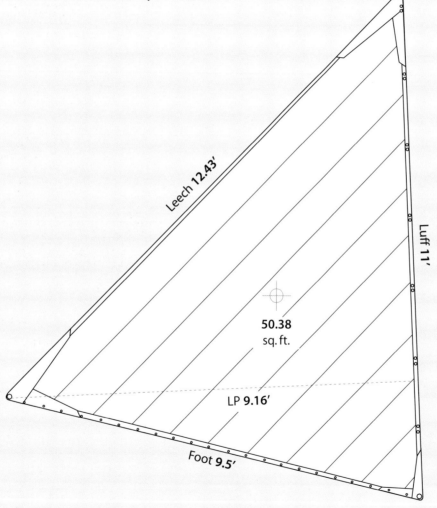

Leech 12.43'

Luff 11'

50.38 sq. ft.

LP 9.16'

Foot 9.5'

Cat-Yawl Rig, Gaff Mainsail and Lateen Mizzen   54 Sq. Ft.

Both of these sails can be of either vertical- or cross-cut construction.
They can have battened roaches, a straight leech, or a slight leech hollow. Draft allowance and bend should be added, though small mizzens
are generally cut with very little draft.

Gaff Mainsail

Head **4.9'**

Batten **12"**

Roach **2.75"**

Leech **10.6'**

Batten **14.5'**

Diag. **8.5'**

Luff **3.95'**

Batten **12"**

34.75
sq. ft.

Foot **7.45'**

Lateen Mizzen

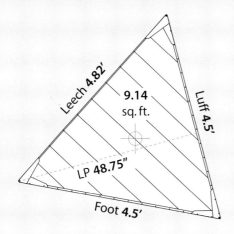

Leech **4.82'**

9.14
sq. ft.

Luff **4.5'**

LP **48.75"**

Foot **4.5'**

Twin Bat-Wing Sails, Mainsail and Mizzen

Figuring out the exact area and C.E. for a bat-wing can take almost as long as it would to build it and probably isn't worth the trouble. It is the equivalent of finding the area and centers of two three-sided sails and two four-sided sails and then finding their combined center of effort. The standard measurement triangle (tack to clew to peak) and its C.E. are what will contribute most of the boat's power and heeling lever when sailing, especially upwind. Since the big roach will twist to leeward somewhat, its

effect can only be estimated. The extra area from the roach will be most noticed when sailing off the wind. If you don't want to figure the total actual area, use the area of the standard triangle and then add 40 to 50 percent as an estimated area for matching sail area to boat size. Bat-wings are generally cut flat, with no luff or foot curves and no spar-bend allowance. The battens must be heavy enough to support the roach.

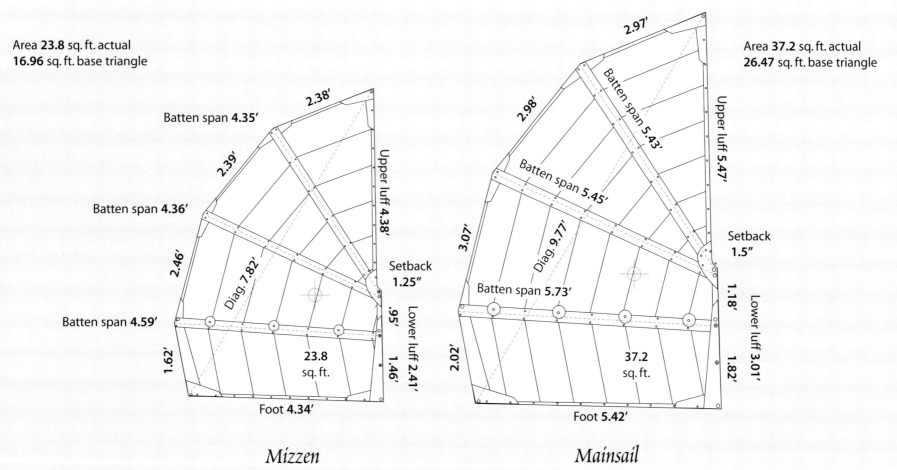

Area **23.8** sq. ft. actual
16.96 sq. ft. base triangle

Mizzen

Area **37.2** sq. ft. actual
26.47 sq. ft. base triangle

Mainsail

Twin Balanced Lugsails, Mainsail and Mizzen

This pair of sails is shown on the decked sailing canoe with the fan centerboard in Chapter Three. The canoe is 14 feet long and the sails total about 46.5 square feet. The mizzen is exactly the same shape as the mainsail, but all linear dimensions are 60 percent of those on the main. Remember, this reduces the mizzen's AREA by 60 percent twice, giving us a bit over 12 square feet. Allowances for draft and spar bend should be added to these base measurements. Draft will be proportional; bend allowance may not.

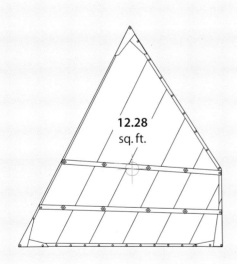

12.28 sq. ft.

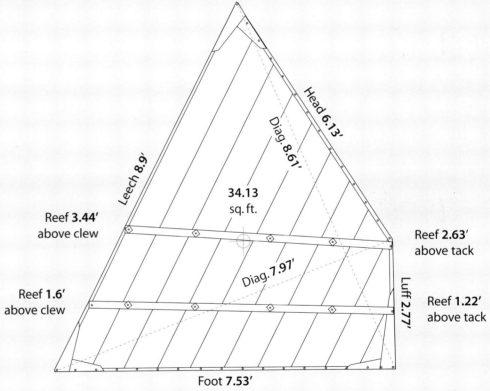

Head **6.13'**

Diag. **8.61'**

Leech **8.9'**

34.13 sq. ft.

Reef **3.44'** above clew

Reef **2.63'** above tack

Diag. **7.97'**

Reef **1.6'** above clew

Luff **2.77'**

Reef **1.22'** above tack

Foot **7.53'**

Chinese-Style Balanced Lugsail, 52 Sq. Ft.

Shown in Chapter Three as 52 square feet on a 14-foot boat, this lug should be a good light-air sail. For higher winds, you might want to reduce it to the 40-to-45-square-foot range. It is paneled like a bat-wing; the battens lie on top of the section-joining overlaps. The sail can be cut flat, but you might want to add some bend allowance for the yard if yours shows a lot of flex.

Battens are external, one on each side, laced through small grommets. A reef could be added, but the sail will start to get quite "horizontal" and might lose a lot of upwind performance when reefed.

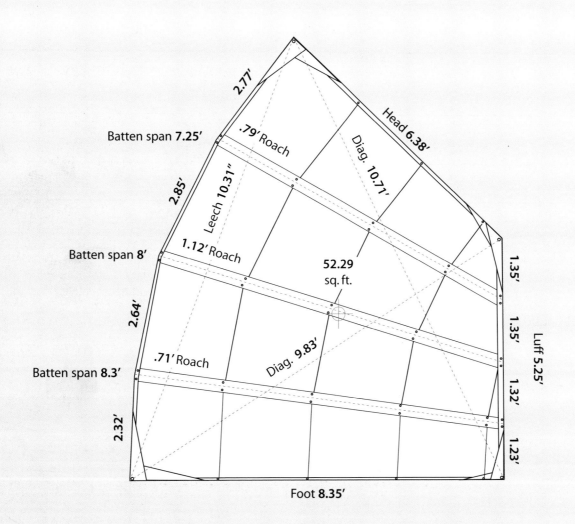

2.77'

Head 6.38'

Batten span **7.25'**

.79' Roach

Diag. 10.71'

2.85'

Leech 10.31"

Batten span **8'**

1.12' Roach

52.29 sq. ft.

1.35'

2.64'

1.35'

Batten span **8.3'**

.71' Roach

Diag. 9.83'

Luff 5.25'

1.32'

2.32'

1.23'

Foot **8.35'**

Balanced Lugsail, 57 Sq. Ft.

This is a workboat-style balanced lugsail designed for the same boat as the sail to the left. The high peak will probably give it better pointing ability, even when reefed. The sail should be cut with both draft and bend allowances, and could be scaled down if desired. Some of the smaller old canoes had more sail area than most people feel comfortable with. Reefed, this sail would be about 40 square feet.

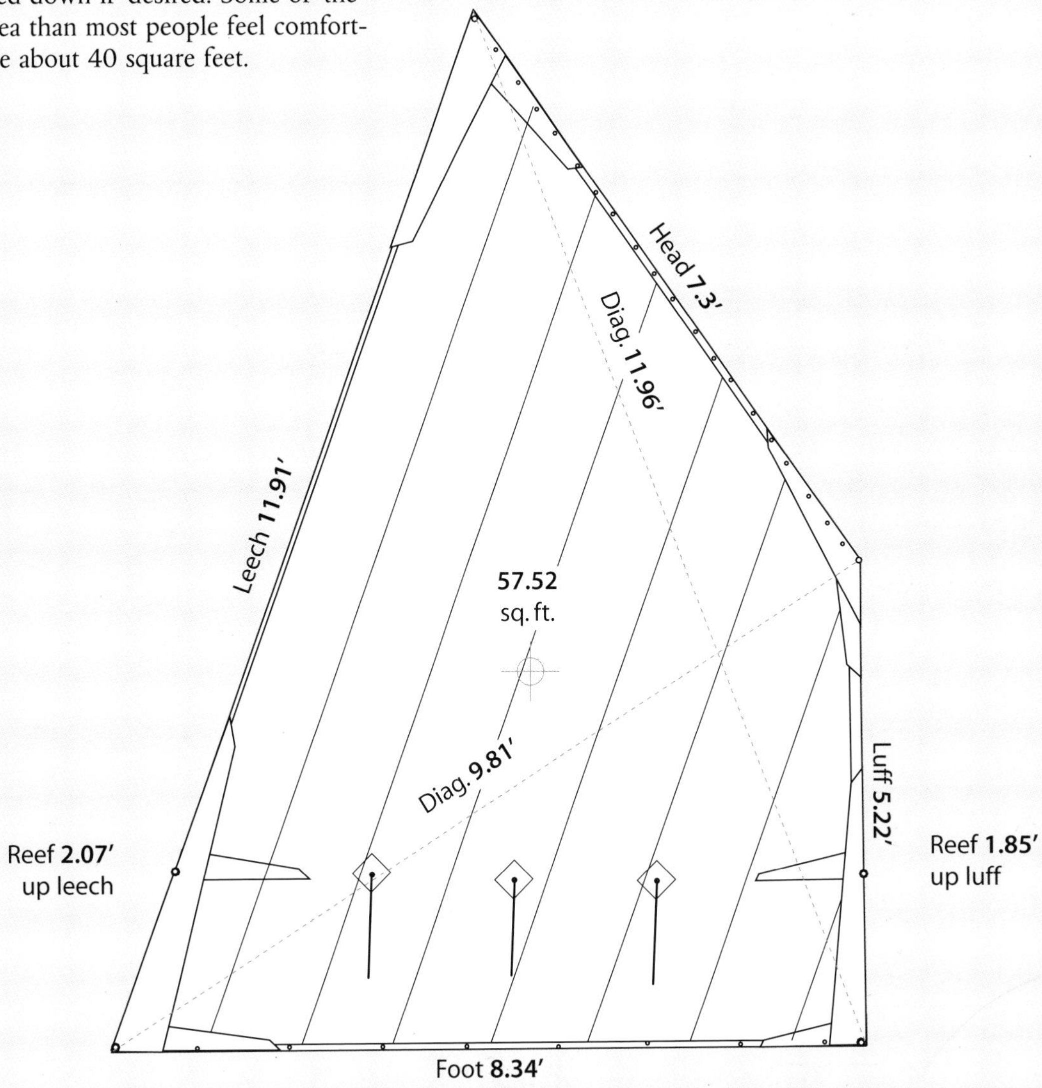

Head 7.3'

Diag. 11.96'

Leech 11.91'

57.52 sq. ft.

Diag. 9.81'

Luff 5.22'

Reef **2.07'** up leech

Reef **1.85'** up luff

Foot **8.34'**

Sprit-Boom Sail, 27 Sq. Ft.

This sail can be mitered or cross-cut. The luff can be laced to the mast, or it can be made with a fabric sleeve that fits over the mast, with a hole for the sprit-tensioning tackle. Since tensioning the sprit tends to bend the mast like an arrow bending a bow, the mast bend should be measured and allowance for it built into the luff shape. Sprit tension will adjust the sail's draft, so it should probably start fairly flat.

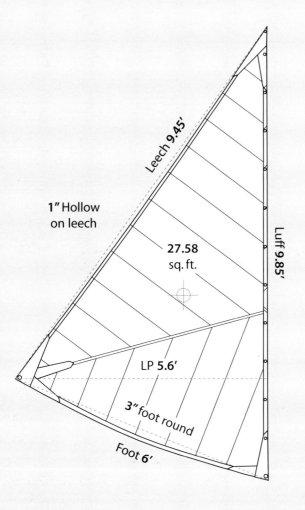

Leech 9.45'

1" Hollow on leech

27.58 sq. ft.

Luff 9.85'

LP 5.6'

3" foot round

Foot 6'

Spritsail, 66 Sq. Ft.

Shown vertically cut with a straight leech, this sail could also be cross-cut. A good, simple sail for any boat.

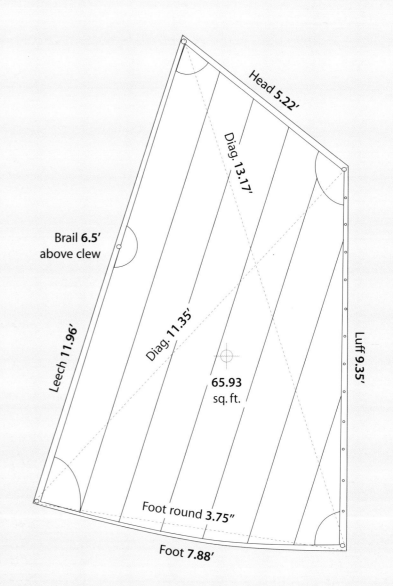

Head 5.22'

Diag. 13.17'

Brail 6.5' above clew

Diag. 11.35'

Leech 11.96'

Luff 9.35'

65.93 sq. ft.

Foot round 3.75"

Foot 7.88'

Standing Lugsail, 46 Sq. Ft.

This is a vertical-cut single-reef lugsail. It could also be made loose-footed (not laced to the boom) or possibly even boomless, though sheet angle might suffer on such a narrow boat as a canoe.

It is a good idea to reinforce the luff of lugsails with roping, an extra layer of fabric, or even light webbing hidden inside the luff tape. Allowances for draft and yard bend should be calculated and added.

Head **6.64'**

Diag. **10'**

Leech **10.6'**

46.4 sq. ft.

Diag. **9.46'**

Luff **4.32'**

Reef **1.66'** above clew

Reef **1.55'** above tack

Foot **7.47'**

Loose-Footed Gaff Sail, 43 Sq. Ft.

The proa Witch Way has two sails like this. Tall short-gaffed mainsails such as this aren't used on boats as much use as they should, as they probably have the highest performance of all gaffers. For normal boats, this one would be fitted with a boom, with the sail set loose-footed. Gaff bend should be minimal; shape would be added to the luff, the head, and the foot.

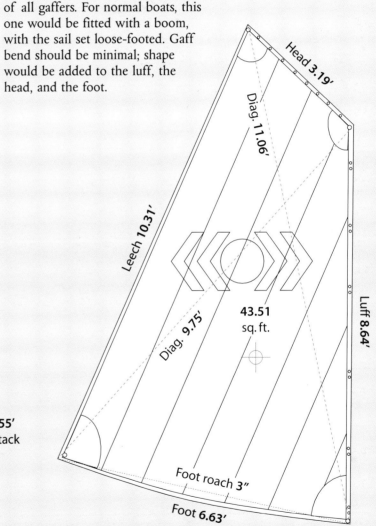

Head **3.19'**

Diag. **11.06'**

Leech **10.31'**

Diag. **9.75'**

43.51 sq. ft.

Luff **8.64'**

Foot roach **3"**

Foot **6.63'**

Ice Scooter-Style Sloop Rig, Mainsail and Jib

These sails are for a rig that could possibly sail without a rudder. The mainsail could provide the power, and trimming the jib could provide the steering. The C.E. (total) should lead the C.L.P. by about 15 percent of waterline length. As long as sailing straight downwind is avoided, it just might work. The boat should pivot on its leeboards, and jib trim should determine the boat's heading by balancing the jib's power to turn the boat against the power of the mainsail. If that didn't work, a small rudder could be fitted to help.

The jib is laced to a jib boom and can be set for self-tacking by using a single sheet run through a centrally mounted fairlead and anchored to the jib boom.

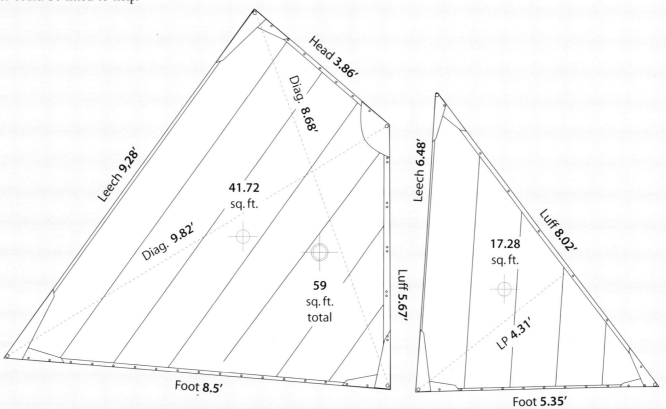

Gaff Schooner Rig, Mainsail and Foresail

These gaff sails should be built with a bit of added draft, but probably won't need an allowance for bend as long as the masts are as stiff as possible. The sheet lead for the boomless foresail should lie on a straight line that would pass from mid-luff, through the sail's clew, and back to a fairlead on the canoe.

Gaff Sloop Rig, Mainsail and Jib

53 Sq. Ft.

These are the sails for our Shallow-Water Special, the 16-footer with the Dutch-style leeboards in Chapter Nine. The high-peaked gaff mainsail should be a good pointer, and the small jib is fun without being so large that it becomes a handful to trim when tacking. Both sails are cross-cut with slightly hollowed leeches; they should have draft calculations added to these basic dimensions.

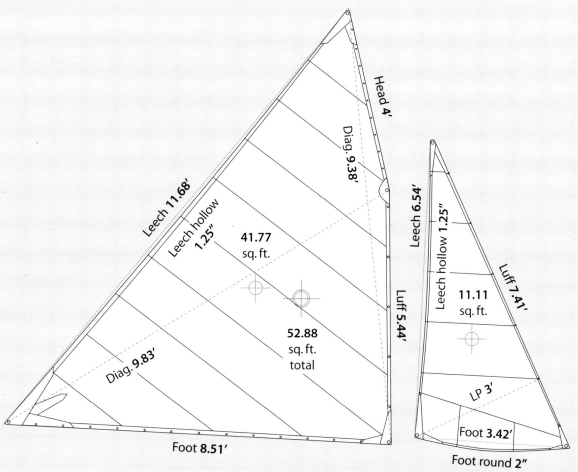

Head 4'

Diag. 9.38'

Leech 11.68'

Leech hollow 1.25"

41.77 sq. ft.

52.88 sq. ft. total

Diag. 9.83'

Luff 5.44'

Foot 8.51'

Leech 6.54'

Leech hollow 1.25"

Luff 7.41'

11.11 sq. ft.

LP 3'

Foot 3.42'

Foot round 2"

Squaresail, 31 Sq. Ft.

With the foot and sides hollowed, this squaresail is less prone to flapping than its simpler cousin to the right. It can be built in a variety of height-vs.-width ratios. Taller versions will catch more wind; shorter ones will make the canoe more stable. A little shape should be built into the bottom by broadseaming the panel seams a bit. A sample broadseaming curve is shown. This is where the foot tapers would begin.

Voyageur's Squaresail, 62.75 Sq. Ft.

It can't get much simpler than this one. Vertical panels, triangular corner patches, and a handful of grommets are all that are needed. You could build it from Dacron or nylon and use it for an extra tarp on canoe trips, just as the originals were. There is no shaping or bend allowance necessary for this utilitarian, but historical sail. Its size could be reduced to 25–40 square feet for use on modern, two-person tripping canoes.

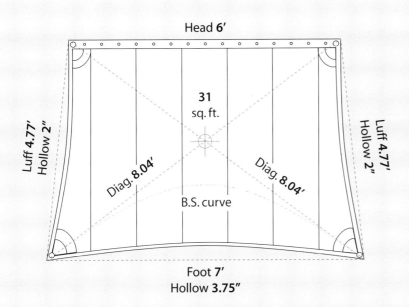

Head **6'**

Luff **4.77'**
Hollow **2"**

31
sq. ft.

Diag. **8.04'**

Diag. **8.04'**

Luff **4.77'**
Hollow **2"**

B.S. curve

Foot **7'**
Hollow **3.75"**

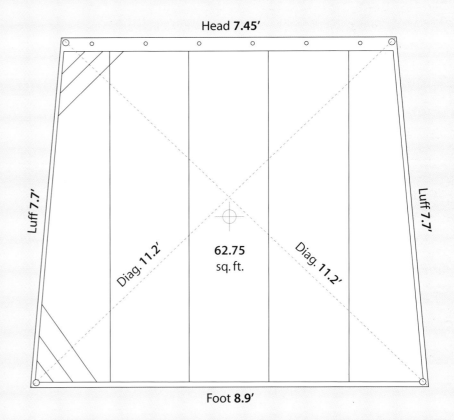

Head **7.45'**

Luff **7.7'**

Luff **7.7'**

Diag. **11.2'**

Diag. **11.2'**

62.75
sq. ft.

Foot **8.9'**

V-Sail, 12.66 Sq. Ft.

Simple to build and use, the V-sail is cut flat, with no bend allowance needed. It is of moderate area but carries most of it up high to catch more wind. Increasing the linear dimensions by a third (133 percent) will yield 8-foot luffs and 25 square feet of sail area. Anything larger might be difficult to handle and stow in a canoe.

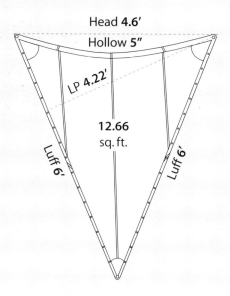

Baidarka Fan Sail

Built from six paneled wedges measuring 44.5 inches on their long sides and 21 inches on their ends, this fan has just under 38 square feet of sail area. Slightly hollowed outer (leech) edges will prevent fluttering, and plenty of reinforcing patches add to its strength. The mast sleeve opens at the bottom, and the six batten sleeves are open along the leech, where there are grommets for the batten ties.

Reef lines allow wedges to be gathered in and tied up to reduce sail area. The two in the center furl the entire sail.

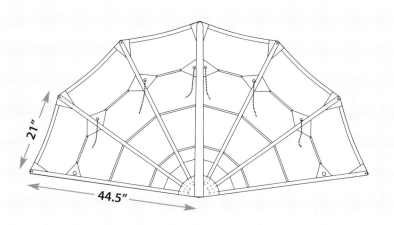

Cutting this sail's wedges with straight sides would yield a flat sail, though the wind would put some draft into it. Cutting wedges with slightly convex sides (with the possible exception of those next to the mast) would create a more spherical, and possibly more stable, shape. The fan sail concept is an interesting and affordable platform for experimentation.

Spinnaker Sizing

Spinnaker measurement and design is more complex than construction and requires more space than we have here to be described. I recommend that you have a kit made up if you want to build one. Yes, you could start from scratch, but I have done it and it's no fun. Let the computer plotters do the work; you build the sail. I wouldn't suggest a canoe spinnaker more than about 6 feet tall.

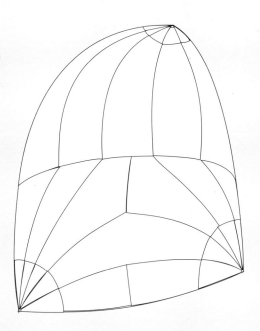

General Sail Construction Notes

The width of panel seams (overlap) is usually ½ inch or ⅝ inch. I have built sails with as little as ⅜ inch seams, but they are tedious to sew. Since seams highlight the narrow-paneled construction, there is no reason to to try and hide or minimize them.

Leech hems are usually the same width as a panel seam. Luff and foot tapes are generally 1-inch or 1¼-inch (2-inch or 2½-inch-wide strips, folded in half) binding the raw edges of the sail.

On twin rigs where the mizzen is significantly smaller than the mainsail, like the twin lateen and twin bat-wing rigs, the corner patches on the mizzen should be scaled down, proportionally to match its smaller sail area. I will also downsize the hardware used for the corner rings.

I keep the fabric panel width, seam width, and the widths of the luff and foot tapes the same as those on the mainsail and use the same size and spacing for the lacing grommets on both sails. Though you may choose to do it differently, I think it helps make the sails look like a matched pair, even though they are different sizes.

Leeboard Patterns

The grid squares here are 1 inch by 1 inch; use them as guides for laying out the shapes of these leeboards full size. Make up patterns and check them against your boat and leeboard brackets to be sure the sizes and locations of the bolt holes will work with your system. There is nothing ultra-scientific about leeboard-profile design, so pick a shape you like and use it as a starting point.

THE END

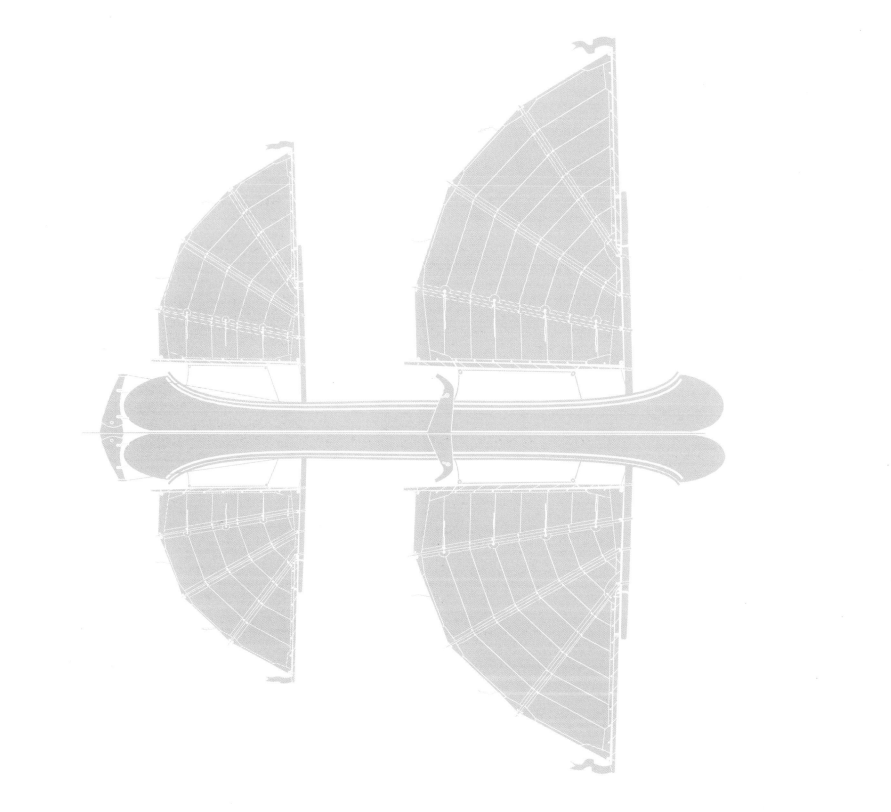

epilogue

I must have been about eleven years old when I first stepped tentatively into a canoe. On an early summer morning I sat on the bottom, as a friend and his father paddled us across a reservoir in Illinois. Small towers of fog slowly migrated across the lake's surface, and the canoe quietly parted the water to let us through, the only sounds being the drips from the paddles between strokes.

I didn't know it at the time, but here were all the ingredients for a very special experience. I would later learn by reading the books of Sigurd Olson that the towers of fog weren't really towers, or blobs or puffs or anything so mundane— they were white horses galloping across the lake, and their home range is north of Lake Superior. With the help of authors like Harry Roberts, I learned the required movements and body posture for an efficient bent-shaft marathon stroke on one page and that, in reality, canoes move mostly by magic on another.

Perhaps sooner or later, I would have figured these things out on my own, but reading the words of all the great canoe authors was a way of finding out that there wasn't anything wrong with me—other people found canoeing as fascinating as I did. Through the books of Eric Morse and Eric Sevareid I went to places that I will probably never go, and authors like John Malo and Bill Mason coached me as I learned to paddle and portage through the wilderness.

Canoe Rig is, in many ways, an effort to give something back to a sport that has given so much to me. Two of my passions, canoeing and sailing, just happened to overlap at the right time and place. An attempt to provide potential customers with an accurate-looking vision of what their finished sail might look like, turned into page after page of drawings, plans, and text.

As I look back to that morning on the reservoir, I can still feel the magic, the slight surge every time matched paddle strokes moved the boat forward. I can still see the white horses. I've been chasing them ever since.